Manazil
28 Mansions
of the Moon

Manazil
28 Mansions of the Moon

Edited and compiled by
Peter Stockinger

Copyright © 2025 Peter Stockinger

All rights reserved. No part of this work may be reproduced, stored in a retrieval system, or transmitted in any form or by any means, electronic, mechanical, photocopying, recording or otherwise without the prior permission of the publisher.

BM Mandrake,
London

The illustrations accompanying most of the 28 lunar mansions are taken from a copy of an anonymous work, held in the Wellcome Collection (Wellcome MS Persian 373). The relevant portion was copied from an earlier work, Nujum al-ulum ('Stars of the Sciences'), dated c. 1570 AD, commissioned by Sultan Ali Adil Shah I of Bijapur, India. It is a compendium of Muslim and Hindu beliefs, considered to be a manual of astrology and astral magic and would explain some of the pictorial references to the 27 Indian Nakshatras. Due to lacunae at the beginning and the end of MS 373, as well as damage to some of the pages, the illustrations for mansions 19, 20 and 22 are seemingly lost.

Contents

Preface 8
Part I Introduction 10
Manazil and Anwa Tradition 10
Alchandreana 14
Choices or Elections 18
Talismans 19
Weather 22
The Qualities of the Lunar Mansions 23
Abu Rayhan Al-Biruni 25
Abu Yusuf Al-Kindi 26
Jafar Indus 26
Muhyiddin Ibn 'Arabi 26
Guido Bonatti 27
Muhammad Al-Qazwini 28
Johannes Stöffler 29
Johannes Schöner 30
Agrippa von Nettesheim 31
Christian Ludwig Ideler 36

Part II 37
The 28 Mansions of the Moon 37
1st Lunar Mansion Al-Sharatan, The Two Signs, The Horns of Aries 37
2nd Lunar Mansion Al-Butayn, The Belly of Aries 43
3rd Lunar Mansion Al -Thurayya, The Many Little Ones, The Rainy Ones 47
4th Lunar Mansion Al-Dabaran, The Follower, The Head or Eye of Taurus ... 51
5th Lunar Mansion Al-Haq'a, The White Spot 55
6th Lunar Mansion Al-Han'ah, The Mark 59
7th Lunar Mansion Al Dhira, The Forearm, Arm of Gemini 63
8th Lunar Mansion Al Nathrah, The Gap or Crib 68
9th Lunar Mansion Al Tarfa, The Glance (of the Lion's Eye) 72
10th Lunar Mansion Al Jabhah, The Forehead or Neck of Leo 75
11th Lunar Mansion Al Zubrah, The Lion's Mane 81
12th Lunar Mansion Al Sarfah, The Changer, The Tail of Leo 85
13th Lunar Mansion Al Awwa, The Barker, Dogs, Cold,
or Winged Ones of Virgo 89
14th Lunar Mansion Al Simak, The Unarmed, Virgo's Ear of Corn 94

15th Lunar Mansion Al Ghafr, The Covering 98
16th Lunar Mansion Al Jubana, The Claws, The Horns of Scorpio 101
17th Lunar Mansion Iklil al Jabhah, The Crown of the Forehead 105
18th Lunar Mansion Al Kalb, The Heart 109
19th Lunar Mansion Al Shaulah, The Sting 112
20th Lunar Mansion Al Na'am, The Ostriches 116
21st Lunar Mansion Al Baldah, The City or Desert 120
22nd Lunar Mansion Al Sa'd al Dhabih, The Fortune of the Slaughterer 123
23rd Lunar Mansion Sa'd al Bula, The Fortune of the Swallower 127
24th Lunar Mansion Sa'd al Su'ud, The Fortunate of the Fortunate 134
25th Lunar Mansion Sa'd al Ahbiyah, The Fortune of the Hidden 134
26th Lunar Mansion Al-Fargh Al-Mukdim, The First Spout 138
27th Lunar Mansion Al-Fargh al Thani, The Second Spout 142
28th Lunar Mansion Batn al Hut, The Belly of the Fish, The Ribbon 145

Part III Source Material 149
Book of Instructions in the Elements of the Art of Astrology, ... 149
The Chronology of Ancient Nations, Al-Biruni 154
Lunar Mansions, from: El-Qazwini's Wonders of Creation 177
Brenner: Das Gross Planeten-Buch, Strassburg, 1559 222
Brenner, Sebastian: Das Grosse Planeten Buch, Frankfurt am Main, 1789 224
Johannes Schöner: Ein nutzlichs Büchlein viler bewerter Ertzney, lang zeyt versamlet und zusammen pracht, Nürnberg, 1528 253
Judgment upon the 28 Mansions of the Moon,
English translation of *Ephemeridum opus ab anno 1532 - 1551*, ... 257
From the Planeten Buch, Straubing 1596: 259
Stöffler's Judgment upon th(e) 28 mansions 262
The Magus or Celestial Intelligencer 264

Bibliography 269
Index 273

Preface

This book is about the Manazil, also known as the Arabic lunar mansions. Other systems, like that of the 27 Nakshatra (Indian lunar mansions), or the Chinese lunar mansions, are not covered here. My intention of writing this book was to gather as much information about the 28 Manazil as I could find, and present them to the reader in an easily approachable way. For this reason, I have divided this book into three parts, providing easy access to core information, but also to supply the interested reader with complete transcripts of hard-to-find source material, some of which has been translated into English for the first time.

The first part provides an introduction into the concept of the lunar mansions. It also traces some of their history, as well as their transmission into Europe. Along a timeline, the most important authors and their texts are introduced. Part one also shows, how the use and portrayal of the lunar mansions has changed over time.

The second part covers the 28 lunar mansions in detail, collating the information found in the core texts, written by the authors introduced in the first part. This part covers all three types of lunar mansions: tropical, sidereal-, and constellational. The tropical mansions are of equal size, beginning with 00* Aries. The size of each mansion is approximately 12*51', which means that the 8th mansion begins with 00* Cancer, the 15th mansion with 00* Libra, the 22nd with 00* Capricorn, and so forth. The sidereal mansions are also of equal size (12*51') but the first mansion begins with the precessed location of Hamal, its determinant fixed star. The constellational mansions are of unequal size, spanning the distance between the mansion's determinant fixed stars. Due to the precession of the equinoxes, the location of these mansions changes over time.

Peter Stockinger

The third part comprises transcripts as well as translations of some of the most important lunar mansion texts. Some of these are hard to find and some were only available in German. These have been translated into English for the first time.

Part I

Introduction

At Orliens in studio a book he say,
 Of magic natural, which his felawe,
 That was that time a bacheler of lawe,
 Al were he ther to learne another craft,
 Hadde privily upon his desk ylaft;
 Which book spak muchel of the operaciouns,
 Touchynge the eighte and twenty mansiouns,
 That longen to the Moone, and swich foyle
 As in oure days is nat worth a flye –
 For hooly chirches feith in our bilevel
 Ne suffreth noon illusiouns to greve.
 (Chaucer, Franklin's Tale)

Manazil and Anwa Tradition

The division of time by the moon's passage through certain parts of the night-sky is probably as old as humanity itself. Looking at the etymology of the English word 'month' we find that it can be traced back to the Proto-Indo-European *meh*, - to measure, referring to the phases of the moon as the measure of time. There are two different cycles which are of interest to us here. The first one, which is known as the synodic month, describes the length of time between two moon-phases, mainly full moon to full moon, or new moon to new moon. One synodic month takes approximately 29.53 days, and therefore 12 synodic months equal 354.37 days. This cycle has been, and still is, the basis for many lunar calendars. Due to the synodic lunar year being approximately 11 days shorter than the solar year, lunisolar calendars usually add a thirteenth month every three years to avoid a shift of the sun's spring equinox point. The other lunar cycle is the sidereal month. This is the length of time it takes the moon to reappear at the same place on the ecliptic in relation to the fixed stars. The sidereal revolution of the moon takes approximately 27.3 days. Archaeological artefacts, like the Austrian Stachelscheibe von Platt, which dates back to the Bronze Age, show that the measurement of time through the division of the ecliptic into 28 equal parts was already common practice as far back as 1500 B.C. The Stachelscheibe (literally "spike disc" named thus because of a circular spike in its center) shows concentric circles, one of them displaying 12 troughs and another one comprising 28 troughs. This has been interpreted as depictions of the 12 tropical months and the 28 lunar mansions or 28 days of a sidereal month, respectively. Much of the details of the lunar mansions' early history is shrouded in mystery, but some scholars have speculated that the system originated with the Babylonians, who passed their knowledge on to the Indians. This conjecture was first made by the German Indologist and historian, Professor Albrecht Weber in his *History of Indian Literature,* 1852. Later, it was Fritz Hommel who tried to connect the 28 mansions with the 24 extra-ecliptic stars, listed by the Ancient Greek historian Diodorus Siculus. His efforts, which were published in the *Deutsche Morgenländische Gesellschaft Zeitschrift,* Vol.45, 1891, were not convincing. Critics soon found several objections to his theory and it was generally refuted. Stefan Weinstock (1901-1971), a British ancient historian, classical philologist and religious scholar of Austro-Hungarian origin, wrote in his important paper *Lunar Mansions and Early Calendars,* that the number of constellations the Babylonians observed were not 28 in number, but that they would mark "a stage in the development from mansions to zodiac." He was convinced though, that "sometimes before that date [the second millennium B.C.] the mansions - perhaps not yet a stable and complete set of them - were observed by the Babylonians (p54) and that "the Babylonian origin of this scheme is established with reasonable certainty." (p69). Possibly around 1000 BC, Indian astronomers either developed or adapted an inherited system, whereby they divided the moon's monthly path into 28 or, later 27 segments, called *Nakshatras*. The name of each *Nakshatra* related to the most visible asterism in each segment. The starting point of the first *Nakshatra* was a point on the ecliptic directly opposite fixed star Spica. In Sanskrit, this point is called *Chitrā,* which is located in *Ashvinī,* an asterism known to us as the constellation of the Ram. At some point before the advent of Islam, the details of this lunar zodiac were passed on from the Indians to the Arabs, in ways and through channels which, to date, are still unknown. It was soon recognised that this system of 28 stars, asterisms, or zodiacal constellations, corresponded with their own list of 28 asterisms along the zodiac belt, which are known as *anwa*. The Bedouins of the Arabian Peninsula devised and used the simple *anwa* system to crudely measure the passage of time. There is still much debate if the name *anwa* actually referred to the acronychal or cosmical setting (that is setting in the west as the sun rises in the east) or the heliacal rising (that is the rising in the east with the sun) of the 28 bright stars or constellations believed to be responsible for rain. This enabled the Bedouins to predict the weather for certain periods. What seems to be fairly certain amongst modern scholars is the notion that a set of stars or constellations delineated the solar year, dividing the ecliptic into 28 segments or periods. Even to this day, some people still retain knowledge of this kind of traditional Arabic star lore. Yemeni farmers still use a calendar which is based on the conjunction of the new moon and the Pleiades. Recognising the similarity between the 28 Nakshatras and their 28 *anwa*, the Arabs combined the two systems. The Arabic name given to the 28 segments of the Indian lunar zodiac was *manazil* (singular *manzil*). The dictionary informs us that the primary meaning of *manzil* is "stage in a journey" also "halting place" or "place of descending". It refers to a dwelling where travellers could stop, dismount, and stay for a rest. Another, secondary, meaning of *manzil* is "house" or "mansion" which has become the default translation used in the West. Although stations of the moon would be more correct, I will use the terms lunar mansion or lunar mansions throughout the text, as this is in keeping with most of the Western source material. Arab scholars slightly adjusted the 28 *anwa* so that they would successfully superimpose the 28 *manazil*. The difference between the two systems was, that the *anwa* system was dependent on the rising or setting of 28 asterisms or fixed star groups, whereas the system imported from India divided the ecliptic into 28 regular segments of 12* 51'. Because one system was based on the achronycal setting and heliacal rising of asterisms, and the other system on a regular division of the ecliptic, the compatibility was not perfect. Another problem was the precession of the equinoxes, which is the westward movement of the equinoxes along the ecliptic, relative to the fixed stars. This meant that the positions of the fixed stars were moving over time in relation to the spring equinox point and could therefore not be perpetually aligned with the *manazil*. At the time of its conception, it was decreed that al-Sharatain, the first lunar mansion in the new *anwa/manazil* system, would be located in the Aries star group and specifically be connected with the fixed stars Sheratan (beta Arietis) and Mesarthim (gamma Arietis). Since then, due to the precession, the stars that originally gave the mansions their names and meanings have long since moved into neighbouring *manazils*, but the original interpretations of the mansions, which are still counted from 0* Aries, have been kept. These lunar mansions are known as the Tropical mansions.

Alchandreana

First, we direct our attention to the use of the lunar mansions in natal astrology. As early as the late 10th century, astrological texts known as *Alchandreana*, began to appear in Europe. These included chapters dealing with the 28 lunar mansions and their interpretations. Here, the particular mansion representative for nature, traits and fate of an individual was depending on the lunar mansion rising at the time of birth, rather than it being the mansion the moon was located in, as one would expect. Also, of interest to note is the fact that in these texts the mansion supposedly 'rising' at the time of a person's birth, was not determined by astrological or astronomical methods but rather by *onomatomancy* (from the Greek *onomatos* ('a name') and *mantia* ('prophecy')). *Onomatomancy* is defined as a method of divination and prophecy by interpreting the number of a person's name. In the case of the mansions, the numerical values of the native's and his mother's name were added up and divided by 28. The resulting number was that of the native's lunar mansion.

This form of fortune telling with the help of the lunar mansions can also be found in the so-called Mondwahrsagebücher (Moon-fortune telling books) which used a complicated system to find answers to specific questions. The querent had to add the number of the question found in listings in the book to the number 28, which represented the number of 'moon-days'. Then the number of days until the next new moon had to be subtracted from the former number. The resulting number pointed to a specific line in the book, which answered the querent's question. No astrological details were included in these books and although the transliterated names of the 28 lunar mansions were listed, it is not entirely clear if the authors knew what it was, they were listing. Dr. Robert Vian, who published a scientific analysis of two Mondwahrsagebücher from the 14th and 15th century, comes to the conclusion, that the authors probably thought the names of the mansions were actually names of Arab prophets.

One of the earliest extant German manuscripts dealing with the lunar mansions in an astrological context is Johannes Hartlieb's *De mansionibus*, written between 1433 and 1435. Hartlieb (1410-1468) was a physician employed by Louis VII of Bavaria and Albert VI of Austria, amongst others. He also published a compendium on herbs and produced German translations of authors like Macrobius or Muscio. His most famous book was the *Puch aller verpoten Kunst, Ungelaubens und der Zauberei* (book on all forbidden arts, superstition, and sorcery) published in 1456, which has been described as "the most important German source of medieval forbidden arts". But let us return to Hartlieb's *De mansionibus*. Although it is generally classed as a Mondwahrsagebuch, implying that it was mainly used for purposes of fortunetelling, only two of the different extant manuscripts include an onomatomantic part, added to the detailed descriptions of the 28 lunar mansions. In the specifically astrological text, the Moon moves through the 28 mansions, providing information about an individual's course of life, depending on the mansion the Moon was in at their time of birth. Research has shown that Hartlieb had access to source material which was originally of Arabic origin, most likely Haly Abenragel's texts on the mansions from the Latin edition, *Praeclarissimus*, as well as Johannes Hispalensis' table of the lunar mansions from *Epitome totius astrologiae*, which Hispalensis compiled in 1142. Frank Fürbeth in his book

Manazil

Johannes Hartlieb, Untersuchungen zu Leben und Werk, makes the case that, judging from Hartlieb's disapproval of necromancy in general throughout his *"Puch aller verpoten kunst"*, it is very likely that he saw the lunar mansion text as a specifically astrological text, rather than something connected to the "forbidden arts". Fürbeth concludes that the onomatomantic parts included in the two manuscripts were later additions.

Another book in the category of the Mondwahrsagebücher, is *Das Grosse Planeten Buch* (The Big Book of the Planets) by Sebastian Brenner. Although this book was very popular, I have not been able to find any biographical information about the supposed author, Sebastian Brenner. His *Planeten Buch* seems to have been in great demand. First published in 1559 it has been more or less continuously in print until the beginning of the 19th century. I had access to the 1559 edition and to the edition published in 1789. It is highly interesting to compare the development of the chapter on the lunar mansions. The 1559 edition lists descriptions of nature, traits, and fate of individuals, born during the rising of a particular mansion, often referred to as a "star". The entry for al-Zubra, the 11th lunar mansion, here referred to as "Alkoraten" is a good example:

> "If a child is born during Alkoraten's rise / it will have a long face / its speech will be soft and ill / uncourtly and nefarious / bad things will happen [to the child] / very often it will be angry / there will be a mark on his loins / but if there is no mark / it will come to much chagrin. If the star rises during the night / who is born / does not care what he does / will be a good orator / [there will be] a mark on his legs / [and he will] also have marks on face and neck. But if it rises in the second hour of the day / who will be born / will have many children by two wives /

but nearly all of them will die / The first child will be a girl / the other one a boy. He will be ill in his eleventh year / if he recovers / he will live healthily for xxiiii years / thereafter he will suffer from illness and will have to work hard / if he survives / he will live lviii years."

When compared to the 1719 edition, it becomes clear that the entries for each of the mansions had been greatly expanded. Added to the natal delineations, we find increased astrological material, but also additional information about lucky and unlucky times (years, months, days), lucky colours, as well as paragraphs on geographical lore. The entry for the 11th lunar mansion, in this edition, here referred to as "Alkratea" reads:

Of the star Alkratea and its effect. This star, also known as Adarf, [and] whose ruler is Neziel, begins in 7 degrees and 20 minutes of Virgo, and reaches with his effect into the 20th degree and 24 minutes of the following signs, and is naturally well tempered, [of] Jupiter and Venus nature, [makes] people happy. If a child is born during Alkratea's rise, it will have a long face, its speech will be soft and ill uncourtly and nefarious, bad things will happen [to the child], very often it will be angry, there will be a mark on his loins, but if there is no mark it will come to much chagrin. Who is born when the star rises during the night does not care what he does, will be a good orator, has a mark on his legs [and he will] also have marks on face and neck. But if it rises in the second hour of the day who will be born then will have many children by two wives, but nearly all of them will die. The first child will be a girl, the other one a boy. He will be ill in his eleventh year, if he recovers, he will live healthily for 24 years, thereafter he will suffer from illness and

Manazil

will have to work hard, if he survives, he will live 58 years. His luck in buying and selling is towards the south and west his front door and the foot-end of his bed and the heads of his livestock in the stable should point towards this country. The time of his luck is September and June, also when the Moon is in the signs of Libra, Gemini, Cancer and Sagittarius, the best days of the week when he shall begin his deeds are Mercury and Venus. The lucky colours of [his] clothes are ice-grey or mixed grey, blue, white and green, horse-grey, dapple-grey and brown. The evil months are January, [Hornung], March, and July, also when the Moon is in Scorpio, Pisces, Leo, and Saturn [?]. The evil weekdays are Saturn and the Sun. The unlucky years are the 5th, 11th, 20th, 22nd, 25th, 30th, 40th, 50th, 60th.

Part two of this book includes the natal information of the mansions; complete translations of both editions are in the third part.

Choices or Elections

Choices or elections are the second important use of the lunar mansions. Here the querent seeks knowledge about what to do or not to do during the Moon's presence in a particular mansion. Some of the earliest printed publications dealing with the lunar mansions in this respect were written by Abu al-Hassan Ali Ibn Ali Ibn Abi al-Rijal, who was also known by the Latinised versions of his name Haly Abenragel, or Haly Albohazen. Abenragel was an Arab astrologer who lived between around 980 and 1037. He was court astrologer to the Tunisian Prince al-Mu'izz Ibn Badis, and his best-known treatise, the *Complete Book on the Judgment of the Stars*, was one of the works translated by scholars working for King Alfonso X of Castile. Later it became an important source of mediaeval astrology in Renaissance Europe and was eventually printed under the title of *Praeclarissimus liber completes in judicious astrorum*, in Venedig, 1485, by Erhard Ratdolt. Abenragel writes extensively on the lunar mansions and he is nearly exclusively dealing with election themes when he is giving topics for the 28 mansions, be that in respect to Hellenistic sources, or Indian lore. His Hellenistic source was Dorotheus of Sidon, an astrologer, who lived in the first century AD. Nearly nothing is known about Dorotheus himself. According to Firmicus Maternus, a Roman Latin writer and astrologer who lived between 306 and 337 AD, Dorotheus was a native of the city of Sidon. It is likely that he lived and worked in Alexandria. He wrote a didactic poem on astrology, which is known as the *Pentateuch*, or as *Carmen astrologicum*. The English translation of this textbook comes from an Arabic translation which is itself a translation of a Persian translation from the original Greek. It is said that Dorotheus also wrote down a complete system of lunar mansions, which is attributed to him until this day. This was already refuted by Haly Abenragel, who claimed that Doronius was the original author. This statement may be misleading though, as Doronius is possibly a misnomer for Dorotheus of Sidon. In more recent times, Wilhelm and Hans Georg Gundel have shown that, apart from *Carmen*, anything said to be written by Dorotheus, including his text on the lunar mansions was not his own work and that only the didactic poem can be attributed to him (Gundel/Gundel: *Astrologumena. Die Astrologische Literatur in der Antike und ihre Geschichte.* Franz Steiner Verlag, Wiesbaden 1966, p119).

Talismans

Another very important use of the lunar mansions is the creation of talismans. Although loosely related to astrological choices or elections, I tend to treat this as an entirely different subject. The most important information about lunar mansion talismans has been transmitted into the West via one of the particularly notorious texts, generally referred to as *Picatrix*. It is the English (or German) translation of a medieval Latin textbook of astral magic which has never been in print until the 20th century. The Arabic text was published in 1933 by Hellmut Ritter. In 1962 Martin Plessner and Hellmut Ritter published their German translation from the Arabic, and Professor David Pingree, published a critical edition of the Latin Picatrix in 1986. The Latin version itself is a translation of the Arabic *Ghāyat al- Hakīm* (The Goal of the Wise), written in the first half of the 11th century. There has been and still is some controversy about the authorship. The Arab historian Ibn Khaldūn (1332-1406) thought the astronomer and mathematician Maslama al-Majriti to be the author, but this has been refuted in recent times. The author is now believed to be Quasim al-Qurtubī, an Andalusian hadīth scholar who lived between 905 and 964. The word "Picatrix" was thought to be the name of the book's original author. In the Latin text's prologue, we read that it is the name of "one wise philosopher, the noble and honoured Picatrix" who "compiled this tome from over 200 books of philosophy and then named it after himself". Sometimes it is also believed to be an attempt to attribute the work to Hippocrates. Picatrix was also the title most commonly known to Western astrologers and magicians. In its prologue, Picatrix states that King Alfonso the X of Castille had the original Arabic text translated into Spanish. This happened at some point between 1256 and 1258. Only a short fragment of the Spanish translation survives and it is not known how long it took for the Spanish version to be translated into Latin. It was this Latin version that was shared widely throughout Europe from the middle of the 15th century. We can see this from manuscripts extant in the libraries of Paris, London, Oxford, Hamburg, and Prague. Marsilio Ficino (1433-1499) read Picatrix and based some of his theories of astral magic on it, which found their way into his *De vita coelitus comparanda*. His contemporary, the Christian Kabbalist Pico della Mirandola (1463-1494) also owned a handwritten copy. In Germany, the Benedictine abbot of Spanheim, Johannes Trithemius (1462-1516) and his pupil, the famous Heinrich Cornelius Agrippa von Nettesheim (1486-1535) owned copies. In his well-known study of occult philosophy, *De occulta philosophia libri tres*, which dealt with elemental, celestial and intellectual magic, Agrippa reproduced much of the information he found in Picatrix. His work was later used by many occultists, and even as late as 1801, Francis Barrett, F.R.C. used Agrippa's lunar mansion descriptions in his book *The Magus or Celestial Intelligencer*. A transcript of the relevant portion is also included in Part three.

Although read and widely used during the Renaissance, Picatrix was vehemently criticised by many. Already in 1456, Johannes Hartlieb wrote in his *Puch aller verpoten kunst, ungelaubens und der zaubrey* (book on all forbidden arts, superstition, and sorcery) that Picatrix was the most complete book in the art of necromancy he had ever seen and that it had led an outstanding number of people into everlasting damnation. Hartlieb wrote this compilation for the Margrave Johann of Brandenburg-Kulmbach (1403-1464), whose physician he was. He warned the margrave to particularly beware of Picatrix, because amongst its sweet work was mixed some bitter poison! Knowing that the Margrave's byname was 'the alchemist' this particular interest of his may not come as a total surprise. Still, so famous was this book, that even the Holy Roman Emperor Maximilian I had two copies in his library. The manuscript which is now held in the British Library was at one time owned by Simon Forman (1552-1611), the infamous Elizabethan astrologer, occultist, and herbalist. Sir Richard Napier (1559-1634), another prominent English astrologer and medical practitioner, who was Forman's pupil, inherited it. Later, the manuscript came into the possession of the astrologer William Lilly (1602-1681) and ended up in Elias Ashmole's collection. Some sources suggest that Ashmole and Lilly swapped copies. There is some confusion about this though, as Ashmole wrote on 5 January 1648: "This evening I delivered to Mr. Lilly Picatrix and was reconciled with him." (MSAshm. 1136, f.184). This seems to have been a peace offering and does not suggest a straight swap. Lauren Kassell, on the other hand, writes in her book *The Economy of Magic in Early Modern England*: "… when he [Ashmole] and Lilly swapped their copies of the Picatrix, an Arabic book of magic" (p55).

It must be noted that in both, the Latin and the Arabic version of the book, there is one whole chapter (Book 1, chapter 4) dealing with the construction of talismans for each of the mansions. Only in the Latin version, there is a second chapter (Book IV, chapter 9) on talismans, or images, which is omitted from the Arabic version. Translations of the relevant portions from the German and the Latin editions are included in Part two.

Weather

There has always been a strong connection between the lunar mansions and weather forecasting, which can be traced back to the anwa tradition. We know of this from source material by ibn-Ezra, al-Kindi, and Jafar Indus. The following is a simplified table from Steinschneider's paper *Über die Mondstationen*. There are 19 mansions, divided into 3 groups, showing rainy, dry, and wet mansions. The remaining mansions seemed to be classed as mediocre, and were therefore not included.

Peter Stockinger

The Qualities of the Lunar Mansions

1. The 10 Rainy Ones

	Jafar/ Bonatti	Al-Kindi	Ibn Ezra
Aldebaran	IV	IV	IV
[Aldirahan]	VII	VII	VII
Algebathan	X	X	X
Algerpha	XII	XII	XII
Alzafra (Algaphata)	XV	XV	XV
Abgebenen	XVI	XVI	XVI
Algard	(XVIII?)	XVIII (XVII)	XVII
Allebra	(XIX)	XIX	XIX
Alnatha	XX	XX	XXI
Alelelach (Alesthadebe)	(XXII?) XXI	XXII	XXII
Alpharga		XVII	XXVII

Manazil

2. The 6 Dry Ones

	Jafar/Bonatti	Al-Kindi	Ibn Ezra
Albotharia	II	II	II
Almuster	V	V	V
Althaif	IX (?)	IX	IX
Altherp	IX (?)	IX	IX
		XVII (XVII)	XVIII
	XVIII	XXIV	
Alesadadabia	XXV	XXV	XXV
Garf alaul	XXVI	XXVI	XXVI

3. The 3 Wet Ones

	Jafar/Bonatti	Al-Kindi	Ibn Ezra
Altoraia	III (VI)	VI	V (VI)
Althimeth	XIV	XIV	XIV
Aleschadebe	XXIV (XXIII)	XXIV	XXIV

Peter Stockinger

What follows, are short biographies of the authors, whose works build the foundation of lunar mansion lore, in chronological order. This timeline begins with al-Biruni, who lived in the 10th Century, in what is now Uzbekistan, and ends with the German Ludwig Ideler, born in 1766.

Abu Rayhan Al-Biruni

The Iranian scholar and polymath Abu Rayhan Al-Biruni (973-1048?) is one of the most important contributors to our understanding of the lunar mansions. He was born in the suburb (Bīrūn, hence the name al-Biruni - of the suburb) of Kath, the capital of the Afrighid dynasty of Khwarezm (Chorasmia) in Central Asia (now part of the autonomous republic of Karakalpakstan in the northwest of Uzbekistan). It is known that al-Biruni wrote 146 books and 95 of those are devoted to astronomy, mathematics, and related subjects. Two of his works are of particular interest to us. These are the *Chronology of Ancient Nations,* written in the year 1000 A.D., and the *Book of Instructions in the Elements of the Art of Astrology*, written in 1029 A.D. In the *Chronology*, al-Biruni gives in-depth explanations how the Arabs worked with the lunar mansions. He also provides detailed information about the astronomical background and the etymology of the 28 individual mansions. The relevant part of the *Book of Instructions* lists the mansions and provides additional information, not found in the *Chronology*. It must be stated that some of the information al-Biruni provides is contradictory. On the one hand, he seemingly approves of the introduction and subsequent use of the tropical mansions (beginning with 0* Aries in the tropical zodiac, rather than using the mansion's determinant fixed stars). In another instance, he writes about a man who associated meteorological changes with the mansions related to the fixed stars. Transcripts of both texts are provided in the third part of this book.

Manazil

Abu Yusuf Al-Kindi

Abu Yusuf al-Kindi (c.796 - 873) who was hailed as the "Philosopher of the Arabs", was polymath, philosopher, astrologer, and musician who was born in Kufa and educated in Baghdad. He wrote hundreds of books on wide ranging subjects, like metaphysics, medicine, logic, philosophy, optics, and on meteorology, astronomy, and astrology. Some of his best-known works on astrology are *De iudiciis astrorum* (The Judgment of the Stars), and *De pluvial, imbribus et ventis, ac aeris mutatione* (Rains, storms, and winds, and Change in the Air). There is also another text, *On the causes [of the forces] attributed to the higher bodies which indicate the origin of rains, by the decree of God,* wherein al-Kindi introduces and lists the lunar mansions in connection with weather prediction.

Jafar Indus

Some scholars believe that Jafar could be identical with Abū Ma'shar (787 - 886) or it could be Abu Ja'far al-Khazin (ca. 900 - 961-971), a mathematician and astronomer, born in Khorasan. Charles Burnett compared texts written by Abū Ma'shar and Jafar Indus and concluded from the textual evidence that the two are not identical.

Muhyiddin Ibn 'Arabi

Compared to what we have seen so far, the philosopher and Sufi Master, Muhyiddin Ibn 'Arabi (1165 A.D. - 1240 A.D.) followed a very different path in his use of the lunar mansions. His approach can be understood as an influential system of correspondences, based on magical symbolism, rather than astrology. Ibn 'Arabi, who was born in Murcia, in the Arab Spain of Al-Andalus, used the lunar mansions as an attempt to organise a chain of being from the uncreated first cause through different levels of celestial manifestation to man.

Titus Burckhardt writes in his *Mystical Astrology According to Ibn 'Arabi,* Fons Vitae, Louisville, 2001, that:

> "Islamic esotericism establishes a correspondence between the 28 mansions of the Moon and the 28 letters or sounds of the sacred language. 'It is not like people think,' - says Muhyiddin Ibn' Arabi, - 'that the mansions of the Moon represent the models of the letters; it is the 28 sounds which determine the lunar mansions." These sounds represent in fact the microcosmic and human expression of the essential determinations of the Divine Breath, which is itself the prime motivation of cosmic cycles. "

Guido Bonatti

Guido Bonatti, whose date of birth and death are unknown, was an Italian astrologer and mathematician. It is believed that he was born around 1207 and died between 1296 and 1300. Historical sources claim that he was the best-known astrologer of the 13th century. He was the advisor of the Holy Roman Emperor, Frederick II and served the governments of Siena, Florence, and Forli. So great was his fame and reputation, that Dante mentions him in his *Divine Comedy*. He confines him to hell, in the eighth Circle, fourth Ring, to be precise. This is where the Fortune Tellers and Diviners are sent to. There, the souls of those who have tried to predict the future are placed, with their heads turned around by 180 degrees, their eyes constantly blinded by tears, which makes it impossible for them to see the future.

Manazil

Bonatti's most celebrated work is *Liber Astronomiae* (The Book of Astronomy). Compiled over 700 years ago, it was and still is one of the most influential works of traditional astrology. The first printed edition was done by Erhard Ratdolt in Augsburg, (1491), followed by the second printed edition, done by Sessa in Venice, (1506), which was followed by a third and last one, printed in Basel, (1550). In 2007, Dr. Benjamin Dykes published a new translation. In his translation, Dr. Dykes identifies many Persian and Arab sources, used by Bonatti. Among them are central authorities, like Abū Ma'shar, Al-Quabīsī, Sahl, Māshā'allāh, Jafar, and Ptolemy.

Muhammad Al-Qazwini

Another knowledgeable person who wrote about the lunar mansions was Abu Yahya Zakariya' ibn Muhammad al-Qazwini (1203–1283), a Persian physician, astronomer, and geographer. Born in Qazvin, Iran, Qazwini served as a legal expert and judge in several localities in Iran and at the city of Baghdad. He was the author of a famous cosmography titled "The Wonders of Creation". This work, was immensely popular and is still preserved today in many copies, some of which are lavishly illustrated. It was translated into his native Persian language, and later also into Turkish and German. In his cosmography, Qazwini wrote that there are always only 14 lunar mansions visible above the earth during the night, and 14 disappear underneath the earth. Every time one of them is setting, the one opposed is rising.

He knew that the Arabs called 14 of these stations "Syriac" and the other 14 were called "Yemeni". Also, the heliacal setting of a star in the west at dawn was called "nun" and the heliacal rising of the opposing one was called "nau". The setting of each star occurs after 13 days, except g'ebha (the 10th lunar mansion in Leo). Thereafter one has to add 14 days, so that the end of the setting of the 28th lunar mansion coincides with the end of the solar year. Then the matter returns to the first state at the beginning of the following year. (A full translation of the relevant portion from al-Qazwini's cosmography, is included in the appendix.

Johannes Stöffler

Johannes Stöffler (1452 - 1531) was a German astrologer, mathematician, and astronomical instrument maker. In 1522, he was elected rector of the University of Tübingen. By that time, he was already very well known for his ephemeris making, continuing the calculations of Regiomontanus. His *Elucidatio fabricae ususque astrolabii* (Explanation of the Construction and Use of the Astrolabe) became a standard work and was published in 16 editions until 1620. In 2007 the first English edition was published. His most famous students were the cosmographer Sebastian Münster, and Martin Luther's great friend, Philip Melanchton, the man who was awarded the honorary title of "Praeceptor Germanie" (Teacher of Germany). We are interested in Stöffler's list of the lunar mansions, which he published in at least two different works. The first one is an almanac he published together with the priest and astronomer Jakob Pflaum of Ulm, entitled *Almanach nova plurimis annis venturis inservientia*, Ulm 1499. The almanac had an extremely wide circulation. It was printed in seven further editions within the first 25 years of its printing. The eighth edition, published in 1522 covering the years 1523 - 1531, was the only edition printed by Lucantonio Giunta, one of Venice's first printers. The almanac received a huge amount of attention, not at least because it contained data of sixteen planetary con-junctions in Pisces during February 1524, predicting a period of unprecedented change and unrest. We find the lunar mansions again in Stöffler's *Ephemeridum opus ab anno 1532 - 1551*, Tübingen, Hulden Morhart 1531. They were eventually translated into German and published in the magazine *Astrologische Rundschau* 3.4 1922 (Dezember-Januar, 12 Jhg). There is also one extant manuscript, known as Beinecke MS 558, which contains an English translation of Stöffler's judgment upon the 28 mansions of the moon. It is held in the Beinecke Rare Book & Manuscript Library, the rare book library and literary archive of the Yale University Library in New Haven, Connecticut. MS 558 is a collection of mainly astrological texts, compiled in England in the 16th century. Compared to the original Latin text, the list in MS 558 omits some details. The mansions' names are missing, and their positions are only given in whole degrees, omitting the minutes included in the original. See Appendix for transcript of relevant portion in MS 558

Johannes Schöner

Johannes Schöner (1477 - 1547) was a German polymath. He was a priest, astrologer, cosmographer, cartographer, geographer, mathematician, and scientific instrument maker. During his life, he enjoyed a Europe-wide reputation as an instrument maker and as one of the continent's leading astrologers. Today he is mainly remembered for playing a part in the events that led up to the publishing of Copernicus's *De revolutionibus orbium coelestium* in 1543. We are mainly interested in two of Schöner's works. The first one is his *Opusculum astrologicum*, printed by Petreius in Nürnberg, 1539. Therein he includes a table of the 28 lunar mansions for the year 1518. The table comprises Latin names of the mansions' determinant fixed stars, the mansions' zodiacal positions and nature (wet/dry/temperate, fortunate/unfortunate). The second work, *Ein nutzlichs Büchlein viler bewerter Ertzney* (A useful booklet of many proven medicines), published in 1528, lists the 28 mansions, their zodiacal positions, their nature (wet/dry/temperate) and the individual choices or elections connected with each of the mansions. The Bavarian State Library holds a book with the title *Planeten Buch aus Grund natürlicher Astrologey* (Planet book based on natural astrology), published in Straubing, 1596, which includes a chapter on the 28 lunar mansions. Although the book has no author is is clearly visible that the section on the mansions is directly copied from Schöner's *Nutzlichs Büchlein*. Both texts are included in Part three.

Agrippa von Nettesheim

Heinrich Cornelius Agrippa von Nettesheim (1486 – 1535) was a German Renaissance polymath. He also was a theologian, physician, and occult writer. Agrippa's academic career began in 1509, when his lectures received attention an he received a doctorate in theology because of them. In the winter of 1509/10, he began to study with Johannes Trithemius at Würzburg. Shortly after, he dedicated the first draft of what would become *De occulta philosophia* to Trithemius. This first draft drew heavily on works by Marsilio Ficino, Pliny, and Pico Della Mirandola. It took until 1531 for the first edition of Book 1 of *De occulta philiosphia libri tres* (Three Books of Occult Philosophy) to appear in print in Paris, Cologne, and Antwerp. The full set of three volumes was first published in Cologne in 1533. This famous work is a significant contribution to the discussion of magic and its relationship with religion. It compiles much of the written occult knowledge of the time, including elemental and celestial magic, numerology, astrology, and cabbalah. The books also include material on the 28 lunar mansions, and we have already mentioned that both, Agrippa and Trithemius had access to one or more copies of Picatrix. There is another important point that I want to discuss here. Due to the transmission of names and lore of the lunar mansions from the Arabic, there are numerous transliterations of the mansion's names in existence. In fact, there

Manazil

are so many that it is nearly impossible to list them all. To give an example of the sheer plethora of transliterations, I have chosen to use Agrippa, because the names of the lunar mansions even differ in the different editions of his *De Occulta*. I had access to three editions, published in 1533, 1651, and 1855. These are as follows:

(Latin): Henrici Cornelii Agrippae ab Nettesheym, De occulta philosophie libri tres, Johannes Soter, Cologne, 1533

(German): Heinrich Cornelius Agrippa's von Nettesheim Magische Werke: sammt den geheimnitzvollen Schriften des Petrus von Abano, Pictorius von Villingen, Gerhard von Cremona, Abt Tritheim von Spanheim, dem Buche Arbatel, der sogenannten Heil. Geist-Kunst und verschiedenen anderen. Zweites Bändchen, Scheible, Stuttgart, 1855.

(J.F.): Three books of occult philosophy written by Henry Cornelius Agrippa of Nettesheim ... ; translated out of the Latin into the English tongue by J.F. (John French) London: Printed by R.W. for Gregory Moule ..., 1651.

The table below shows the different names of the 28 lunar mansions as printed in the Latin, German, and English editions.

Mansion	Latin	German	J.F
#1 al-Sharatan	Alnath	Alnath	Alnath
#2 al-Butain	Allothaim Albochan	Albothaim Albocham	Allothaim Albochan
#3 al-Thurayya	Achaomazone Athoraye	Achaomazone Athoraye	Achaomazon Athoray
#4 al-Dabaran	Aldebram Aldebaram Aldelamen	Aldebram Aldebaram Aldelamen	Aldebram Aldebaram Aldelamen
#5 al-Haq'a	Alchataya Albachia Albachaya	Alchataya Albachia Albachaya	Alchatay Albachay
#6 al-Han'ah	Alhanna Alchaya	Alhanna Alchaya	Alhanna Alchaya
#7 al-Dhira	Aldimiach Alarzach	Aldimiach Alarzach	Aldimiach Alarzach
#8 al-Nathrah	Alnaza Anatrachya	Alnaza Anatrachya	Alnaza Anatrachya
#9 al-Tarfa	Archaamuel Alcharph	Archaam Alcharph Achaam Alchaam	Archaam Arcabp
#10 al-Jabbah	Algelioche	Ageliache	Algelioche

Manazil

	Algebh	Aglebh	Albgebh
		Algeliache	
		Aglebh	
#11 al-Zubrah	Azobra	Azobra	Azobra
	Ardaf	Ardaf	Ardaf
#12 al-Zarfah	Al Zarpha	Al Zarpha	Al Zarpha
	Alzarpha	Alzarpha	Alzarpha
	Azarpha		Azarpha
#13 al-Awwa	Alhayre	Alhayre	Alhaire
#14 al-Simak	Achureth	Achureth	Achureth
	Arimes	Arimes	Arimes
	Arimet	Arimet	Arimet
	Azimeth	Azimeth	Azimeth
	Alhumech	Albumech	Alhumech
	Alcheymech	Alcheymech	Alcheymech
#15 al-Ghafr	Agrapha	Agrapha	Agrapha
	Algarpha	Algarpha	Algarpha
#16 al-Jubana	Azubene	Azubene	Azubene
	Ahubene	Ahubene	Ahubene
#17 Iklil al Jabhah	Alchil	Alchil	Alchil
#18 al-Kalb	Alchas	Alchas	Alchas
	Althoh	Althoh	Althoh
	Altob	Altob	Altob
#19 al-Shaulah	Allatha	Allatha	Allatha
	Achala	Achala	Achala
	Hycula	Hycula	Hycula

#20 al-Na'am	Abnahaya	Abnahaya	Abnahaya
#21 al-Baldah	Albeda Abeda Albeldach	Albeda Abeda Albeldach	Albeda Abeda Albeldach
#22 al-Sa'd al Dhabih	Zodeboluch Zandeldena Sadahacha	Zodeboluch Zandeldena Sadabecha	Zodeboluch Zandeldena Sadabacha
#23 Sa'd al Bula	Zobrach Sabadola	Zobrach Sebadola	Zobrach Zabadoia
#24 Sa'd al Su'ud	Sadabath Chadezoath Chadezoat	Sadabath Chadezoath Chadezoat	Sadabath Chadezoath Chadezoat
#25 Sa'd al Ahbiyah	Sadalabra Sadalachia	Sadalabra Sadalachia	Sadalabra Sadalachia
#26 Al-Fargh al-Mukdim	Alpharg Phtagal Mocaden	Alpharg Phtagal Mocaden	Alpharg Phtagal Mocaden
#27 al-Fargh al Thani	Alcharya Ahhalgalmoad Alhalgalmoad	Alcharya Ahhalgalmoad Alhalgalmoad	Alcharya Ahhalgalmoad Alhalgalmoad
#28 Batn al-Hut	Albotham Alchalh	Albotham Alchalh	Albotham Alchalcy

Manazil

Christian Ludwig Ideler

Christian Ludwig Ideler (1766 – 1846) was a German chronologist and astronomer. We are only interested in his work *Untersuchungen über den Ursprung und die Bedeutung der Sternnamen* (Investigation on the origin and significance of the names of stars). His book was groundbreaking at the time, and still offers valuable information today. Ideler drew on the works of al-Qazwini, Ulugh Beg, and al-Farghani, as well as those of Ptolemy, Manilius, and many others. Any relevant information is included in the second part of this book.

Peter Stockinger

Part II

The 28 Mansions of the Moon

There are twenty-eight principal parts or stars through which the fate of all are disposed and pronounced indubitably, future as well as present. Anyone may with diligence forecast goings and returnings, origins, and endings by the most agreeable aid of these horoscopes.
(London, British Library Ms. Add. 17808, fold. 85v-99v, *Mathematica summi astologi*, fol.90r)

1st Lunar Mansion Al-Sharatan, The Two Signs, The Horns of Aries

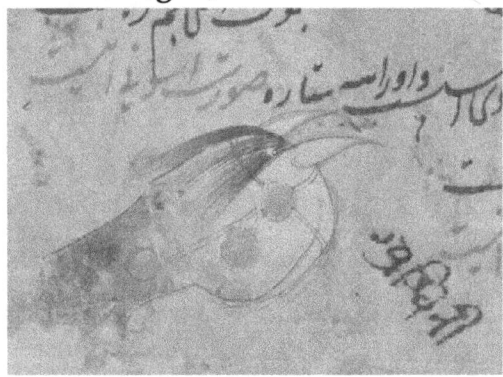

The first lunar mansion is al-Sharatan, al-Sharatain, or al-Saratan. It is also called the Two Signs, the Horns of Aries, the Two Tokens, the Two Signals, the Two Portents, the Butting, or the Butters. An alternative name for this mansion is al-

Manazil

Nath, sometimes transliterated in the West as Alnath, Alnacha, Almach, or Ilnath. Ideler connects this with alpha-Arietis, which is called el-Nathi, the Butter, or el-Nath, which means to butt. Al-Qazwini writes that this name refers to the two horns of the Ram. He possibly means the two stars in question to be alpha-Arietis, and beta-Arietis. Today, the determinant stars of this lunar mansion are thought to be Sheratan (beta-Arietis), and Mesarthim (gamma Arietis). Kunitzsch writes that, in recent times, Nath was given to beta-Tauri and eventually changed to Elnath. Also, according to Kunitzsch, the name Sheratan has only been applied in recent times. Some scholars think that it means "two" of something, which could be the "Two Signs," again referring to the first lunar mansion. Al-Qazwini states that these were the two stars indicating the beginning of the year. Ideler writes that it means "the two horns of the Ram," referring to *al-hamal*. Hamal is another name for alpha-Arietis, applied in recent times from the constellation name al-hamal (the Lamb), which was another name for Aries. [Also see Aldebaran (alpha-Tauri)]. Concerning gamma-Arietis, Ideler and Kunitzsch agree that the name Mesarthim is derived from a Latin transliteration of al-Sharatan, which Johann Bayer, a German celestial cartographer, who produced the first atlas to cover the entire celestial sphere, wrongly connected with a Hebrew word for servants.

We can also see from Chaucer's *Franklin's Tale*, written in 1374, that Alnath was not only one of the names of the first lunar mansion, but also the name of a fixed star in the constellation of the Ram. The longitude of this fixed star served as reference point, indicating the location of the first as well as all subsequent lunar mansions. In the *Franklin's Tale,* Chaucer reveals important information concerning the understanding and use of the mansions at the time. In Chaucer's tale, we learn about a book of natural magic (... a book of *"magyk natureel"*) which included the lunar mansions:

Peter Stockinger

> "...] Which book spak muchel of the operaciouns,
> Touchynge the eighte and twenty mansiouns,
> That longen to the Moone,"

We also find out about the Franklin's considerable astronomical knowledge, as well as his mathematical capabilities, as it is stated that:

> "...] He knew ful wel how fer Alnath was shove
> Fro the heed of thilke fixe Aries above
> That in the ninthe speere considered is.
> Full subtilly he calculated al this
> When he had founde his first mansioun,
> He knew the remenaunt by proporcioun".

In Chaucer's days, the cosmological model used was the Ptolemaic model, which is also known as the Heavenly- or Celestial Spheres model. It was a geocentric model, wherein the seven planetary spheres, the sphere of the fixed stars, and the sphere of the zodiac, were moving in concentric circles around the Earth. The spheres were made of a transparent material, called quintessence. The 9th sphere, which was furthest away from the Earth, was known as the *Primum Mobile*. This was the sphere that generated the primary motion, carrying the planets and the stars around the Earth. The *Primum Mobile* also contained the 12 signs of the Zodiac. Below the *Primum Mobile* was the sphere of the fixed stars, also known as the *Firmament*. This was the 8th sphere, sometimes also called the *Stellar Sphere*, containing the stars and constellations. Due to what is known to us as the Precession of the Equinoxes, over time the fixed stars and constellations change their position in regards to the signs of the Zodiac. The rate of this apparent forward movement is about 1 degree per 72 years. Chaucer's Franklin knew how

Manazil

far fixed star Alnath, which had once been located at 00* Aries, had moved. From its location at the time, he could calculate the longitudes of the remaining 27 mansions.

The tropical boundaries for the first lunar mansion are 0* Aries and 12*51'26" Aries.

The sidereal boundaries, given in tropical Zodiac longitude, precessed for 2024, are 3* Taurus and 18 Taurus. The modern longitudes (2024) of the determinant fixed stars are 4*18' Taurus for beta-Arietis (Sheratan), and 3*31' Taurus for gamma-Arietis (Mesarthim). Alpha-Arietis, which is Chaucer's Alnath, but is nowadays known as Hamal, is currently located at 8*00' Taurus. In general star lore, it is said that fixed star Sheratan is of the nature of Mars and Saturn, causing injuries, defeat, or destruction. Elsbeth Ebertin writes that World War I soldiers who had this fixed star in prominent position in their birth charts, were acting in particularly bold and daring ways. According to Ptolemy, determinant fixed star Hamal, which was originally known as Alnath, is of the nature of Mars and Saturn. It causes violence brutishness, cruelty, and premeditated crime. Also, according to Ptolemy, Mesarthim is of the nature of Saturn and Mars. The reversal of order seems to indicates a lessening of the impulsive aggressive nature of Alnath.

The are different names for the lord or angel of this mansion. Ibn al-Hatim calls him Haris; in the Picatrix we find the name to be Geriz, and Agrippa gives the name as Geniel.

According to Abenragel quoting Dorotheus, this mansion is suitable for buying tame animals, and for journeys or voyages. Also, for making arms, planting trees, cutting hair or nails, or putting on new clothes. It is unsuitable for contracting marriage, entering partnerships of any kind, or buying slaves, who will be bad, disobedient, or run away. If one was to be captured during this mansion, prison will be bad and strong. Abenragel also writes that the Indians, who called this mansion Al Sharatain, or Ilnath, say it would be good to take medicines, and pasturing livestock if the Moon is in this mansion.

Al-Biruni writes that this mansion causes discords and journeys. With Moon here, buy cattle, plant and take voyages.

The Arab Picatrix informs us that this mansion is favourable for journeys and for taking laxatives. It is a favourable time to construct talismans for travellers to protect them from dangers of travel. When the Moon is in this mansion, one can also make talismans to separate spouses or friends through alienation or enmity. Another suggestion is to create talismans to enable a slave to escape or flee wherever he wants to, and destroy the companionship of comrades. It is said that this lunar mansion is mischievous and fiery. In all operations which are aimed at doing good, let the Moon be free of bad luck planets [the malefics, Mars and Saturn] and of being combust. If, on the other hand, used for evil operations let her be burnt and malevolent.

In the Latin edition, we additionally find that, according to Pliny, Alnath is useful for destroying and depopulating. One should make an image of a black man wrapped and cloaked in a garment of hair, standing on his feet, with a spear in his right hand in the manner of a warrior. The image should be engraved on an iron ring and suffumigated with liquid storax. A seal of black wax should be made with the ring, saying:

> "You, O Geriz, kill [name] son of [name] woman swiftly and quickly! Destroy them!"

Ibn al-Hatim writes that the image connected with this mansion would be that of a black lion, wrapped in garments of hair and with a lance in his hand. Agrippa

Manazil

writes that the image was that of a black man in a garment made of hair, and girdled round, casting a small lance with his right hand. Giordano Bruno has the image as an Ethiopian in an iron chair, casting a javelin, girded with cables.

Ibn Arabi calls the mansion the Two Signs; its attribution is the First Intellect, or the Pen. Its divine attribute is Divine Essence.

Bonatti and Jafar note that this mansion is temperate and brings bad luck and misfortune.

From a natal perspective, Brenner writes in his 1559 edition that a child, male or female, born when Alnacha is rising in the first hour of the day, will have a mark near its mouth, and as well near the eyes, [and] will have a beautiful nose. It will come into possession of property but will be of cloudy mood. Whatever he wishes for or wants will happen. He will have a frightful face and will do bad things everywhere, so that he will be feared. He will also be judging over country and people, will be tall and ill in his heart, and bad tempered. It will be hard for him to get friends and nobody will love him. But if he should have a wife, he will have two children by her. Both of them will be male, all because of this star rising at the time. He will also be black and have long teeth. He shall protect himself from being burnt by fire and from being struck by iron. He is said to use the art of magic, or an evil spirit would be inside him. He has a mark on his upper thigh between his legs, or another was on both shoulders close to the sides. He is big and has pretty feet. Dignified he will be in whichever land he will travel, and he will rise higher from one to the other. He will have a good voice, rough and not uncovered. He will get to the age of 23 years. These are the attributes of a child which is born when Alnacha rises early with the Sun of the first hour. If the star rises in the second hour and a child will be born, be it female or male, it will be poor throughout its life and without property, and shall have misery and no sympathy. They shall have many children and would like to own and wear pretty clothes, like to eat spices. They will be intelligent, well brought up, and are of soft predisposition. His enemies and master will give him a lot of trouble and he will not escape this. If a child is born at a different hour than this one, be it day or night, it will be beaten to death by the might of the star. God may prevent us from that.

2nd Lunar Mansion Al-Butayn, The Belly of Aries

The second lunar Mansion is al-Butayn, the Belly of Aries. In the West, it is known as al-Botein, al-Butani, or Albocain, amongst other transliterations. Its three determinant stars are Botein (delta-Arietis), as well as epsilon-Arietis, and rho-Arietis, which are both unnamed. There is some confusion, with Al-Qazwini stating that: What is meant by that is the belly of the Ram, consisting of three dark stars (epsilon, delta, and rho) which have the triangular shape of hearthstones. Al-Biruni substituted pi for rho, others thought it to be zeta. There was also the opinion that the determinant stars of this mansion were the three dark stars of Musca, a faint triangle above the constellation of the Ram. The name of Botein is derived from Al

Manazil

Butayn, which is the diminutive of Al Batn, "The Little Belly." This mansion is also known as the Belly of Aries or the Belly of the Ram.

The tropical boundaries for the 2nd lunar mansion are 12*51'26" Aries and 25*42'52" Aries. The sidereal boundaries, given in tropical Zodiac longitude, precessed for 2024, are 18* Taurus and 00* Gemini. The modern longitudes (2024) of the determinant fixed stars are 21*11' Taurus for delta-Arietis (Botein), and 18*48' Taurus for epsilon-Arietis. Ptolemy wrote that the fixed stars in the front and back parts of Aries, which are Botein, Hamal, Sharatan, and Mesartim, can denote abnormal sexual behaviour when Venus is with them and she is afflicted by the Moon and Saturn.

The are different names for the lord or angel of this mansion. Ibn al-Hatim calls him Anakhil; in the Picatrix we find the name to be Enedil, and Agrippa gives the name as Enediel.

According to Abenragel, quoting Dorotheus, it is neither good to marry, nor to buy slaves, if the Moon is in this mansion. It is also bad for boats and prisoners, like what was said about al-Nath, above. Abenragel writes that the Indians, who called this mansion Al Butain, or Albethain, say it would be a good time to sow and to make journeys.

According to al-Biruni, this mansion is good for the finding of treasures and the retaining of captives. With Moon here, one should buy and sell but avoid the sea.

The Arab Picatrix tells us that al-Butain, is used to make talismans to dig wells and channels, and to find missing items as well as buried treasure. It is also good to make talismans for abundant growth of crops. The mansion can also be used to make talismans to prevent marriage of certain people before they come together. Also, the making of all salacious talismans is encouraged, because this mansion brings good luck and is fiery. The mansion is also used to free slaves and to tighten bonds of a prisoner if you want to torture him.

In the Latin edition, we additionally find that this mansion, which is called Albotain, can be used to destroy the buildings of households. One can also create a talisman to make one man rage against another. Or it can be used to make a prison stronger and more secure for its captives.

According to Pliny, Albotayn is for removing anger. One has to take white wax and mastic gum, blending them over a fire. Use the blend to make the image of a crowned king and suffumigate with aloe wood, saying:

> "You, O Enedil, cast away the anger of [name] from me, reconcile him towards me, and bestow my requests towards him."

Agrippa writes that one should make talismans against the wrath of the prince, and for reconciliation with him, seal in white wax and mastick the image of a crowned king, and perfume it with Lignum Aloes.

Ibn al-Hatim writes that the image connected with this mansion would be that of a crowned king. Agrippa agrees, and Giordano Bruno has the image as a king on a throne, and a man prostrate on the ground, lifting a sceptre.

Ibn-Arabi gives this mansion the name the Belly of Aries. Its attribution is the Universal Soul, or the Preserved Tablet. Its divine attribute is the One Who Calls Forth.

Bonatti and Jafar note that this mansion is temperate, and more fortunate than unfortunate.

From a natal perspective, Brenner writes in his 1559 edition:

If a child, man or woman, is born during Albokain rising, it will be happy and good. God is making him happy through riches and anybody who sees him or

Manazil

knows him will come to love him. He is quite dark and beautiful, and has a round face. Who is born during the night will be different. He is rough, with a huge beard that is strong and hard. His friends he will be talkative. He will have watery eyes and a beautiful nose, large eyebrows, white teeth, and pretty cheeks. Who is born in the evening when the cattle is taken off the fields will like to fence and argue, hate and envy his innocent neighbours. He will love other men's wives and other men will love his wife. He will be secretly molested. He will use up his estate and will nourish himself in a sinful way. He will not amass riches, but he will have to work hard to strife towards it. And he will live his life with a lot of pain. He will take on a profession, will give up on it due to an accident, and will therefore not save enough money during his lifetime to pass anything on to his children. It will cause him to take what he has not put there. Proud and red he will come to sadness. His days will be miserable or he will be dead due to magic trickery. His enemies will trouble him, honour and virtue make him sick. His face shall be marked with two signs; one is above the eyes. He will be bitten by dogs and be wounded by iron, and he will in back and lumbar region. But if one would be born in the early hours of the morning when the star is rising, then this child will be blind due to the power of Albokaim. Or white spots will cover the eyes so he will only be able to see a little bit. He will have intercourse with many women. He will have a mark on his mouth, will inherit property, and will have a temper. He will have three marks, one on the neck, the other one on the head, the third one on the [duennen?]. He will live healthily for 40 years. Then he will be weak. If he recovers, he will live 80 years or thereabouts. I tell you this according to the stars.

Peter Stockinger

3rd Lunar Mansion Al-Thurayya, The Many Little Ones, The Rainy Ones

The third lunar Mansion is al-Thurayya, the Many Little Ones, or the Rainy Ones. In the West, it is known as Alcoreia, Athoriae, and Achaomazone, amongst other transliterations. Its determinant stars are the Pleiades, also known as the Seven Sisters, a nebulous cluster, situated on the shoulder blade of the Bull. The Arabs compared the Pleiades to a bunch of grapes. In Greek mythology, they eternalise the seven daughters of Atlas and Pleione, daughter of Oceanus - Maia, Taygete, Electra, Alcyone, Asterope, Kelaino and Merope.

Determinant fixed star is Alcyone (eta Tauri), a greenish-yellow star is the brightest of the stars. Located in the centre of the cluster, Alcyone is generally taken as a reference point for the group. Al-Biruni writes that the mansion's name would be a diminutive of Tharwâ, which is originally identical with Tharwa, i.e. a collection and great number of something. Some people maintain they were called so because the rain, which is brought by their Nau,' produces Tharwa, i.e. abundance. They are also called Alnajm (i.e. the Star).

Manazil

The tropical boundaries for the 3rd lunar mansion are 25*42'52" Aries and 8*34'18" Taurus.

The sidereal boundaries, given in tropical Zodiac longitude, precessed for 2024, are 00* Gemini and 10* Gemini. The Pleiades are among the first fixed stars identified in astronomical literature. References can be found from as early as the 3rd millennium BC. At this time, Alcyone marked the vernal equinox. The star's modern longitude (2024) is 00*19' Gemini. The origin of the name Pleiades is unclear, but some scholars are of the opinion that it originates from the term meaning 'full' or 'many'. According to Ptolemy the Pleiades are of the nature of Mars and the Moon They are said to make their natives wanton, ambitious, turbulent, optimistic, and peaceful; to give many journeys and voyages, success in agriculture and through active intelligence; and to cause blindness, disgrace, and a violent death.

The are different names for the lord or angel of the mansion. Ibn al-Hatim calls him Abulsith; in the Picatrix we find the name to be Annuncia, and Agrippa gives the name as Amixiel.

According to Abenragel, Dorotheus said that this mansion was good for buying domesticated animals and for hunting, for all matters involving fire, and for doing good. It would be bad for forming a marriage union, and making partnerships, especially with those more powerful. It would also be bad for buying cattle or flocks, for planting trees, sowing, or putting on new clothes. If captured, prison would be strong and long. It also suggests that journeys by water will bring fear and danger. Abenragel writes that the Indians who called this mansion al Thurayya, or Athoraie, say it would be good for trade and for revenge on enemies when the Moon is in this mansion. It is indifferent for travel, though.

According to al-Biruni, this mansion is profitable to sailors, huntsmen, and alchemists. With the Moon here in the case of an election, plant and sow but do not marry or travel by water.

The Arab Picatrix tells us though, that when the Moon is in al-Turaija, one should make talismans for sea travellers to free them from harm. It is also used to destroy associations and cooperatives, as well as to loosen ties and chains of prisoners. Sometimes one can create talismans for success of alchemical operations, the handling of fire, for hunting, and to cause love between married couple. It is also useful to harm sheep, cattle, and slaves, so they will be lost by their master. Reason is because this mansion is lucky but also partially unlucky.

The Latin edition recommends that in this mansion, which is called Azoraya, to make talismans for sailors at sea so that they may return safely. It is also useful to reinforce prison cells, and to accomplish works of alchemy. One can also carry out any work done with fire, and for hunting expeditions on land. This mansion is also good to create affection between husband and wife.

According to Pliny, Azoraye is for the acquisition off all good things. One should make the figure of a seated woman dressed in clothes, holding her right hand above her head. Suffumigate with musk, camphor, mastic gum, and aromatic. Say:

"O Annuncia, make [request the good you desire to do] to happen"

Make this figure on a silver ring whose flat part should be a square table and worn on your finger.

Ibn al-Hatim writes that the image connected with this mansion would be that of a clothed girl, putting her right hand on her head. Agrippa generally agrees with the Picatrix, but adds to seal the talisman, and perfume it with musk, camphor, and calamus aromatics [aromatic oils]. It gives happy fortune and every good thing.

Manazil

Giordano Bruno has a more detailed image, showing a woman dressed in finery, sitting in a chair, her right hand raised over her head, entwined in her flowing hair.

Ibn-Arabi gives this mansion the name the Many Little Ones. Its attribution is Universal Nature. Its divine attribute is called the Interior.

Bonatti and Jafar note that this mansion is wet, unlucky, and unfortunate.

From a natal perspective, Brenner writes in his 1559 edition:

> If Alcoreia is rising at the birth of a child, it will be a great thinker, much loved, with grey hair and dog eyes. But if the star is rising with the Sun and in the seventh hour the planet Mars is also rising, who is tempting some to do evil, and a child is born, be it man or woman, they will experience much in their youth and will have much work to do. They will be poor in old age and will have four wives, many children, and he will be a fine fellow when it comes to play and companionship. But if this star is rising in the evening when it gets dark and a child will be born, it will have enough on its table throughout its entire life. It will have a small head and a big nose. What he purchases in foreign lands will not last long. He will live 54 years, and nourish himself. Thereafter he will get seriously ill; if he will recover, he will live 80 years.

4th Lunar Mansion Al-Dabaran, The Follower, The Head or Eye of Taurus

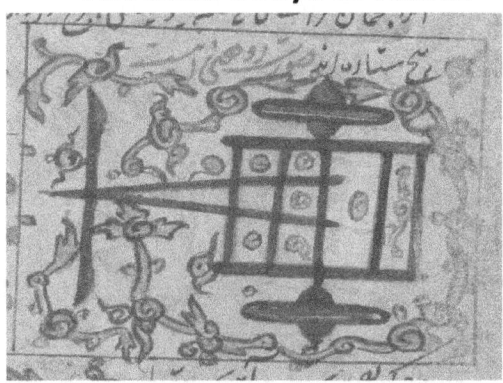

The 4th lunar mansion is al-Dabaran, also Aldebaran, or Aldebram, amongst many other transliterations. It is also known as the Follower, or the Head or Eye of Taurus. Al-Biruni writes that this mansion would also be called Alfanik, which is a great camel-stallion, not used for riding. It is thought that this mansion is called the Follower because of its determinant fixed star Aldebaran (alpha Tauri), who is following the Pleiades. Alternatively, it could be the name for all the Hyades, following after the Pleiades, who were the determinant stars of the 3rd lunar mansion. Kunitzsch writes that Aldebaran would be one of the oldest Arabic star names applied in the West (since the 10th century).

The tropical boundaries for the 4th lunar mansion are 8*34'18" Taurus and 21*25'44" Taurus.

The sidereal boundaries, given in tropical Zodiac longitude, precessed for 2024, are 10* Gemini and 24* Gemini. The modern longitude (2024) of the determinant fixed star Aldebaran is 10*07' Gemini. This fixed star is known as the bright right, or southern eye in the constellation of Taurus Ptolemy named it Lampauras, the torch. Ideler lists the names of this fixed star as *el-debaran, Ain el-thaur,* the bull's eye, *Tali el-nedschm*, the one following the Pleiades, *Hhadi el-nedschm*, herder of the Pleiades, and *el-fenik*, the large camel, compared to the other, surrounding stars belonging to the Hyades. These are called el-Kilas, the small camels.

Aldebaran is also one of the so-called Royal Stars, which, in the past, marked the two Equinoxes and two Solstices. Aldebaran was marking the 00* Aries point in 3044 BC. For more about the Royal Stars, see lunar mansions 10 and 18.

Ptolemy writes that Aldebaran is of the nature of Mars, but Alvidas states that it would be similar to Mercury, Mars, and Jupiter conjoined. It is supposed to give honour, eloquence, steadfastness, intelligence, integrity, courage, and popularity. Public honours, as well as wealth through others, and a gain of power are also attributed. The caveat is that the benefits are seldom long lasting. On the downside, there is also a danger of violence or sickness.

The are different names for the lord or angel of this mansion. Ibn al-Hatim calls him Iswawis; in the Picatrix we find the name to be Assarez, and Agrippa gives the name as Azariel.

According to Abenragel, Dorotheus said that this mansion was good to build a house, which will be solid. It is good for building in general, to dig a ditch, to buy slaves who will be loyal and honest, and to buy livestock. It is also good to be with kings and lords, for receiving power or honours. It is bad to contract marriage, since woman will prefer another, or to enter partnerships, especially with those more powerful. Voyages will involve big waves. If captured, the captivity will be long but, if captured for skills, the captive will be released through goodwill. Abenragel writes that the Indians, who called the mansion al Dabaran, or Addauennam, say it would be good for sowing, for putting on new clothes, and for receiving women and feminine things. It would also be good for demolishing a building or starting a new one, for making a journey, except for the third part of day.

According to al-Biruni, the mansion causes the destruction and hindrances of buildings, fountains, wells, gold mines, the flight of creeping things, and begetting of discord. With the Moon in this mansion, it is good to pursue business, travel, marry and take medicine.

The Arab Picatrix recommends to make talismans to harm a city, to quash hope of continuation or the good state of a building, to harm young plants, to keep a master's slaves, and to split up or separate married couples. Also to make talismans that will bring adversaries to well-diggers or people who seek for hidden treasures. It is also used to make talismans that will cause wreck and ruin, or to banish snakes and scorpions.

The Latin Picatrix tells us that in this mansion, which is called Aldebaran, to create a talisman to condemn a city or a village or some building one would want to destroy. It is also used to make a master abhor his slave, to instils discord between a husband and his wife, and to contaminate wells and springs. It is also used to find buried treasures, or to kill or bind all kinds of reptiles or poisonous animals.

According to Pliny, Aldebaran is used to create enmity. One should take red wax, shaping from it the image of an armed soldier who is riding a horse, holding a serpent in his right hand. Suffumigate with red myrrh and storax and say:

> "You, O Assarez, make it so for me, and fulfil my request." Asking for animosity, division, and ill will from the pertinent people.

Manazil

Ibn al-Hatim agrees with the Picatrix, and adds that the talisman should be buried in the house of the one whom you wish; she will be infatuated. Giordano Bruno has a fuller description of the image. According to him it shows a knight riding a horse, holding a snake in his right hand, pulling a black dog along with his left.

Ibn-Arabi's attribution for this mansion, he calls al Dabaran, or the Follower is Universal Substance, or prima materia. The Divine Attribute is called the Last.

Bonatti and Jafar note that this mansion is wet, unlucky, and unfortunate.

From a natal perspective, Brenner writes in his 1559 edition:

> A child that is born during Aldaboran rising likes to laugh and is red, rich and will be angry with his parents. He shall have many duties and make a living from them. He will bequeath everything to one of his friends and only few thoughts shall confuse him throughout his life. He shall love his wife like his own body. He shall not like to eat and drink and shall beckon to two wives, and find goods beneath the earth. But if it rises during the night and a child will be born, it will be as quiet as a lazy woman and will live under its own roof, and will not travel anywhere where he is allowed to travel. And if Aldaboran is rising in any hour and somebody will be born, he shall be poor and an animal will bite him. Many coughs come out of his chest. He is angry and afraid, and he will be wounded by iron. Rarely or not at all shall he be happy and he will never be lucky. A son will hurt him, he will break a bone, he will die in a foreign country and nobody will be there to bury him. When he is 40 years old, he will become ill. If he recovers, he will be 20 years old.

Thereafter, he will be ill again; if he recovers, he will live 48 years, then he will be ill again and if he survives, he will get to the age of 88.

5th Lunar Mansion Al-Haq'a, The White Spot

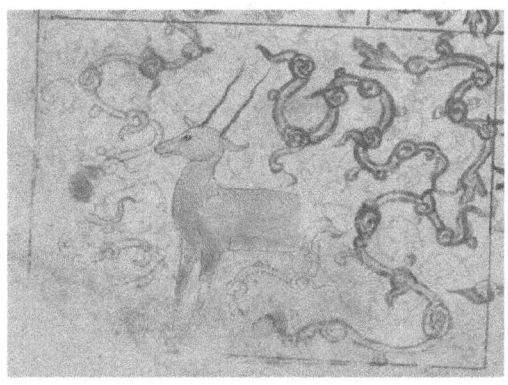

The 5th lunar mansion is called al-Haq'a, the White Spot, or Circle of Hair (on a horse). Transliterations are Alhathaya, Albachaia, Aluxer and Almusin, amongst others. Determinant stars of this mansion are lambda-, phi1-, and phi2 Orionis. Ideler wrote that the constellation of Orion was known to the Arabs as *el-dschebbar*, the Giant. This is a man, girded with a sword, carrying a staff. The three stars on his face are called *el-hek'a*, which resembles the name of the 5th lunar mansion. Kunitzsch, on the other hand, wrote that the asterism *al-jauza'* was a feminine figure which represented Orion. It corresponded to what was known to be Gemini in other cultures. Therefore, the Arabs used the name for both, Orion and Gemini. This led to some confusion regarding star names between the two constellations. The names for lambda Orionis are an example for this confusion. Meissa, one name commonly used for lambda Orionis, comes from the Arabic *al-*

maisian, for gamma-, or xi Gemini. Kunitzsch wrote that it could mean "the Sparkling One" or "the Proudly Marching One" but gamma-, and xi Gemini are stars of the 6th lunar mansion, al-Han'a. Due to a confusion of the 5th and the 6th mansion, Meissa was wrongly applied to lambda Orionis. In fact, lambda Orionis should really be Heka, from *al-haq'a*, which is the Circle of Hair on the side, foot, or neck of a Horse, comprising lambda-, phi1-, and phi2 Orionis.

The tropical boundaries for the fifth lunar mansion are 21*25'44" Taurus and 4*17'10" Gemini. The sidereal boundaries, given in tropical Zodiac longitude, precessed for 2024, are 24* Gemini and 9* Cancer. The modern longitude (2024) of the determinant fixed star lambda Orionis (Heka/Meissa) is 24*02' Gemini.

Manilius wrote about Orion:

"Near neighbour to the Twins (Gemini), Orion may be seen stretching his arms over a vast expanse of sky and rising to the stars with no less huge a stride. A single light marks each of his shining shoulders, and three aslant trace the downward line of his sword: but three mark Orion's head, which is imbedded in high heaven with his countenance remote. It is Orion who leads the constellations as they speed over the full circuit of heaven." [Manilius: *Astronomica*, 1st century AD, p35]

> "Orion will fashion alert minds and agile bodies, souls prompt to respond to duty's call, and hearts which press on with unflagging energy in spite of every trial. A son of Orion's will be worth a multitude and will seem to dwell in every quarter of the city; flying from door to door with the one word of morning greeting, he will enjoy the friendship of all." [Manilius: *Astronomica*, 1st century AD, p305]

Peter Stockinger

The are different names for the lord or angel of this mansion. Ibn al-Hatim calls him Iqbal; in the Picatrix we find the name to be Cabil, and Agrippa gives the name as Gabiel.

According to Abenragel, Dorotheus said that this mansion was good for buying slaves who will be good and loyal. It is also good for building, for travel by water, for washing the head, indeed general washing, and for hair cutting. It is bad for partnerships. If captured, imprisonment will be long, unless captured for skills, when the captive will escape. Abenragel writes that the Indians, who called this mansion al Hak'ah, or Alhathayasay, say it would be good for contracting marriage, for putting boys to study laws, scriptures, or writing. Also, for making medicines, or for making a journey.

According to al-Biruni, the mansion helps the return from a journey, the instruction of scholars, building. It also gives health and goodwill. With the Moon here, begin war but do not sow or undertake any good.

In the Arab Picatrix we are informed to make talismans to guarantee that boys turn out well and make progress in being taught Islam, in writing, and their skills. Also to make talismans for safety and welfare of travellers, and the fast progress of journeys by sea. Furthermore, to make talismans to secure buildings, and to destroy cooperatives. This is because this mansion also partakes in misfortune. Furthermore, make talismans to establish concord and harmony between married couples, when the Moon and the Ascendant are in a human sign. Make sure that it is under good circumstances, free from the malefics and from combustion. (Human signs are: Gemini, Virgo, Libra, Sagittarius, and Aquarius).

The Latin Picatrix, who calls this mansion Almices, tells us to make talismans for children who are learning a craft or a profession, also to make them to protect those who are on journeys, so they may return quickly and to protect those travelling by sea. One can also make talismans to improve buildings, or to destroy the alliance of two people. Furthermore, make talismans to instil affection between a husband and his wife.

According to Pliny, Almizen (al-Haq'a) allows you to be well received by kings and by officials. Make a silver sigil on which the head of a man without a body should be sculpted. Write the name of the Lord of this mansion on this head, and write your request on the sigil. Suffumigate with sandalwood and say:

> "You, O Cabil, make it so for me and fulfil my request, namely that kings and officials should receive me well and in the best possible manner."

Place this sigil under your head when you go to sleep, and keep your desire in your mind. You will receive the answer you seek.

Ibn al-Hatim writes that the image should be a head without a body, with a large crown on it. He also writes that the talisman should have the name of the king engraved on his throat. It should be kept on your person. He continues that:

> "You will not enter into the presence of kings and nobles but that your desire will be satisfied and the evil (caused by) your enemy will be postponed."

Giordano Bruno has a different description of the image. According to him, it shows a silver prince on his throne, having a rod in his right hand and embracing a girl with his left.

Ibn-Arabi's attribution for this mansion, which he calls the White Spot, is called Universal Body. The Divine Attribute is called the Manifest.

Bonatti and Jafar note that this mansion is wet, lucky, and fortunate.

From a natal perspective, Brenner writes in his 1559 edition:

A child being born during Almusin rising will have a big forehead and will be bald and without hair, and will have lots of strange thoughts. But if he is born during the night, he will have to live with a lack of power, in misery and toilsomeness. Many women will surround him, he will have a sign on one arm and as well on the [?dien]. He will be wounded by a stone, hurt by iron, and a dog will bite him. Women will love him and find him and he will get two more signs, one on his heart, and one on his arm. He will break a bone, or fire will burn him. He shall be lucky with women and beasts, but it will take time to give his wife a child. He will live healthily for 35 years. Thereafter he will become ill; if he recovers, he will get to 60 years.

6th Lunar Mansion Al-Han'ah, The Mark

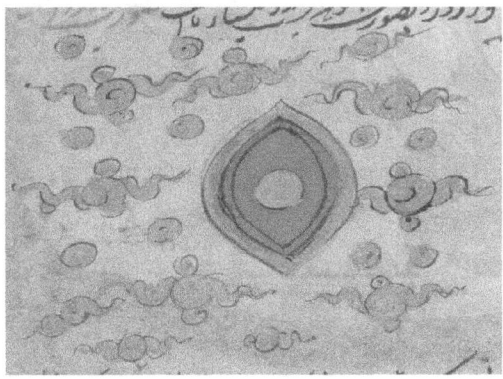

The 6th lunar mansion is called al-Han'ah, the Mark, the Brand, or the Scar. Agrippa called this mansion the Little Star of Great Light. Alhana, Atabuen, Alchaia, or Athaya are some of the many transliterations this mansion was given in the West. The mansion comprises two determinant stars, gamma Gemini (Alhena), and xi Gemini (Alzirr), at the feet of Pollux the Eastern Twin in the constellation of the Twins. Al-Qazwini writes that one of them is called *ezzirr*, (button), the other one *elmaisan* (one who walks proudly). Others claim that the mansion has five determinant stars, gamma (Alhena), mu (Tejat Posterior), nu (nu), eta (Propus), and xi (Alzirr). Al Biruni translated the name of the mansion as Winding, as if the stars of this station were winding around each other, or curving from the central star. We have already discussed that one of the names for the 5th mansion was *el-tehhai*, which, by mistake, was allocated to the feet of the Twins. Ideler thinks that after the mix-up, the name changed to *el-nuhattai*. It is likely that, due to the similarity of the names of the 5th and 6th mansions, *al-ha'qa*, and *al-han'ah,* many errors have been made.

The tropical boundaries for the 6th lunar mansion are 4*17'10'' Gemini and 17*08'34'' Gemini. The sidereal boundaries, given in tropical Zodiac longitude, precessed for 2024, are 9* Cancer and 20* Cancer. The modern longitude (2024) of the determinant fixed star gamma Gemini (Alhena) is 9*26' Cancer. Xi Gemini's (Alzirr) longitude is 11*32' Cancer. Gamma Gemini (Alhena) is a brilliant white star, located at the left foot of Pollux, and xi Gemini (Alzirr) is a star on his right foot. Alhena (or *al-Han'ah*) is usually translated as a Brand, or Mark, on the right side of a camel's, or horse's neck. According to Ptolemy, Alhena is of the nature of Mercury and Venus. Alvidas gives Moon and Venus instead. It is thought to bestow imminence in art, but can also denote an affinity to accidents of the feet. Elsbeth Ebertin wrote that Alhena supposedly has a Venusian nature, combined with a Jupiterian influence. This bestows an artistic inclination, but also an interest in the sciences.

The are different names for the lord or angel of this mansion. Ibn al-Hatim calls him Anari; in the Picatrix we find the name to be Nedeyrahe, and Agrippa gives the name as Dirachiel.

Peter Stockinger

According to Abenragel, Dorotheus said that this mansion was good for partnerships and ventures. It also causes that associates will agree and be honest and loyal. It is good for hunting, for journeys by water, but may cause delays. The mansion is bad for taking medicine and for treating wounds. New clothes put on at the time the mansion is active will soon tear. If captured, release takes place within three days. If not, expect very long imprisonment. Abenragel writes that the Indians, who called this mansion al Han'ah, Alhana, or Atabuen, say it would be good for kings to declare war, enrolment of armies and cavalry, as well as for knights seeking better pay. It is also good for the successful siege of a city, or for smiting enemies and evildoers. It is bad for sowing, for seeking a loan, or for burial.

According to al-Biruni, the mansion is favourable for hunting, besieging towns, and the revenge of princes. It can be used to destroy harvests and fruits, and can hinder the operation of a physician. With the Moon here, plough, sow, but do not travel.

The Arab Picatrix tells us to make talismans to besiege a city or destroy it. It is also used to punish kings and it can bring all kinds of problems and evil upon your enemies. One can also make talismans to destroy seeds, deposits, or all sorts of goods that have been entrusted to somebody for safekeeping. The mansion is also useful to establish a good relationship between comrades, was well as for luck with hunting. Lastly, one can make talismans to counteract effects of medicines taken.

The Latin edition suggests to make talismans, in this mansion called Atahya, to destroy cities or even whole villages, to position armies around them, and to enable the king's enemies to exact revenge. It is also used to destroy harvests, as well as trees. Also, to spark friendship between two associates, and to improve hunting. Lastly, it is used to curse medicines so that they will fail to work.

Manazil

According to Pliny, Achaya is used to create love between two people. Make two white wax images embracing each other, wrap them in white silk and suffumigate with aloe wood and amber, and say:

> "You, O Nedeyrahe, join (name) and (name), and place between them friendship and love."

Ibn al-Hatim agrees with the Picatrix, but also writes that the talisman should be suffumigated with camphor and damp aloe-wood. Giordano Bruno has a different description of the image. According to him it shows two men in armour, bareheaded, casting down their swords and embracing each other.

Ibn-Arabi's attribution for this mansion, which he calls the Mark, is Form. The Divine Attribute is called the Wise.

Bonatti and Jafar note that the mansion is common, unlucky, and unfortunate.

From a natal perspective, Brenner writes in his 1559 edition:

> A child born during Alkaia's rise will be rich, honest, keep his own, and do well with it. It will have grey hair, thick eyebrows, and a cleft above the nose. His adornment will be red, and he will suffer from an illness in his back. An evil spirit will haunt him, and women will love him very much. But if the star rises in the second hour after sunrise, and a child will be born, it will have spots in its eyes, will lose many teeth, and will have grey hair. But if it rises in the third hour, who will be born will be of high rank, and will achieve deeds of wonder of which an equivalent is hardly found in any kingdom. And who will be born if it rises in the fourth hour, shall be healthy, and if Mars rules shall have to sell meat. He will let blood and his livelihood shall be made through buying. He

will live healthily for ten years, then he will be ill. If he recovers, he will live 44 years, thereafter he will be ill again. If he recovers, he will reach the age of 90.

7th Lunar Mansion Al Dhira, The Forearm, Arm of Gemini

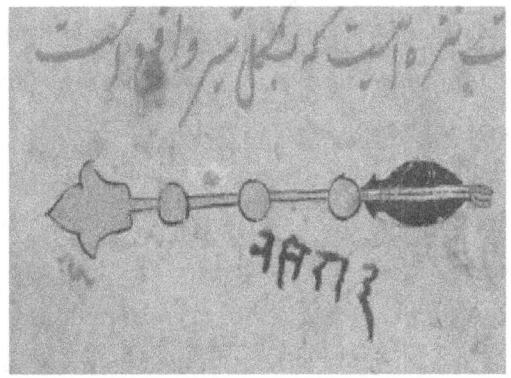

The 7th lunar mansion is called al-Dhira, or el-Dsira, the Forearm, or the Arm of Gemini. There are many Western transliterations, like Addirach, Alarzach, Aldyrabe, or Aldimiach, to name only a few. Al-Qazwini writes that it is the retracted paw of the Lion *d'ira'lassad elma.kbu.da*. The Lion has two paws, the retracted one, *ma.kbu.da*, and one stretched out, *mabsu.ta*. The latter is directed towards the south, the former towards the north, and the Moon moves into the former. It consists of two determinant stars, alpha-Gemini (Castor), and beta-Gemini (Pollux), as well as the stretched-out paw. Al Biruni contradicts Al-Qazwini, when he writes that this mansion is represented by the retracted paw. Al-Biruni writes that according to the astronomers, the outstretched arm is the head of Gemini, and the other arm belongs to the stars of Alkalb Almutakaddim (Procyon).

Manazil

Ideler agrees with Al-Biruni, saying that the stretched-out paw is aligned through the head of Gemini, and that the two stars of Canis Minor are placed in the retracted paw.

The tropical boundaries for the 7th lunar mansion are 17*08'34" Gemini and 00* Cancer. The sidereal boundaries, given in tropical Zodiac longitude, precessed for 2024, are 20* Cancer and 7* Leo. The modern longitude (2024) of the determinant fixed star Castor is 20*34' Cancer. Pollux' longitude is 23*32' Cancer. The first determinant fixed star alpha Gemini (Castor) was named Al Ras al Taum al Mukaddim, the Head of the Foremost Twin by the Arabs, although the Arabian astronomer Al Tizini claimed that the early and indigenous term was Al Awwal al Dhira' the First in the Paw or Forearm. This refers to the big Lion, known as Asad to the nomads, which is mentioned above. The second determinant fixed star beta Gemini (Pollux) is a yellowish or reddish star positioned on the head of the Southern Twin (eastern), also known as the Immortal Twin. The early Arabs' named Pollux Al Thani al Dhira, the Second in the Forearm. Later this changed to Al Ras al Taum al Mu'ahar, the Head of the Hindmost Twin, and Al Ras al Jauza', the Head of the Twin.

Castor is of the nature of Mercury, according to Ptolemy. It is said to bestow distinction, a keen intellect, success in law and many travels, sudden honour, or fame, which may be followed by loss of fortune and disgrace. It is also a pointer towards sickness and trouble. Pollux is of the nature of Mars, according to Ptolemy. This fixed star bestows a subtle, crafty, spirited, brave, audacious, cruel, and rash nature, a love of boxing, dignified malevolence, and relates to poisons.

The are different names for the lord or angel of this mansion. Ibn al-Hatim calls him Sha-lika; in the Picatrix we find the name to be Siely, and Agrippa gives the name as Seheliel, or Scheliel.

According to Abenragel, Dorotheus said that this mansion was good for partnerships which will be good and useful, with loyal and agreeable associate. It is useful for the washing of the head, hair cutting, and for putting on new clothes. Also, good for buying slaves and livestock, for smiting or making peace with enemies. Furthermore, for voyages towards destination, but delays on return. It is bad for buying land, and for giving up medicine. If captured, unless he escapes in three days, the captive will die in prison. Likewise, if he has escaped something he fears, he will encounter it again. Abenragel writes that the Indians, who called the mansion Al Dhira or Addirach, say it would be good for ploughing and sowing, for putting on new clothes, for women's jewellery, and for cavalry. This mansion is bad for journeys, except in last third of the night.

According to al-Biruni, it is favourable for gain and friendship, as well as for lovers. It can also be used to destroys magistracies. With the Moon here, it is advised to travel and to take medicine.

The Arab Picatrix suggests to make talismans to increase and to bless commerce, and to increase the growth of seeds. It is also good for prosperity and for the safety of all people travelling at sea. Talismans can also be made to create a good relationship between friends and companions. One can bind flies, so that they cannot come to a particular place. On the downside, alchemical operations, which are undertaken during this mansion, will fail and will therefore have to be repeated. Make talismans to get what you want from a ruler or mighty man you would like to connect with. Also make talismans to guarantee that an escaped slave will be well. Last, it is useful to withdraw land, goods, or houses, from their owner.

The Latin Picatrix, which calls this mansion Aldirah, tells us to make talismans to increase trade and profit and to travel safely. Also, of use to increase harvests, to sail safely, to generate friendships between your friends and your associates. Talismans can be made to prevent flies from entering a location, and to ruin someone's career. It is also effective to go before a king or some other notable person, to gain royal favour, or to get that you wish from a particular lord.

According to Pliny, Aldira is for acquiring all good things. One should make a silver sigil onto which should be sculpted the image of a man, dressed in his clothes, stretching his hands towards the heavens in the manner of a man praying and pleading. Write on his chest the name of the lord of this mansion, Selehe. Suffumigate with good smelling things and say:

"You, O Siely, do (name) a thing and fulfil my request."

Ibn al-Hatim agrees with the Picatrix, adding that the talisman should be suffumigated with wax, mixed with mastic or perfume. Giordano Bruno's image is that of a man kneeling with both hands raised to heaven attending a person dressed in finery on a silver throne.

Ibn-Arabi's attribution for this mansion, which he calls the Forearm, is the Throne. The Divine Attribute is the All-Encompassing.

Bonatti and Jafar note that this mansion is wet, lucky, and fortunate.

From a natal perspective, Brenner writes in his 1559 edition:

Who is born during the rise of Aldira shall teach and know a lot. He will drink a lot and his heart will be very mild. He will find treasure beneath the earth, and he will be very angry. And if he cannot get revenge, he will not believe his eyes. His first wife will be ugly and dark. Nature will provide him with two or slightly more children. Very often he will be annoyed with his father and mother, which he and his brothers will outlive. He shall be in a way that no man shall outdo him if he was not of high rank. He will be wounded on his head, and on his arm shall be a mark, and one in his groin, and two on his genitals between his legs, and another one on his mouth. He will live naturally for 44 years. Thereafter he will die from an illness on his neck.

Manazil

8th Lunar Mansion Al Nathrah, The Gap or Crib

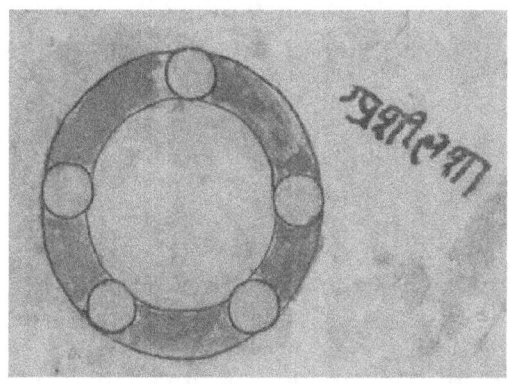

The 8th lunar mansion is called al-Nathrah, the Gap, or Crib. Other transliterations include Alnaza, Abiatra, Alamiathra, and Anatrachaya, to name only a few. Al-Qazwini calls the mansion Ennet'ra, the brattice, which is the Crib in the Crab. He writes that it consists of three stars next to each other. One of them looks as if it would be a little cloud. This may be the reason why Agrippa calls this mansion misty, or cloudy. It is the nose of the giant Lion, anf-elasad, mentioned the entry about the 7th lunar mansion, above. Al-Biruni provides more details, he writes that the determinant stars are M44 (Praesaepe), the Beehive in the Crab's shell, as well as gamma, and delta Cancri (the two Aselli). He states that this is the place between the mouth and the nostrils of the Lion, also called Allaha (the uvula), and consists of two stars, between which there is a nebula, the whole belonging to the figure of Cancer.

The tropical boundaries for the 8th lunar mansion are 00* Cancer and 12*51'26" Cancer. The sidereal boundaries, given in tropical Zodiac longitude, precessed for

2024, are 7* Leo and 18* Leo. The modern longitudes (2024) of the determinant fixed stars are 9*03' Leo for delta Cancri (Asellus Australis), 7*51' Leo for gamma Cancri (Asellus Borealis), and 7*32' Leo for M44 (Praesaepe). Praesaepe, the Beehive cluster was also called the Crib and the two Asellis were known as the two Asses or Donkeys. According to Ptolemy both the Aselli are of the nature of Mars and the Sun. It is thought that they provide care and responsibility. They also bestow a charitable and fostering nature, but there is also the possibility of serious accidents and burns, or even a violent death.

The are different names for the lord or angel of this mansion. Ibn al-Hatim calls him Aqaris; in the Picatrix we find the name to be Annediex, and Agrippa gives the name as Amnediel.

According to Abenragel, Dorotheus said that this mansion was good for voyages, and for swift on outwards- and return journeys. Marriages contracted will be harmonious for a while, then discordant. A slave bought will be deceitful, accuse his master, and then run away. A partnership started will involve fraud on either side. If captured under this mansion, the captive can expect a long imprisonment. Abenragel writes that the Indians, who called this mansion Al Nathra, or Aluayra, say that it would be good for taking medicine, for cutting new clothes, for women's jewellery and for putting them on. During this mansion, rain will bring benefit not damage. The mansion is bad for travel though, except for last third of the night.

Al-Biruni, writes that this mansion causes love, friendship, and society between fellow travellers. It drives away mice, afflicts captives, and causes their imprisonment. With the Moon in this mansion, it is good to navigate.

The Arab Picatrix tells us to make talismans of love and friendship between those who hate each other. It is also good to make a talisman for the prosperity of a traveller, and to establish good relations between comrades. Also to make talismans so that prisoners and captives will be in bonds for a long time and to make slaves evil. Talismans can also be made to expel mice as well as all kinds of bugs.

In the Latin Picatrix we find that we should make talismans for love and friendship under this mansion which they call Annathra. Also, make talismans to ensure whoever goes through villages in a wagon may proceed safely. Furthermore, make talismans to spark friendship between two associates. It is also good to reinforce a prisoner's cell, to curse and afflict captives, and to expel mice and bedbugs.

According to Pliny, this mansion he calls Annathra, is for acquiring victory. Make a tin image of a man with the face of an eagle. Write on his chest the mansion's lord's name, Annediex. Suffumigate with sulphur (Agrippa calls it brimstone) and say:

> "You, O Annediex, do (specify) for me and fulfil (specify) request for me."

Hold the image before an army and you will conquer and achieve victory.

Ibn al-Hatim tells us to make the image of an eagle with the face of a man. The talisman should be engraved in lead. Who wishes to be victorious in battle should use the talisman. Giordano Bruno has a different description of the image. According to him it should be a man riding an eagle, carrying reins which bind another two eagles in front.

Ibn-Arabi's attribution for this mansion, which he calls the Gap, or Crib, is the Footstool. The Divine Attribute is the Grateful.

Bonatti and Jafar note that this mansion is wet, lucky, and fortunate.

From a natal perspective, Brenner writes in his 1559 edition:

Peter Stockinger

A child born during Abiatra rising will learn to fence and fight. He will reject all the teachings of his elders. He does not love his friends, often gets angry, which often shows his foolish immodesty. He will become a drinker and a glutton, a rouge, reveal secrets, and will be very angry. He will have a mark on his face etc. Similar will happen to the one born during the day. Who is born during the night must live a diabolical life. He will mercilessly punish the ones to be chastised. He will arrive in the country of a lord which will bring him little piety and his end will be hard and bitter. He will better his life during old age. His head will become ill and he will suffer from pressure on his heart and in his back. Otherwise, he will stay healthy for 30 years. Thereafter he will get ill. If he recovers, he will become an old man and will reach ninety years.

Manazil

9th Lunar Mansion Al Tarfa, The Glance (of the Lion's Eye)

The 9th lunar mansion is called al-Tarfa, which, according to al-Qazwini, comes from *tarf-elesad*, the eye of the lion. For this reason, this mansion is also known as the Glance of the Lion's Eye. Western transliterations are Attraaif, Atars, and Arcaph, to name only a few. The determinant stars are two little stars in front of *el-g'ebha* (the Lion's forehead), similar to the *far.kadain* (the two calfs in Ursa major), but they are of less brilliance than the latter, in a somewhat crooked line. Al-Biruni writes that this mansion was known as the Eye of Leo, two stars close to each other, one belonging to Leo, the other to the stars outside the figure of Cancer. In front of them there are stars called *Al'ashfar*, which were known as the Eyebrows of Leo. Kunitzsch states that lambda Leonis is known as Alterf, which has been applied only in recent times. It covers xi Cancry, which is nameless, and lambda Leonis, which he associates with the asterism al-asad, the big Lion we have mentioned before.

Peter Stockinger

The tropical boundaries for the 9th lunar mansion are 12*51'26" Cancer and 25*42'52" Cancer. The sidereal boundaries, given in tropical Zodiac longitude, precessed for 2024, are 18* Leo and 00* Virgo. The modern longitude (2024) of the determinant fixed star Alterf is 18*12' Leo. Alterf is of the nature of Mercury and Saturn and is said to cause discord and hindrance to travellers.

There are different names for the lord or angel of this mansion. Ibn al-Hatim calls him Rawyal; in the Picatrix we find the name to be Raubel, and Agrippa gives the name as Barbiel.

According to Abenragel, Dorotheus said that this mansion was good for voyages, both away and return. It is also good for reinforcing doors and making locks, for making beds and putting up bed-curtains, and for transplanting wheat. This mansion is bad for partnerships, which will involve fraud on either side. It is also bad for cutting hair, or putting on new clothes. Putting on new clothes may lead to drowning in them. If captured, a long time of imprisonment should be expected. Abenragel also writes that the Indians, who call this mansion Al Tarf, or Attraaif, say that it would be bad for sowing, for journeys, or for entrusting anything to anyone, as well as seeking to harm anyone.

According to al-Biruni, the mansion hinders harvest and travellers can cause discord. With the Moon in this mansion, it is good to plant, build, or marry, but not to travel.

The Arab Picatrix tells us to make talismans to harm crops, to harm land travellers and others you want to harm. Also to expose and to separate comrades, and to capture and harm your opponent in a court case.

In the Latin Picatrix we are advised to make talismans in this mansion called Atarf, to ruin harvests, to curse travellers and all those seeking to do harm. Also to

Manazil

cause divisions and enmities between allies, and to force a man to defend himself from another one who wants something from him.

According to Pliny, this mansion, he calls Atarfa, is useful for causing sickness. We should make a lead image of a man without a penis, who is holding his hands over his eyes. Write on his neck Raubel, the name of the lord of this mansion. Suffumigate with pine resin and say:

> "You, O Raubel, make (name), daughter of (name) fall ill, or make her blood flow."

Ibn al-Hatim partially agrees with the Picatrix, in that the image is that of a man who has his hand placed over his two eyes, but he omits the missing penis. He continues that the image should made of black wax, or of lead if you do not cauterise. A small, hot nail should be made and driven into one eye. The talisman should be suspended in the wind from its head at the rising of Mars or Saturn. The name Rawyal should be engraved on the figure's head, together with the name of the affected person. The speciality of this talisman is to remove ophthalmia, disease of the eyes, and blood flow. Giordano Bruno has a fuller description of the image. According to him it shows an eunuch with his hands blocking his eyes, standing before a filthy bed.

Ibn-Arabi's attribution for this mansion, which he calls the Glance, is the Self-Existing Ultimate Sphere, the Starless Sky, the Zodiacal Towers. The Divine Attribute is the Independent, the Rich.

Bonatti and Jafar note that this mansion is common, lucky, and fortunate.

From a natal perspective, Brenner writes in his 1559 edition:

A child being born when Alkarphes is rising will be sad and cry. Many children will come from it, but they will not live long. He will commit unchastity and he will be repulsive to many, but most lovely to his masters. He will be much ill, innocent, and shapely. He will have a wound on the head, and a mark on the back, the bite of an animal on one leg, and two marks between the legs on the genitals, one of which is caused by fire. He will have enough property, both land and plough. And if he escapes, which he will not want, he will return, which is of great benefit to him. And the time he was away will lead to his ruin. He is tough enough to live fresh and healthily 44 years. Thereafter he will get ill. If he recovers, he will be well until he reaches ninety years, then he will die in a foreign land.

10th Lunar Mansion Al Jabhah, The Forehead or Neck of Leo

The 10th lunar mansion is called al-Jabhah, the Forehead or Neck of the Lion. Transliterations include Alglebh, Algerische, Alzezal, and many more. Al-Qazwini writes that this mansion consists of four stars in a crooked line. The names of these stars are alpha Leonis (Regulus), gamma Leonis (Algieba), zeta Leonis (Adhafera), and eta Leonis (Al Jabhah). They are positioned in oblique direction from south to north. The Arab astronomers called the southerly star *kalb-elasad*, the Heart of the Lion, which is known to us as Regulus.

The tropical boundaries for the 10th lunar mansion are 25*42'52" Cancer and 8*34'18" Leo. The sidereal boundaries, given in tropical Zodiac longitude, precessed for 2024, are 00* Virgo and 11* Virgo. The modern longitude (2024) of the most important determinant fixed star, Regulus, is 0*10' Virgo. In general star lore, Regulus is of the nature of Mars and Jupiter, according to Ptolemy. This fixed star signifies violence, and destructiveness, and has a connection to military honour of short duration, which is likely to fail. Imprisonment, and a violent death are also likely. On the other hand, there is also the possibility of success, which can make a person magnanimous and generous.

Regulus is one of the four so-called Royal Stars, being considered their main star because its location in the constellation of the Lion, lending it the power of the animal it represents. The other three Royal Stars are nowadays thought to be Aldebaran (see LM 4), Antares (see LM 18), and Fomalhaut. The latter is not a determinant fixed star of any of the lunar mansions, and therefore not of interest to us in this context.

In 1945, the journal *Popular Astronomy* published an article by George A. Davis, Jr. with the title *The So-Called Royal Stars of Persia*. In his article, Davis traces the history of the 'Royal Stars of Persia.' He writes that the conundrum of these stars began in 1771, when the French Orientalist Antequil-Duperron published the first translation into French, one of the Persian's sacred books, the Zend-Avesta (*Zend-Avesta, ouvrage de Zoroastre*). In this work, he attempted to identify two of the four prominently mentioned 'stars'. Four years after this publication, Jean Sylvester Bailly published *Histoire de l' Astronomie Ancienne.* In his book, the author attempts to prove that the astronomy of the Persians began about 3209 B.C. He also writes that as Aldebaran, Antares, Regulus, and Fomalhaut roughly marked the equinoxes and solstices at that time, they had to be the four 'great stars' mentioned by the Persians. Baily was followed by another French writer who, having views of his own, gave the four stars in question the denomination of Royal Stars. In 1861, yet another French author wrote in *Astronomie Populaire*, that the Royal Stars were "without doubt the four guardians of the heavens of the Persians in the year 3000 B.C." Davies writes that the thesis of these French writers may be summed up as follows:

> "Aldebaran, Antares, Regulus, and Fomalhaut marked the equinoxes and solstices in the year 3000 B.C.; *therefore*, these four stars were the ones mentioned by "Zoroaster" in the sacred books of the Persians; *therefore*, they were the four "royal stars"; and *therefore*, Persian astronomy existed at least as far back as 3000 B.C. It was as simple as that. Or was it?" (p150)

Davies continues to say that Richard Hinkley Allen, in his *Star-Names and Their Meanings* (London 1899), as well as Wiliam Tyler Olcott in his *Star Lore of All Ages* (New York and London, 1911), used countless references to these stars, with many of the second-hand authorities they consulted being entirely unreliable. Davies concludes that:

> "Practically all writers on the constellations since 1900 have followed Allen without asking any questions or examining the original records."

Manazil

Davies then moves on to give quotes from the *Bundahshi*, or Original Creation, a collection of fragments, relating to the cosmogony, cosmology, mythology, and legendary history of the ancient Persians and the worship of Ahura Mazda. What interest us here is the passage that, after Auharmzad created the twelve constellations of the zodiac, (Ahktar) and the 28 lunar mansions, "] they have ordained every single constellation of those 6480 small stars as assistants: and among those constellations four chieftains, appointed on the four sides, are *leaders*. [...] As it is said that Tishtar is the chieftain of the east, Sataves the chieftain of the south, Vanand the chieftain of the west, and Haptokring the chieftain of the north." (p152)

Without going into too much further detail here, I skip to the conclusion Davies comes to at the end of his learned article. He writes:

> "In the first place, Aldebaran and Regulus cannot be found among the four leaders or chieftains, and Sirius and Ursa Major are not mentioned in the tradition at all. In the second place, the four "royal stars" instead of being merely guardians, turn out to be four chieftains, preparing their forces for battle against Ahriman and his myrmidons of evil; and there is not the slightest evidence in either the sacred or secular literature that any king of Persia, either historical or legendary, ever claimed for himself, or had appropriated for him, any particular stars or constellations. Thirdly, we find only one star among the four leaders and three constellations. And, lastly, when we talk of the stars and constellations which were known to the Persians of 3000 B.C., we are dealing not only with vague and uncertain inferences, but also with an

utterly unknown quantity, and such speculations have no historical value whatsoever in researches of this kind." (p158)

According to Abenragel, Dorotheus said that this mansion was good for buildings which will last, and for partnerships, benefiting all parties. If captured, due to the command of a great man, or because of a great deed, and will have a long, hard imprisonment. Abenragel also writes that the Indians, who called this mansion Al Jabah, or Algebhe say that it would be good for contracting marriage, for sugar and what is made with it. He also writes that it is bad for journeys and entrusting anything, for putting on new clothes or for women's jewellery.

According to al-Biruni, the mansion strengthens buildings, promotes love and benevolence. It also helps against enemies. With the Moon here, sow, plant, release prisoners, but take no purgatives.

The Arab Picatrix suggests to make talismans to establish a good relationship between spouses, as well as to send nasty things to enemies and travellers. Also to make talismans to strengthen the bonds of prisoners, and to give longevity to buildings. It is also possible to make talismans so that comrades are in harmony and are useful for each other.

The Latin Picatrix tells us to make talismans, in this mansion called Algebha, to incite love between husband and wife, or to curse enemies and travellers. It is also good to make talismans to reinforce the prison of captives, and to reinforce and complete buildings. It is also good to make talismans to create benevolence between associates.

According to Pliny, this mansion, he calls Algebha, is for healing the sick or to make a woman give birth easily. Make a gold or brass image of a lion's head and write on it Aredafir, which is the name of the mansion's lord. Suffumigate with amber and say:

"You, O Aredafir, lift the pains, sufferings, and illnesses from my body and the body of anyone who drinks the liquid in which this sigil has been washed."

Give the sigil to a sick man to carry with him, or wash it in any liquid you will give to drink to a sick man, or a woman feeling the pains of childbirth.

Ibn al-Hatim agrees with the Picatrix regarding the image, and includes that the talisman is for entering into the presence of a king. It can cure diseases and extract a foetus. Whoever engraves this image on a seal of gold or red copper, and engraves on it the name of a king, and daily fumigates it with musk and walnut, and prays in the name of the lord of this mansion, and keeps it with him, will see wonders. During the stay of the Moon in this mansion, one should not put on new clothes, or travel. Giordano Bruno has a fuller description of the image. According to him it is that of a woman giving birth in front of a golden lion and a recovering invalid.

Ibn-Arabi's attribution for this mansion, which he calls Al Jabbah, or the Forehead, is the Sky of the Fixed Stars, the Sphere of the Stations, the Sun of Paradise, the Roof of Hell. The Divine Attribute is the Powerful.

Bonatti and Jafar note that this mansion is temperate, lucky, and fortunate.

From a natal perspective, Brenner writes in his 1559 edition:

> If Algebla is rising when a child is born, it will be pale, most lovely, proud, and boisterous. He will think of himself as mighty and that he would be a king's companion. Therefore, many will try to kill him but no harm will come to him, because due to his wisdom he will escape. And he will come from one virtue to the next through which he will win a lot

but lose it all soon after. Iron will wound him and his head will be unhealthy. He will suffer from smallpox, which will make him recognisable. He will be a well-repeated man and a great illness will befall his head. And if his anger will lead him, he will be raging and mad. He will have a big nose; his shoulders will be high and his loin will be well formed. When he is ten years old, he will be at the mercy of a master. Thereafter he will get ill. If he recovers, he will live 40 years, thereafter he will have to deal with a great illness. If he recovers, he will live 68 years, but he will die from a great illness at last.

11th Lunar Mansion Al Zubrah, The Lion's Mane

The 11th lunar mansion is called al-Zubrah, the Lion's Mane. Azobrach, Azobre, Ardaf, and Alkoraten are some of the mansion's transliterations. Al-Biruni writes that it is located at the shoulder of the Lion, the place where the neck begins. According to Alzajjaj, it is the place of the mane on his neck, because the mane bristles up when he is in wrath. According to Alna'ib Alamuli, Zubra is a piece of iron by which the two shoulder-blades of a lion are imitated. Al-Qazwini also notes that the determinant stars are called *kâhil-elasad,* interscapilium leonis. Another name is *elhurtân,* the two eyes of needles. Al-Biruni has another etymology, namely that they are called the Two Khurt, i.e. holes, as if each of them was penetrating the interior of the Lion, one of them on the root of the tail.

The tropical boundaries for the 11th lunar mansion are 8*34'18" Leo and 21*25'44" Leo. The sidereal boundaries, given in tropical Zodiac longitude, precessed for 2024, are 11* Virgo and 21* Virgo. The modern longitude (2024) of determinant fixed star delta Leonis (Zosma) is 11*39' Virgo, that of theta Leonis (Coxa) is 13*45' Virgo.

I have come across another name for theta Leonis, which is Chort (Arabic for "small rib"), or Chertan. Ideler writes that this is the singular of el-Chortan. Apparently, Tizini called delta Leonis the northern-, and theta Leonis, the southern star of the Chortan. In general star lore, Zosma is said to be of the nature of Saturn and Venus. It can cause selfishness or egotism, and unhappiness of mind.

There are different names for the lord or angel of this mansion. Ibn al-Hatim calls him Aqlul liqabul; in the Picatrix we find the name to be Necol, and Agrippa gives the name as Neciel.

According to Abenragel, Dorotheus said that this mansion was good for buildings and foundations which will last. It is also good for partnerships from which associates will gain. Lastly, it is also good for cutting hair. The mansion is bad for new clothes. If captured, it will be at the command of a leader, and signifies long imprisonment. Abenragel also writes that the Indians, who called this mansion Azobrach, or Al Zubrah, say that it would be good for sowing and planting, as well as for besieging. It is also indifferent for trade and journeys, but bad for freeing captives.

According to al-Biruni, the mansion is good for voyages, gain by merchandise, and the redemption of captives. With the Moon here, plant, marry but do not navigate.

The Arab Picatrix tells us to make talismans to free prisoners and captives and to besiege cities. Talismans can also be made for prosperity of commerce and for the benefit of a traveller. Also, for the longevity of buildings, and to create a harmonious relationship between comrades.

In the Latin Picatrix we are told to make talismans, in this mansion called Azobra, for the liberation of captives and to position armies outside cities and villages. Furthermore, make talismans to organise trade and the wealth it yields. Talismans can also be made to protect travellers on the road. There is the possibility to make talismans to reinforce buildings for stability and to increase the wealth of friends.

According to Pliny, in this mansion, named Azobra, make the talismans that you may be feared and well-received. Make the image of a man riding on a lion on a golden tablet, holding a spear in his right hand and holding his left hand over the lion's ear. Write Necol, the name of the lord of this mansion, in a straight line on the image and say:

> "You, O Necol, grant me glory so that I may be feared by men and that everyone may tremble when beholding me. Placate the hearts of kings, lords, and noblemen, that they may receive me well and honour me."

Agrippa recommends to suffumigate with good odours and saffron.

Ibn al-Hatim agrees with the Picatrix, except that, in the image, he replaces the spear with a slingshot. Giordano Bruno has the same description of the image.

Manazil

Ibn-Arabi's attribution for this mansion, which he calls Al Zubrah, or the Mane, is the First Heaven, the Sphere of Saturn, the Sky of the Visited House and Lotus of the Extreme Limit, the Abode of Ibrahim (Abraham). The Divine Attribute is the Lord.

Bonatti and Jaffar note that this mansion is temperate, lucky, and fortunate.

From a natal perspective, Brenner writes in his 1559 edition:

If a child is born during Alkoraten's rise, it will have a long face and its speech will be soft and ill, uncourtly, and nefarious. Bad things will happen to the child and very often it will be angry. There will be a mark on his loins, but if there is no mark, it will come to much chagrin. If the star rises during the night, who is born does not care what he does. He will be a good orator and there will be a mark on his legs and he will also have marks on face and neck. But if it rises in the second hour of the day, who will be born will have many children by two wives, but nearly all of them will die. The first child will be a girl, the other one a boy. He will be ill in his eleventh year. If he recovers, he will live healthily for 24 years, thereafter he will suffer from illness and will have to work hard. If he survives, he will live 58 years.

Peter Stockinger

12ᵗʰ Lunar Mansion Al Sarfah, The Changer, The Tail of Leo

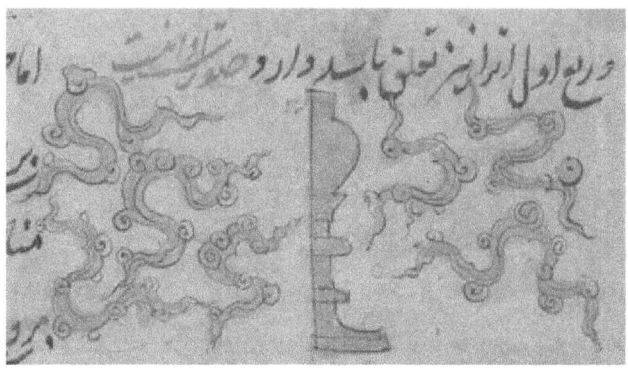

The 12ᵗʰ lunar mansion is called al-Sarfah, the Changer, or the Tail of the Lion. Some of the mansion's transliterations are Azarpha, Atorsiana, or Discordia, to name a few. Al-Biruni writes that it is a bright star near to some very dim ones, called the Claw of the Lion. It stands on the end of the Lion's tale, and is called so because the heat turns away when it rises, and the cold turns away when it disappears. Al-Qazwini agrees with al-Biruni, and adds that its rise takes place on 9. ailûl (September) and its setting on 9. ad'âr (March). During the rising of this star, the Nile begins to swell and the last days of winter fall in its nau. The determinant fixed star in question is Denebola, also known as beta Leonis. Ideler writes that el-Serfa derives from the root word saraf, which is used to describe a change in the weather.

The tropical boundaries for the 12ᵗʰ lunar mansion are 21*25'44'' Leo and 4*17'10'' Virgo. The sidereal boundaries, given in tropical Zodiac longitude, precessed for 2024, are 21* Virgo and 27* Virgo. The modern longitude (2024) of determinant fixed star beta Leonis (Denebola) is 21*57' Virgo. In general star lore, according to Ptolemy, Denebola is of the nature of Saturn and Venus. This fixed star is said to bestow swift judgment, but also disgrace, as well as misfortune from the elements of nature.

There are different names for the lord or angel of this mansion. Ibn al-Hatim calls him Adhbisha; in the Picatrix we find the name to be Abdizu, and Agrippa gives the name as Abdizuel.

According to Abenragel, Dorotheus said that this mansion was good for buying slaves and livestock, but only once the Moon is out of Leo. Reason for this is that the Lion is a great devourer. (If he eats a lot, it leads to stomach pains, power, boldness, and obstinacy). What is lent will not be returned, or only with great effort and delay. Voyages will be long, hard, and dangerous, but not fatal. Abenragel also writes that the Indians, who call this mansion Azarfa, or Al Sarfah, say that it would be good for starting all building, for arranging lands, sowing, and planting. It is also good for marriage, for putting on new clothes, for women's jewellery, and for making a journey in the first third of the day.

According to al-Biruni, this mansion gives prosperity to harvest and plantation, and hinders seamen. It is good for the bettering of servants, captives, and companions. With the Moon here, travel, navigate, sow, plough, marry and send messengers.

The Arab Picatrix suggests to make talismans for the prosperity of crops and plantations, to destroy a person's belongings so he will be harmed, also to sink ships, and to establish a good relationship between comrades. During the Moon's stay in this mansion, alchemical operations will be successful. Lastly, make talismans to bring slaves into the right condition, so that they will remain how one wants them to be.

Peter Stockinger

The Latin Picatrix tells us to make talismans in this mansion called Acarfa, to improve harvests and plants. It is also to ruin someone financially, to curse ships, or to bolster allies, authorities, captives, and slaves that they may be stable and prosperous.

According to Pliny, this mansion he calls Azarfa is for separating two lovers from each other. Make a black lead image of a dragon fighting with a man. Write Abdizu, which is the name of the lord of this mansion, in a straight line on that image. Suffumigate with lion fur, mixed with asafoetida, and say:

> "You, O Abdizu, disjoin and separate (name) from (name). "

Bury this image in the place you want, and what you desire will be.

Ibn al-Hatim generally agrees with the Picatrix, but his image depicts a snake, rather than a dragon. He also advises that the talisman should be made of wax, or on a plate of lead. The name of the lord of this mansion should be engraved on the snake's head. Giordano Bruno has a fuller description of the image. According to him it depicts a leaden and blackened seat, in which a dragon fights with a man.

Ibn-Arabi's attribution for this mansion, which he calls Al Sarfah, or the Changer, is the Second Heaven, the Sphere of Jupiter, the Abode of Musa (Moses). The Divine Attribute is the Knowing.

Bonatti and Jafar note that this mansion is dry, lucky, and fortunate.

From a natal perspective, Brenner writes in his 1559 edition:

> If a child is born during Alsarpha's rise, it will be of placid nature and have much honour and property. He will be well established with great masters, who will give him much. He will be lucky and if he chooses, he will be a farmer and winemaker. But he will not be lucky and move

Manazil

from one town to another. After he will find a wife, he will get some property and he will be busier than he ever was before. And will neither be concerned with riches, nor with unrighteous indulgence. Nobody can catch him out in his wisdom. He will suffer from a serious illness which he will endure with patience. He will be very modest and talkative. To be a merchant will only serve him during wintertime. He will rule over much land, be modest in the amount of food he eats. His hair is beautiful and curly. He will have a son who will be a thief and run away from his master. He will break a bone and have many marks on his body. One from iron, one from fire, on the belly or the leg, or one each of his legs, on the neck and on his] hands. He] will die in a foreign land. When he is 44 years of age, he will be ill and weak. If he recovers, he will live ninety-seven years. Thereafter nobody can prevent it, be it man or woman, they must die.

13th Lunar Mansion Al Awwa,
The Barker, Dogs, Cold, or Winged Ones of Virgo

The 13th lunar mansion is called al-Awwa, the Barker, also known as Dogs, Cold, or the Winged Ones of Virgo. Other names for this mansion are Alone, Alama, or Algane, to name only a few. Al-Biruni writes that it consists of five stars in a line, the end of which is turned. And therefore, the Station is called so because the verb 'Awa means to turn. They stand on the breast and wing of Virgo. Al-Qazwini writes that these are four stars, following sarfa, [the 12th lunar mansion] similar to an aleph, whose bottom end is bent a little backwards, just like the Kufic way of writing, [...]. They are seen as dogs, following the Lion, and some say that they would be warakâ'lasad, the Lion's hips. Their rising takes place on 22. ailûl (September), and their setting on 22. ad'âr (March), and their nau is depleted of rain. Ideler wrote that the stars on the left shoulder of the Virgin would be called al-Auwa, the barkers. He also knows that some say the stars along the body and armpit of the Virgin belong to al-Auwa, too. They see them as dogs, barking after the Lion. Additionally, he writes that an alternate name for this mansion is al-Bard, the Cold. Reason for this name is the idea that rising and setting of this mansion takes place in cold weather. In a footnote, Ideler questions this idea, referring to the rising and setting dates, which according to al-Qazwini, are March and September. Ideler thinks that therefore, the name al-Bard would not be justified for the Arabic climate. The determinant stars of this mansion are thought to be Zavijava (beta Virginis), Zaniah (eta Virginis), Porrima (gamma Virginis), Auva (delta Virginis), and Vindemiatrix (epsilon Virginis). It must be noted that there are uncertainties, regarding the mansion's exact number of stars. Al-Qazwini wrote that the four stars Zavijava, Zaniah, Porrima, and Auva, would be the determinant stars. In other sources, he also included smaller stars. According to Fergani, the 13th mansion would contain five stars, including Vindemiatrix. Concerning Zavijava, Al Firuzabadi, a 14th Century Arabian lexicographer, included the star with the 12th lunar mansion, Al Sarfah.

The tropical boundaries for the 13th lunar mansion are 4*17'10" Virgo and 17*08'34" Virgo. The sidereal boundaries, given in tropical Zodiac longitude, precessed for 2024, are 27* Virgo and 24* Libra. The modern longitudes (2024) of the five fixed stars are 27*30' Virgo for beta Virginis (Zavijava), 5*10' Libra for eta Virginis (Zaniah), 10*28' Libra for gamma Virginis (Porrima), 11*48' Libra for delta Virginis (Auva), and 10*16' Libra for epsilon Virginis (Vindemiatrix). According to Ptolemy, fixed star Zaniah is of the nature of Mercury and Venus. It is thought to bestow refinement, honour, congeniality, order, and a lovable nature. Porrima is of the nature of Mercury and Venus, according to Ptolemy. This star is thought to give a courteous, refined, and lovable character. It bestows the native with prophetic instincts. In general astrological star lore, Vindemiatrix is of the nature of Saturn and Mercury, according to Ptolemy. This star is said to indicate a fall into disgrace, and can cause its natives to become widows.

There are different names for the lord or angel of this mansion. Ibn al-Hatim calls him Asarub; in the Picatrix we find the name to be Azerut, and Agrippa gives the name as Jazeriel.

According to Abenragel, Dorotheus said that this mansion was good to buy a slave who will be good, loyal, and honest. Also, to start building, to give oneself to pleasures and jokes, and to come before a king or famous man. It would be good to take medicines, to cut new clothes, to wash or cut hair. It is also not bad to marry a corrupted woman and, if marrying a virgin, the marriage will last a while. A voyage undertaken during this mansion will involve a delay in return. If captured, the person will be injured in prison, but the captivity will end well. Abenragel also writes that the Indians, who called this mansion Aloce, or Al Awwa, say that it would be good to plough, sow, make a journey, marry, or free captives.

According to al-Biruni, this mansion gives benevolence and gain, is good for voyages, harvests and freedom of captives. With the Moon here, sow, plant, take medicine, but do not travel or marry.

The Arab Picatrix tells us to make talismans for the prosperity of businesses and of seeds, for the benefit of a traveller, for the agreement of marriage between two partners, as well as for the release of captives. Also make talismans to connect with kings and greats.

The Latin Picatrix suggests us to make talismans, in this mansion called Alahue, to increase trade and profits from it, to increase harvests and to protect travellers by road. Also make talismans to complete buildings, to free the imprisoned, or to charm noblemen for your own benefit.

According to Pliny, this mansion he called Alahue, is good for relaxing a man who is unable to spend time with a woman as well as for inducing love between man and wife. Make a red wax image of a man with an erection, and a white wax image of a woman. Join both images in the way that they are embracing each other. Suffumigate with aloe wood and amber. Immerse them in rosewater and wrap them in a cloth made of white silk. Write the name of the man you want on both images. If a woman carries these, she will appear very attractive to the man named on the image at the moment he sees her. If a person is under the effect of a binding spell and unable to spend time with a woman, they should carry these images. It will relax the man and enable him to have sex with the woman. The name of the lord of this mansion is Azerut.

Ibn al-Hatim agrees with the description in the Picatrix, but specifies that the images of this talisman should be that of a man spread out opposite a woman. He omits the inclusion of the erection. He also recommends to wrap both figures in a red rag for love and the excitation of sexual intercourse. Giordano Bruno has an entirely different description of the image. According to him it shows a stallion, mounting a frenzied mare, while a shepherd stands with a fixed expression and both hands on his staff.

Ibn-Arabi's attribution for this mansion, which he called Al Awwa, or the Barker,

Is the Third Heaven, the Sphere of Mars, the Abode of Harun (Aaron). The Divine Attribute is called the Victorious.

Bonatti and Jafar note that this mansion is dry, unlucky, and unfortunate.

From a natal perspective, Brenner writes in his 1559 edition:

If a child is born when Algane is rising, it will collect many goods and treasures, but he will not keep them. He will have many children, but few will survive. He will be of pleasant appearance and when he will be 36 years of age, he will be honoured and everybody will be pleased for him. Much honour and many good things will be the result. If he decides to be a merchant instead, he will make more money if he nurtures it. But he will have a great sorrow, and there will be a mark on his elbow. He will have a mark on his belly or his genitals, which is caused by fire, etc. He will live 36 years. But if a child is born when the star is rising in the second hour of the day, he will be ruler over his dynasty. Tersely nothing will be to his detriment and he will not fail or falter. But if it happens in the third hour, it will be the child of a king. And if he is from a lineage in the Holy Roman Empire, he will be emperor. Should he be a poor man who will not have such dignity, he will still be the ruler of his line. And he will rise above his peers, with honour, with riches, with property, and with respectability etc. If he is born with Algane in the fourth hour, he will die from all illnesses. And if a child is born with the star in the fifth hour, it will be rich, ever unhealthy, but will live forty years longer than the others due to this star's power.

14ᵗʰ Lunar Mansion Al Simak, The Unarmed, Virgo's Ear of Corn

The 14ᵗʰ lunar mansion is called al-Simak, the Unarmed. It is also known as the Virgo's Ear of Corn. Transliterations of this mansion's name are Azimech, Arimes, Azimel, and many others. According to al-Biruni, it is also called the Calf of the Lion, and Alsimak Alramih is his other calf. This Simak is called 'A'zal (i.e. bare), because whilst the other Simak Alramih (the shooter) is accompanied by a star said to be his lance, this one has no such accessory, and is therefore said to be bare of weapons [unarmed]. According to Sibawaihi, a Persian grammarian who live between c.760 and 793, Simak is called so on account of it rising high, or, according to others, because the moon does not enter this Station. But if that were the case, Alsimak Al'a'zal would not deserve the name of a lunar mansion, for, of course, the moon enters and frequently covers it (so as to make it disappear). The determinant star is a brilliant star on the left palm of Virgo, which some people call Sunbula (the ear). But this is wrong, because the Ear (Spica) is Alhulba, (i.e. hog's bristle), which Ptolemy calls Aldafira, i.e. Crines plexi. This is a number of small stars behind the tail of the Great Bear, very much like the leaf of Lublab, i.e. helxine. The whole zodiac sign is also called so (i.e. Spica). According to the Arabs, Alhulba (the hog's bristle) stands on the end of the Lion's tail, being the small hairs on the end of the tail. Al-Qazwini adds that the rising of simâk el'azal occurs on 5. tis'rîn elawwal (October), and its setting on 4. nîsân (April). Its nau brings plenty of rain, and it is very rare that it fails to rain. Ideler knows that Firuzabadi gave the 13th and 14th mansion the common epithet of al-anharan, which means those who bring water, due to their rising during the rainy season.

The tropical boundaries for the 14th lunar mansion are 17*08'34'' Virgo and 00* Libra. The sidereal boundaries, given in tropical Zodiac longitude, precessed for 2024, are 24* Libra and 4* Scorpio. The modern longitude (2024) of the determinant fixed star Spica is 24*11' Libra. Spica, the brightest star in the constellation Virgo stands at the Ear of Wheat shown in the Virgin's left hand. This is why Agrippa calls this mansion Virgo's ear of corn. In traditional astrological star lore, Spica is of the nature of Venus and Mars, according to Ptolemy. This fixed star is said to bestow success and riches, as well as a sweet disposition, and a love of art and science to the native. There is also the possibility of unscrupulousness to be taken into consideration.

There are different names for the lord or angel of this mansion. Ibn al-Hatim calls him Anah; in the Picatrix we find the name to be Erdegel, and Agrippa gives the name as Ergediel.

According to Abenragel, Dorotheus said that this mansion was good to start a voyage and a partnership, which will be profitable and harmonious. It is also good to buy a slave, who will be good, honest, and respectful. On the downside, marriage with a virgin will not last long, but it is not bad to marry a corrupted woman. If captured during this mansion, the captive will soon escape or be released. Abenragel also writes that the Indians, who called this mansion Azimech, or Al Simak, say that it would be good for marrying a woman who is not a virgin, for medicines, as well as for sowing and planting. This mansion is bad for journeys or entrusting something to someone. According to al-Biruni, the mansion causes marital love, cures the sick, helps sailors, but hinders journeys by land. With the Moon here, one should dig but not marry or travel.

The Arab Picatrix suggests to make talismans for a good relationship between spouses, and to achieve complete healing through medical treatment. It also recommends to make talismans to harm seeds and plantations, to destroy deposits and to make it that evil hits travellers. Lastly, make talismans for the welfare of kings and seafarers, and for the establishment of harmony between comrades.

The Latin Picatrix tells us to make talismans in this mansion called Azimech, to instil love between man and wife. It is also advisable to make talismans to heal the infirm with knowledge of the body and medicine. On the contrary, during this mansion, there can also be talismans made to curse harvests and plants. Talismans can also be made to empower kings so that they may be strong and take the throne. Also make talismans to protect those sailing, and to win the friendship of associates.

According to Pliny, this mansion he called Azimech, is for separating a man from a woman. Make a red bronze image of a dog catching its own tail with its mouth. Suffumigate with dog and cat hair (Agrippa specifies this to be a black dog or cat) and say:

"You, O Erdegel, separate and divide (male name) from (female name) through enmity and ill will."

Name the persons you want to divide and bury the image wherever you wish.

Ibn al-Hatim describes the image as a dog, biting the end of its paw. He tells the reader to engrave the image on a plate of red copper, and to fumigate it with a dog hair. Giordano Bruno seemingly combines the two images. He gives it as a man holding a dog suspended by its tail, with the dog biting its own paw.

Ibn-Arabi's attributions for this mansion, which he called Al Simak, or the Unarmed, are the Fourth Heaven, the Sphere of the Sun, and the Abode of Idris (Enoch, Hermes). The Divine Attribute is the Light.

Bonatti and Jafar note that this mansion is dry, lucky, and fortunate.

From a natal perspective, Brenner writes in his 1559 edition:

Who is born during Alchimech's rise shall benefit much from women, all of whom will die, but all his affairs shall continue He has beautiful white hair and his advice will be good. A dog will bite him, his beard will be long and his face broad and not thin. Nature will give him children who will not live long. He will not get old and rather die than reach a proper age. On the upper lip near the nose, he will have a mark. He will live 42 years and that would be the longest he will live naturally. But if he is born during the night, he will pass on much property to his children. Legally he shall have two wives. He shall be affable, with a burn mark on his belly. He will travel to a master's land, buy many things. He will die and other people will own what he inherited. They will keep his property, who have little courage. He will get ill in his 14th year, if he recovers, he will live 30 years and will get 53 years old. Thereafter will be his end and nobody can prevent that.

15th Lunar Mansion Al Ghafr, The Covering

The 15th lunar mansion is called al-Ghafr, the Covering. Transliterations are Algarf, Algalia, and Algarf, to name only a few. Agrippa called it the Covering, or Flying Covered. According to al-Biruni, this mansion consists of three not very brilliant stars on the rain and the left foot of Virgo. It is called Ghafr, because the light of its stars is imperfect, from the verb Ghafara, i.e. to cover a thing, or, because it rises above the claws of Scorpio and becomes to it like a Mighfar (i.e. coat of mail). According to Alzajjaj, the name is derived from Ghafar, i.e. the hair on the end of the Lion's tail.

Al-Biruni also writes that, according to the Arabs, it is the best of the Lunar Stations, because it stands behind Leo and before Scorpio. The evil of the Lion lies in his teeth and claws, the evil of the Scorpion lies in its venom and the sting of its tail. A Rajaz poet says:

"The best night for ever
Lies between Alzubana and Al'asad (Leo)."

Peter Stockinger

Al-Qazwini writes that the rising of the determinant stars takes place on 18. tis'rîn elawwal (October), and their setting on 18. nîsân (April).

The tropical boundaries for the 15th lunar mansion are 00* Libra and 12*51'26'' Libra. The sidereal boundaries, given in tropical Zodiac longitude, precessed for 2024, are 4* Scorpio and 15* Scorpio. The determinant stars are iota Virginis (Syrma), kappa Virginis, and lambda Virginis. The modern longitude (2024) of the determinant fixed star Syrma is 4*09' Scorpio. Ptolemy made the observations that the stars in the head of Virgo operate like Mercury and somewhat like Mars. Syrma is said to be connected to occult sciences, and bestows secret wisdom, as well as a sharp, penetrating mind that has the ability to extract hidden truths.

There are different names for the lord or angel of this mansion. Ibn al-Hatim calls him Aqalidh; in the Picatrix we find the name to be Achalich, and Agrippa gives the name as Ataliel.

According to Abenragel, Dorotheus said that this mansion was good for moving house, for adapting or preparing a house, its owner and site. It is also good to seek to do a good deed, to buy and sell, but only to sell slaves not livestock. Reason for that is because Libra is a human sign. The mansion is bad for both land and sea journeys. Marriage will not last in harmony, or only for a while. Partnerships entered will lead to fraud and discord. Money lent will not be returned. It is also bad for cutting hair. Abenragel also writes that the Indians, who called this mansion Algarf, or Al Ghafr, say that it would be good for digging wells and ditches, to cure illnesses to do with wind, but not others. They also say that it is bad for journeys. According to al-Biruni, the mansion is favourable for extracting treasures, or digging pits. It helps divorce, discord, the destruction of houses and enemies, and hinders travellers. With the Moon here, it is unfortunate for anything.

Manazil

The Arab Picatrix tells us to make talismans for digging wells and treasures, and to get hold of them. Also to prevent a traveller from going on a journey, to separate a married couple and to destroy the good relationship between friends, to make enemies out of comrades, to expel enemies and to remove them from their country of origin, as well as for the destruction of homes and houses.

In the Latin Picatrix we find to make talismans for digging wells, in this mansion called Algafra. Make talismans to seek buried treasure, and to impede travellers on their journeys. Also make talismans to put a division between a husband and his wife so that they may never have sex. Other reasons to make talismans in this mansion are to induce discord between friends and associates, to scatter enemies from their positions, or to destroy their homes.

According to Pliny, Algafra, which is the Latin name of this mansion, it is good to make talismans for gaining friendship and goodwill. Make an image out of enqueon (?) which you should draw the figure of a seated man, holding a paper in his hand as if he was reading. Suffumigate with incense (Agrippa specifies it to be frankincense) and nutmeg and say:

"You, O Achalich, do (such and such) a thing for me, and fulfil (such and such) a request for me."

Ask for things that pertain the to the joining of friendship, love, and goodwill. Carry this image with you.

Ibn al-Hatim agrees with the Picatrix, but states that the image should be drawn on a seal of qal (?). Giordano Bruno describes the image a man sitting, reading a letter, who is smiling to flatter the courier.

Ibn-Arabi's attribution for this mansion, he called Al Gahfr, or the Cover, are the Fifth Heaven, the Sphere of Venus, and the Abode of Yusuf (Joseph). The Divine Attribute is the Form-Giver.

Bonatti and Jafar note that this mansion is temperate, unlucky, and unfortunate.

From a natal perspective, Brenner writes in his 1559 edition:

Who is born during Algaphar's rise, all his children will die. He will be handsome and affable, have burning eyes, will be charming. He will be captured due to the envy of a lord. A dog will bite him, or he will get burned. He will have a mark on his face, on his head, at his heart. His gallbladder will be unhealthy. But if the same hour is on a Monday, as may well occur, who will be born then will be master of his house. But it will not be of any use to him. When he reaches 15 years, he will get ill and shapeless. If he recovers, he will get 38 years old. Thereafter he will get ill again. If he escapes, he will live for ninety years. Then he will suffer from death

16th Lunar Mansion Al Jubana, The Claws, The Horns of Scorpio

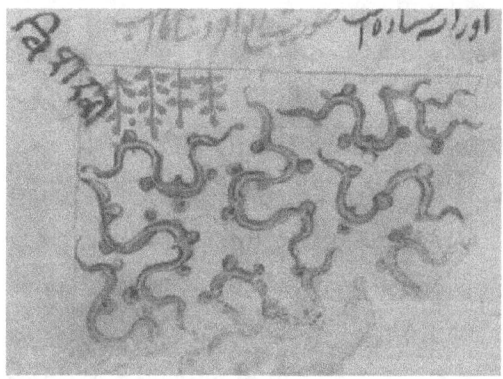

The 16th lunar mansion is called al-Jubana, also known as the Claws, or the Horns of Scorpio. Some transliterations are Alcibene, Ahubene, or Alzibinin, to

name only a few. Al-Biruni writes that this mansion consists of two brilliant stars. He refers to Zuben Elgenubi and Zuben Eschemali. These two stars are standing in a place where the two claws of Scorpio might be; they belong, however, to Libra. The word is also derived from zabana (i.e. to push), as if the one of them were being pushed away from the other, not united with it. Al-Qazwini writes that the determinant stars rise on 31. tis'rîn elawwal (October) and set on 29. nîsân (April). He also knew that the Arabs accredit bad winds to their nau, particularly the strongest north wind, which is hot in the summer.

The tropical boundaries for the 16th lunar mansion are 12*51'26" Libra and 25*42'52" Libra. The sidereal boundaries, given in tropical Zodiac longitude, precessed for 2024, are 15* Scorpio and 3* Sagittarius. The determinant stars are alpha Librae (Zuben Elgenubi), and beta Librae (Zuben Eschemali). The modern longitudes (2024) of these fixed stars are 15*25' Scorpio for Zuben Elgenubi, and 19*43' for Zuben Eschemali. According to Ptolemy Zuben Elgenubi is of the nature of Saturn and Mars. It is said to cause malevolence, obstruction, crime, and disgrace. Zuben Eschemali is of the nature of Jupiter and Mercury, according to Ptolemy. It is said to bestow good fortune, honour, riches, as well as permanent happiness.

There are different names for the lord or angel of this mansion. Ibn al-Hatim calls him Asarut; in the Picatrix we find the name to be Azeruch, and Agrippa gives the name as Azeruel.

According to Abenragel, Dorotheus said that this mansion was good to buy slaves because they would be good, loyal, and honest. This mansion is bad for marriage, which will only last in harmony for a while. It is also bad for partnerships, which will lead to dishonesty and mutual suspicion. If somebody is captured during this mansion, he will soon be out of prison, if God wills. Abenragel also writes that the Indians, wo called this mansion Azebone, or Al Jubana, say that it would be bad for journeys, trade, and medicines. It is also bad for sowing, women's jewellery, for cutting or putting on new clothes. According to al-Biruni, this mansion hinders journeys and marriage, harvest, and merchandise. It is favourable for the redemption of captives. With the Moon here, you should buy cattle but should not navigate.

The Arab Picatrix indicates to make talismans to harm business deals, plantations, and crops. Also make talismans to separate friends or married couples, as well to punish a woman as wished by her husband. One can also make talismans that make sure that evil will befall an enemy on a journey. It is also used to separate comrades and to free a prisoner from his shackles.

The Latin Picatrix tells us to make talismans during this mansion called Azubene, to curse merchandise, harvests, and plants. It is also used to sow discord amongst friends, or between man and wife. Talismans can also be made to curse a woman you desire, or to impede those on a journey in a way that it might fail. Lastly, make talismans to sow discord between friends, and to free captives from prison cells.

According to Pliny, Azebene is for gaining amounts of profit in the business of buying and selling. Make the figure of a man sitting on a throne, holding scales in his hands on a silver lamella. Suffumigate with odorous items (Agrippa recommends well smelling spices), and show the image to the stars every night for seven nights, while saying:

"You, O Azeruch, do [...] for me, and fulfil my request for [...]."

Ask for things pertaining to the purchase and sale of goods.

Manazil

Ibn al-Hatim agrees with the Picatrix. Giordano Bruno has a fuller description of the image. According to him the image shows a silversmith, having a balance in one hand, an abacus on the table.

Ibn-Arabi's attributions for this mansion, which he called Al Jubana, are the Sixth Heaven, the Sphere of Mercury, and the Abode of Isa (Jesus). The Divine Attribute is called the Numberer.

Bonatti and Jafar note that this mansion is temperate, and more fortunate than unfortunate.

From a natal perspective, Brenner writes in his 1559 edition:

Who will be born when Alzibinin rises will be proud and ostensive. He will be a king's chancellor or scribe and he will judge people. He will be a wealthy man, but he will also be useless and a burden for many, but useful and good for himself. His heart shall be diseased and he will get burnt, break a bone, and will have a mark on his face. He will have a wise wife and will inherit much from his father and mother. In his youth he will be devilish, but in his old age he will be good. When he is sixteen years of age, he will get ill. If he recovers, he will get to the age of 36 years. Thereafter, he will have to die from a great illness, or be killed by iron.

17th Lunar Mansion Iklil al Jabhah, The Crown of the Forehead

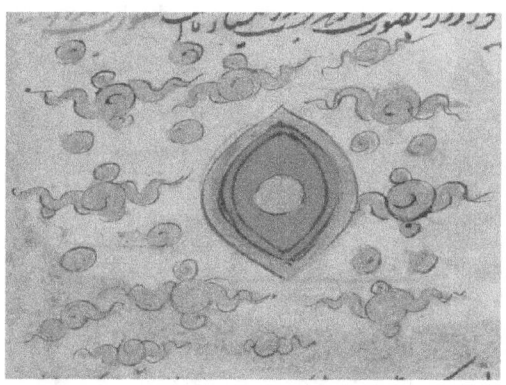

The 17th lunar mansion is called Iklil al Jabhah, also known the Crown of the Forehead. Agrippa called it the Crown of Scorpio. Transliterations are Alchil, Alactil, al-Iklil, amongst many others. Al-Biruni claims that it is the head of Scorpio, consisting of three stars which form one line. Ibn-Alsufi declares this to be impossible, and maintains that it consists of the 8th star of Libra and the 6th one of the stars outside Libra, as also Ptolemy has it in his Almagest. According to Ibn-Alsufi, those who consider the three bright stars in one line as Al'iklil are mistaken, for he says that the Crown, (i.e. Al'iklil) could not be anywhere but upon the head. However, theview of the Arabs in general - in opposition to that of Ibn-Alsufi - is this, that the three stars in one line are Al'iklil. The Arabs have a proverb applicable to this subject, saying: "The two contending parties were content, but the judge declined to give a judgment." Al-Qwazwini writes that the Crown's rising takes place on 13. tis'rîn (November), and their setting on 13. ajâr (May). In this nau, numerous rain showers and thick clouds appear. The mansion's determinant fixed stars are beta Scorpius (Acrab or Graffias), delta Scorpius (Dschubba), and pi Scorpius which does not seem to be of known astrological significance.

The tropical boundaries for the 17th lunar mansion are 25*42'52" Libra and 8*34'18" Scorpio. The sidereal boundaries, given in tropical Zodiac longitude, precessed for 2024, are 3* Sagittarius and 10* Sagittarius. The modern longitude (2024) of the determinant fixed stars are 3*32' Sagittarius for Acrab/Graffias, and 2*54' Sagittarius for Dschubba. According to Ptolemy, Acrab/Graffias is of the nature of Mars and Saturn, and is thought to indicate malevolence, crime, pestilence, and contagious diseases. Dschubba is also of the nature of Mars and Saturn, according to Ptolemy. This fixed star is believed to indicate malevolence, immorality, and shamelessness.

There are different names for the lord or angel of this mansion. Ibn al-Hatim calls him Aryath; in the Picatrix we find the name to be Adrieb, and Agrippa gives the name as Adriel.

According to Abenragel, Dorotheus said that this mansion was good for starting to erect a building, which will be solid and durable. It is also useful for settling a dispute between two people, as well as to foster love. Love begun during this mansion will be absolutely solid and last for ever. It is also good for all medicine. Voyages started during this mansion will bring anxiety and sorrows, but who does so will survive. Partnerships started will bring discord, and he who marries, will find his wife impure. This mansion is bad for selling slaves or cutting hair. Abenragel also writes that the Indians, who called this mansion Alidil, or Iklil al Jabhah, say that it would be good to buy flocks and livestock, to change their pasture, to put on new jewellery and to besiege towns. According to al-Biruni, the mansion improves misfortune, makes love durable, strengthens buildings and helps seamen. With the Moon in this mansion, build, sow, plant, navigate but do not marry.

Peter Stockinger

In the Arab Picatrix we are told to make talismans for good condition and life of pets, for the besiegement of towns and the steadfastness of buildings, as well as for the security of see travellers. All agree that friendship made during the time the Moon is in this mansion will not cease. This is why it is chosen to create talismans of friendship in this mansion.

The Latin Picatrix tells us to make talismans in this mansion called Alichil, to heighten the level of deception, so that one might excel through it. Also, to position armies around cities and villages. It can also be used to make talismans to reinforce and stabilise buildings, and to protect those travelling on water. The Moon should be in this mansion while forging friendships. This friendship will last and will never be destroyed. In this mansion, make everything for the arrangement of lasting love.

According to Pliny, this mansion, which he calls Alichil, is for preventing a thief from breaking into a house to steal something. Make the image of a monkey on an iron sigil with its hand above his shoulder. Suffumigate with monkey hair, as well as the hairs of a female mouse, and wrap the talisman in the monkey's pelt. Bury it in your house and say:

"You, O Adrieb, guard all my things and everything present in that house, lest any thief enters it."

Additionally, Ibn al-Hatim writes that the image should be that of two apes, the left hand of one of which is on its head while the right is in its image (sic). The other of the two has likaffi (?) the palms of his hands on his shoulders. His name is Adhniyab. It should be engraved on a seal of iron or red wax and wrapped in the skin of an ape. Fumigate it with the hair of an ape and the slough of a snake. Giordano Bruno has a different description of the image. According to him it shows a man carrying an ark, followed by a monkey.

Manazil

Ibn-Arabi's attributions for this mansion, which he called Ilkil al Jabhah, are the Seventh Heaven, the Sphere of the Moon, and the Abode of Adam. The Divine Attribute is the Evident.

Bonatti and Jafar note that this mansion is temperate, unlucky, and unfortunate.

From a natal perspective, Brenner writes in his 1559 edition:

If Alactil rises and a child will be born, it will be hairy, and he will always be an ill man. He will have a mark on his hand, or elsewhere, and he will never get rid of his illness. He will be poisoned, or worry greatly. His tongue will be loose, he will talk much, which will be both serious and badmouthing. His eyebrows will be growing together and he will be full of hate and envy, but not arguing quickly. He will be of good complexion and recover from a great illness. Then he will become wealthy and defer one after the other. He shall be indebted to many and being very honourable, he will inherit his father's estate and have a good time with his wife of whom he will have four. When he is 14 years, he will get ill. Thereafter he will be healthy until his 17th year. Thereafter he will get ill; if he recovers, he will get to the age of 65. Thereafter he will die on the bed in his house.

18th Lunar Mansion Al Kalb, The Heart

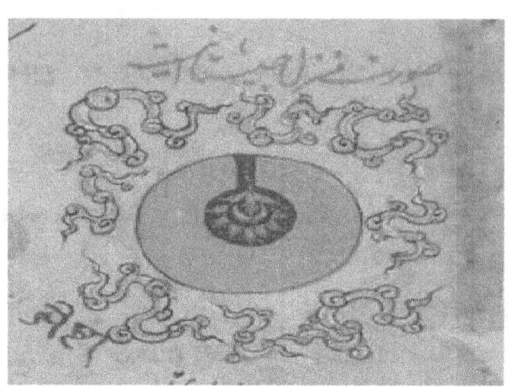

The 18th lunar mansion is called al-Kalb, the Heart. Agrippa called it the Heart of Scorpio. Known transliterations are Alcab, Altoh, and Arcaro, to name a few. Al-Biruni does not have to say much about this mansion, apart from the fact that its determinant fixed star is a red star behind Al'iklil and between two other stars called Alniyat (Praecordia). The star he is talking about is alpha Scorpius, also known as Antares, the Heart of the Scorpion. Antares is generally thought to be a derivative of anti - Ares, "similar to," or the "rival of," Mars, in reference to its colour. The fixed star is one of the four so called Royal Stars of Persia (see LM 10). Oriel (Antares) supposedly was the Watcher of the West. It is thought that at one time the four stars marked the two Equinoxes and two Solstices, whereby Antares marked 00* Libra in 3052 BC. According to Ptolemy, Antares is of the nature of Mars and Jupiter. This fixed star is said to denote malevolence and destructiveness, but also liberal thinking, and broad-mindedness.

The tropical boundaries for the 18th lunar mansion are 8*34'18" Scorpio and 21*25'44" Scorpio. The sidereal boundaries, given in tropical Zodiac longitude, precessed for 2024, are 10* Sagittarius and 24* Sagittarius. The modern longitude (2024) of determinant fixed star alpha Scorpius (Antares) is 10*06' Sagittarius.

Different names are given to the lord or angel of this mansion. Ibn al-Hatim does not give a name, but see below for the names of the two scorpions. In the Latin Picatrix we find the name to be Egribel, and Agrippa gives the name as Egibiel.

According to Abenragel, Dorotheus said that this mansion was good for building work to be undertaken, which would be solid. This mansion is also good for planting and for taking medicines. If a man gets married and Mars is with the Moon in this mansion, the man will find her not to be a virgin. If he enters a ship, he will get off it again. This mansion is bad for selling slaves, new clothes, or cutting hair. Partnerships will result in discord. Abenragel also writes that the Indians, who called this mansion Alcalb, or Al Kalb, say that it would be good for building, for arranging lands and buying them. It would also be good for receiving honours and power. If it begins to rain during this mansion, it will be wholesome, useful, and good. Eastwards journeys are favoured during the Moon's stay in this mansion. According to al-Biruni, the mansion causes discord, sedition, and conspiracy against princes and rulers. It also indicates revenge from enemies, but frees captives and helps building. With the Moon in this mansion, plant, sow, travel, and go to war.

The Arab Picatrix tells us to make talismans to raise flags for kings, so they can defeat their enemies. Also make talismans for the longevity of buildings. Who marries a woman when the Moon is with Mars in this mansion, the wife will lose her husband. The same goes for the mansion before this one. Also make talismans for the escape of slaves, for the growth of crops, and the secure travel of seafarers. Talismans to separate comrades should also be made in this mansion.

The Latin Picatrix suggests to make talismans during this mansion they call Alcalb, to rouse conspiracy against kings. Talismans can also be made to inflict vengeance upon desired enemies or to build and reinforce buildings. Lastly, make talismans to free captives from prison cells, and to divide friends.

According to Pliny this mansion, which he calls Alcab, is for removing fever and abdominal pain. Make a bronze image of an adder holding its tail above its head. Suffumigate with the horn of a stag, and say:

> "You, O Egribel, guard this house of mine, so that neither an adder nor any other harmful beast may enter it."

Place the image in a vase and bury it under your house.

I am slightly confused by Ibn al-Hatim's description of the talisman image and subsequent use of the talisman. According to him, the image is that of two scorpions, named Ahbiyal and Aghiyal. The latter of the two has spikes implanted in its eyes. In what follows, Ibn-al-Hatim seems to conflate snakes and scorpions and their actions. For this reason, I am omitting his description to avoid further confusion. Giordano Bruno has more of a straight forward description of the image. According to him it shows a brass man, bearing a snake in his hand which chases away many serpents.

Ibn-Arabi's attributions for this mansion, which he called the Heart, are the Sphere of Ether, Meteors, and Fir. The Divine Attribute is the Seizer.

Bonatti and Jafa note that this mansion is dry, lucky, and fortunate.

From a natal perspective, Brenner writes in his 1559 edition:

Who is born when Alcab is rising will do many bad things. He is handsome, imposing, angry, and reddish brown. He experiences hardship and sorrow, has evil urges and is quick to seek revenge like a fool. His back and his head are always unhealthy. If somebody is born when the star is rising in the first hour of the day, he will have much to cry and hardship which will continue. He will have heart problems and pain in one leg, which will never be healed. He will be accused of magical cunning. Who will be born in the second hour of the day will receive sorrow and hardship. He will become a wealthy man through building and working. His heart and his bravery are based on a small amount of property due to his success as a merchant. Other people will become merchants also due to his wares. His property will increase and grow and get more and more all the time. He will have pain in his belly. At the age of sixteen he will get ill and heavy, and if he recovers, he will live 30 years. Thereafter he will get unwell, unhealthy, and weak. If he recovers, he lives 48 years. Then he will die and get killed by iron, suffering death of unforeseeable misery.

19th Lunar Mansion
Al Shaulah, The Sting

Vignette missing, this is 2nd version of Mansion 4

The 19th lunar mansion is called al-Shaula, the Sting. Agrippa called it the Tail of Scorpio. In the West, it is also known as Axala, Alsebra, or Exaula, to name only a few transliterations. Al-Biruni calls this mansion the Sting of Scorpio. It consists of two bright stars near each other on the top of the tail of Scorpio. These are lambda

Scorpius (Shaula) and nu Scorpius. Al-Qazwini and all other sources I have investigated agree that the other determinant star is upsilon Scorpius (Lesath). Al-Qazwini writes that these two stars are close, nearly touching each other; they are the tail of the Scorpion. They are called s'aula, similar to the lifted part of the tail, because of their elevation, and in Arabic, one says: s'âla bid'anabihi, it has lifted its tail. Behind it is the real Scorpion's Sting, looking like a little cloud. They rise on 9. kânûn elawwal (December) and set on 9. hazîran (June). Ibn al-Hatim includes another shining one under which are three.

The tropical boundaries for the 19th lunar mansion are 21*25'44" Scorpio and 4*17'10" Sagittarius. The sidereal boundaries, given in tropical Zodiac longitude, precessed for 2024, are 24* Sagittarius and 13* Capricorn. The modern longitude (2024) of determinant fixed star lambda Scorpius (Shaula) is 24*56' Sagittarius. Upsilon Scorpius' (Lesath) longitude is 24*22' Sagittarius. Elsbeth Ebertin writes that Lesath (upsilon Scorpius) is in close conjunction with Shaula (lambda Scorpius), and that both determinant stars have a Mars nature blended with Mercurian influence.

There are different names for the lord or angel of this mansion. Ibn al-Hatim does not give a name; in the Latin Picatrix we find it to be Annucel, and Agrippa gives the name as Amutiel.

According to Abenragel, Dorotheus said that if a man gets married when the Moon is in this mansion, he will find his wife not to be a virgin. This mansion is bad for voyages, which will end in shipwreck, for partnerships, which will be discordant, for selling slaves, and very bad for a captive. Abenragel also writes that the Indians, who called this mansion Al Shaula, say that it would be good for besieging towns and encampments, for disputing against enemies, for making a journey, for sowing and for planting trees. The mansion is also bad for entrusting something to somebody.

According to al-Biruni, this mansion helps in besieging cities, taking towns, and driving men from their places. It is also used for the destruction of seamen and captives. With the Moon here, buy cattle, hunt but do not marry.

The Arab Picatrix shows us to make talismans to besiege cities, to be victorious over enemies, and to destroy the possessions of a person. It is also used for splitting up and separating of people or couples. Furthermore, one can make talismans for the benefit of travellers, for the growth of seeds, for the escape of a slave from his master, and for the sinking of ships and shipwrecking. It is also used to separate comrades and for the escape of imprisoned people and prisoners.

The Latin Picatrix tells us that this mansion, named Exaula, is used to make talismans to position an army around cities and villages. Also, to enter and take them, seize what you will, to ruin the wealth of whoever you please. Furthermore, make talismans to drive men from a place, to benefit men going through a village in wagons, to increase harvests, to make prisoners escape, to destroy and to break up ships, to divide and ruin the riches of associates, and to kill prisoners.

According to Pliny, Axaula is for promoting menstruation. Make a talisman out of zinc on which is shown the outline of a woman, holding her hand in front of her face. Suffumigate with liquid storax and say:

"You, O Annucel, make the blood of (name) flow."

If a woman holds this talisman to her rear, she will give birth easily and without danger.

Ibn al-Hatim writes that the image is that of two women. One of them has her hand placed over her vulva. The other one is spread out like a river. The names of the women are Adhniyal and Abriyal. This talisman should be made of white wax or lead, suffumigated with liquid storax, and wrapped in a cotton rag. The talisman should be hung in a stream of water, or set up over the patient's vulva. Giordano Bruno has a short description of the image. According to him it shows a woman with her hands over her face and extended.

Ibn-Arabi's attribution for this mansion, which he calls Al Shaula, is Air. The Divine Attribute is the Living One.

Bonatti and Jafar note that this mansion is temperate, lucky, and fortunate.

From a natal perspective, Brenner writes in his 1559 edition:

> Who is born under the star Alsebra, he will be a fake and a liar who likes to spin new tales. His intention is evil in hidden and open ways. He likes to insult his neighbours and is a fraud. If he can bring about confusion and hostility amongst people, he will do so all the time. He has small and bright eyes, handsome eyebrows and is well formed. He is quite a pretty man with a slim body. He will be going to war on horseback. He will have four wives and the fourth will be the prettiest. He will have two marks on his neck, and two on the shoulders. He is optimistic and evil, does not care what he is doing and a dog or another animal will bite him. And if he will be born in winter, he will be black. In summer he will be white perry and clear. He will have curly hair, nearly red complexion and will win many treasures. He will wound and kill many people, which will cause much hardship. He shall have two children with his wife and will be their enemy. He will receive a spot on his eye and another mark on one of his fingers. When he is seventeen years of age, he will get ill. If he recovers, he will live healthily until 36

years. Then he will get ill again. If he recovers, he will live 56 years. Thereafter he will receive bad things and iron will kill him, which rarely happens.

20th Lunar Mansion Al Na'am, The Ostriches

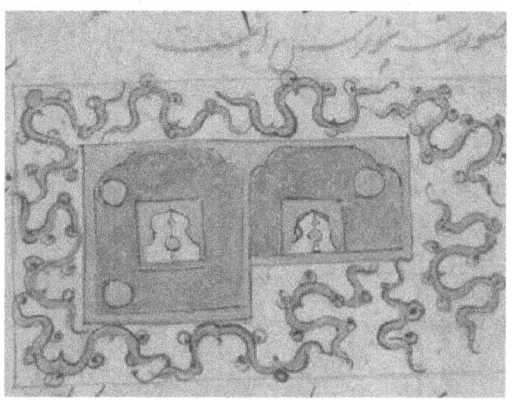

*Missing Vignette,
this is another version of mansion 7*

The 20th lunar mansion is called al-Na'am, the Ostriches. Agrippa called it the Beam, or Transom. In the West, it is known as Alnagin, Nahaim, or Alkanaim, to name only a few of the existing transliterations. Al-Biruni writes that this mansion consists of eight stars, four of them lying in the Milky Way in a square, which are the Descending Ostriches, descending to the water, which is the Milky Way; and four of them lying outside the Milky Way, also in a square, which are the Ascending Ostriches, ascending and returning from the water. The stars were compared to ostriches, as if four of them were descending, four ascending. The Descending

Ostriches stand on the bow and arrow of Sagittarius, and the Ascending Ostriches stand on his shoulder and breast. Al-Qazwini agrees with al-Biruni and adds that their rising takes place on 22. kânûn elawwal (December), and their setting on 22. hazîrân (June). The eight stars forming this lunar mansion are gamma, delta, epsilon, eta, sigma, phi, tau, zeta Sagittarius.

The tropical boundaries for the 20th lunar mansion are 4*17'10'' Sagittarius and 17*08'34'' Sagittarius. The sidereal boundaries, given in tropical Zodiac longitude, precessed for 2024, are 13* Capricorn and 16* Capricorn. The modern longitude (2024) of determinant fixed star zeta Sagittarius (Ascella) is 13*59' Capricorn. The other most noteworthy determinant star is sigma Sagittarius (Nunki) at 12*44' Capricorn. Gamma Sagittarius (Alnasl) is at 01*37' Capricorn, delta Sagittarius (Kaus Medius) is at 4*56' Capricorn, epsilon Sagittarius (Kaus Australis) is at 05*26' Capricorn. The westernmost of the determinant stars, gamma Sagittarius (Alnasl), delta Sagittarius (Kaus Medius), epsilon Sagittarius (Kaus Australis), and eta Sagittarius, were Al Na'am al Warid, the Going Ostriches. The easternmost stars, sigma Sagittarius (Nunki), zeta Sagittarius (Ascella), phi Sagittarius, and tau Sagittarius, were Al Na'am al Sadirah, the Returning Ostriches, passing to and from the celestial river, the Milky Way. Some also thought that the star lambda Sagittarius (Kaus Borealis) was their keeper.

There are different names for the lord or angel of this mansion. In the Picatrix we find the name to be Queyhuc, and Agrippa gives the name as Kyriel.

According to Abenragel, Dorotheus said that this mansion was good for buying small animals, but bad for partnerships and captivity. Abenragel also writes that the Indians, who called this mansion Alimain, or Al Na'am, say that it would be good for buying animals. Rain will be good and will do no harm. It is also indifferent for journeys.

Manazil

According to al-Biruni, the mansion helps the taming of wild beasts, and strengthening of prisons. It destroys the wealth of societies and compels man to come to a certain place. With the Moon here, build, ask favours but do not marry.

The Arab Picatrix tells us to make talismans to bring to order a hard to tame animal (for riding or carrying of burden). It is also useful for the fastness and shortening of a journey, to attract a wanted person and for friendship. Otherwise, it can be used to make it harder for prisoners, and to spoil the good relationship between comrades.

The Latin Picatrix suggests to make talismans during this mansion they call Nahaym, to domesticate wild, untamed beasts. Also to make talismans to cause travellers by carriage to return quickly. Furthermore, make talismans to make a man come to wherever you wish him to be, also to associate good men with each other, and to strengthen cells for prisoners. Also, to bring evil and ruin upon wealthy friends.

According to Pliny, this mansion, which he calls Alnaym, is for hunting. Make on a tablet of tin an image with the head and the hands of a man, and the body of a tailed, four-footed horse, with a bow in his hands. Suffumigate with fox hair (Agrippa says with the head of a wolf) and say:

> "You, O Queyhuc, grant me all the game of the land, coming to me at once."

Giordano Bruno has a slightly different description of the image. According to him it shows a centaur with a hunter's bow and quiver on the left, and a dead fox on the right.

Ibn-Arabi's attribution for this mansion, which he called Al Na'am is Water. The Divine Attribute is the Live-Giver.

Peter Stockinger

Bonnati and Jafar note that this mansion is wet, lucky, and fortunate. From a natal perspective, Brenner writes in his 1559 edition:

> Who is born under the star Alkanaim will be black, have a big nose, will be quick and have a small head. He will inherit his father's estate after his death, and will fall into water. He will have short teeth and an ill heart. He will lose his best friend, will have an evil tongue. He will also have an evil tongue to gossip and slander. He will have two wives, but it happens that he will not like to be with women, which happens due to an impediment of his nature. But he will have enough children which may also apply at times to women who are born under this star. He will receive many goods, will lose some of them at times, but luck will have it that they will increase day by day. He will have a heavy heart due to fright, be slim, and because of a woman or something else he will be at the mercy of an enemy. He will have five marks on him and when he reaches 20 years, he will fall ill. If he escapes, he will get to the age of 51 years. Thereafter he will get ill again. If he recovers, he will become an old man of 80 years. Thereafter it will not continue. He must perish and die miserably.

21ˢᵗ Lunar Mansion Al Baldah, The City or Desert

The 21ˢᵗ lunar mansion is called al-Baldah, the City, or Desert. In the West it is known as Albeda, Alneda, or Albeldach, to name only a few of this mansion's transliterations. According to al-Biruni, this mansion is a desert district of heaven without any stars, at the side of the Horse, belonging to Sagittarius. Al-Qazwini agrees and adds that the lunar mansion's rising takes place on 4. kânûn elâhâr (January) and their setting on 4. tamûz (July). Ideler writes that Firuzabadi summed it up stating that al-Baldah (the City) would be a place in the sky wherein there are no stars. Sometimes the Moon avoids this space and moves into al-Kilada, the Necklace, or Bow, instead. These are six stars in a circle and Albaldah (pi Sagittarius) is the brightest of them. The stars set together with the sun at the shortest day of the year.

The tropical boundaries for the 21ˢᵗ lunar mansion are 17*08'34'' Sagittarius and 00* Capricorn. The sidereal boundaries, given in tropical Zodiac longitude, precessed for 2024, are 16* Capricorn and 4* Aquarius. The modern longitude

(2024) of the determinant fixed star pi Sagittarii (Albaldah) is 16*35' Capricorn. As far as I am aware, there is no astrological interpreation connected to this fixed star.

There are different names for the lord or angel of this mansion. Ibn al-Hatim calls him Kawyakifah; in the Picatrix we find the name to be Bectue, and Agrippa gives the name as Bethnael.

According to Abenragel, Dorotheus said about the significance of this mansion, that a woman whom a man dismisses or who is divorced or widowed will not marry again. It is indifferent for slaves bought, since they will think much of themselves and will not humble themselves to their masters. Abenragel also writes that the Indians, who called this mansion Albeda, or Al Baldah, say that it would be good for starting any building, for sowing, for buying lands or livestock, for buying and making women's jewellery and clothes. It is indifferent for journeys.

According to al-Biruni, the mansion is favourable for harvest, gain, buildings, and travellers, but causes divorce. With the Moon there, take medicine, navigate, and put on new clothes.

The Arab Picatrix tells us to make talismans for the steadfastness of buildings, and for the growth of crops. It is also good for making talismans to keep goods, farm animals and animals for riding or carrying being owned constantly by one master. Also, make talismans for the safe journey of travellers. One can make talismans for a woman, that she will be dismissed by her husband, in the way that she will never marry again.

In the Latin Picatrix we find that under this mansion, which is called Elbelda, it is good to make talismans for the reinforcement of buildings. It is also used to increase the yield of harvests, to retain profits, to protect those travelling through villages, and to separate a wife from her husband.

Manazil

According to Pliny, Albelda is for destruction. Make the image of a man with two faces, one in front, and the other one facing backwards. Suffumigate with sulphur and carob, saying:

"You, O Bectue, desolate the place of (name) and destroy him."

Place the image in a small bronze container. Add sulphur and carob and some hairs, and bury it wherever you desire. Agrippa suffumigates with brimstone and either jet, or yellow amber, depending on the translation. Both of words are derivatives from the original Latin 'carabe' from the Arabic 'kharuba'.

Ibn al-Hatim generally agrees with the Picatrix, but adds that the talisman should be suffumigated with sulphur, amber, and the hair of a man for three nights. It should be buried in a place whose people you wish to separate. Its speciality is misfortune, emptiness, and emigration. Giordano Bruno has a different description of the image. According to him it shows two men together, one watching while the other shaves off his gathered hair.

Ibn-Arabi's attribution for this mansion, which he calls the City, is Earth. The Divine Attribute is the Death-Giver.

Bonatti and Jaffar note that this mansion is dry, unlucky, and unfortunate.

From a natal perspective, Brenner writes in his 1559 edition:

> Who is born under the star Alneda will have much grief. He will ride much and will be a strong sword fighter or an archer who is useful to himself. With his weapons and his piety, he will win much. He will burn himself on iron, being careless be it good or bad, and will be wealthy. And if Saturn joins also, this star is not beneficial to humans. And all path he rides or walks on will be dull [?]. He will cough and his head will

be numbed by an illness which is unlikely to cease. But if a person is born when the star is rising in the second hour of the day, their forehead will be big and bold. He will have two children. He is lusting after women in an evil way, will have a handsome body, all over. And he will recover from great illness. His possessions will be increasing and decreasing as luck will have it. He will fall into poverty and die a strange death, killed by a bite. If he gets to the age of twenty-one years, he will get weak. Then he will be ill for four years. If he recovers, he will get to the age of 70. Then he will die from the bite of a poisonous animal.

22nd Lunar Mansion Al Sa'd al Dhabih, The Fortune of the Slaughterer

Missing, this is Mansion 14 b

The 22nd lunar mansion is called al-Sa'd al Dhabih, the Fortune of the Slaughterer, or the Slaughterer's Joy. Agrippa called this mansion the Shepherd. Other names in the West are Sadabacha, Zandeldena, or Caalbeda, to name only a few of the existing transliterations. Al-Biruni writes that this mansion consists of two stars, the one to the north, the other to the south, distant from each other about one yard. Close to the northern one there is a small star, considered as the sheep which he (Sa'd) slaughters. The two stars stand on the horn of Capricorn. Nowadays, they are known as alpha1 Capricorni (Giedi Prima), and alpha2 Capricorni (Giedi Secunda). Giedi Secunda was known by the Arabs as al-scha, the Sheep. The other determinant fixed star is beta Capricorni (Dabhi) which was known as al-dsabih, the Slaughterer. Ideler also thinks that the name of this mansion refers to a sacrificial, or some other ceremony, which nomadic Arabs used to perform during the heliacal rising of this fixed star.

The tropical boundaries for the 22nd lunar mansion are 00* Capricorn and 12*51'26'' Capricorn. The sidereal boundaries, given in tropical Zodiac longitude, precessed for 2024, are 4* Aquarius and 11* Aquarius. The determinant stars are alpha1 Capricorn (Giedi Prima), Alpha2 Capricorn (Giedi Secunda), and beta Capricorn (Dabhi). The modern longitudes (2024) of the fixed star alpha1 Capricorn (Giedi Prima) is 04*06' Aquarius. Alpha2 Capricorn (Giedi Secunda) is very close at 04*12' Aquarius. Beta Capricorn (Dabhi) is located at 4*23' Capricorn. According to Ptolemy, Dabhi is of the nature of Saturn and Venus. Giedi Prima is of the nature of Venus and Mars, according to Ptolemy, and it is thought to signify sacrifice and offering. Giedi Secunda is said to be associated with piety and self-sacrifice.

There are different names for the lord or angel of this mansion. Ibn al-Hatim calls him Ufit Aranit; in the Picatrix we find the name to be Geliel, as we do in Agrippa.

According to Abenragel, Dorotheus said that this mansion was good to entering a partnership, which will bring profit and usefulness. Also good for entering a ship, though there will be great anxieties from a strong desire to return and the like. A man who becomes engaged will break the engagement before the wedding and die within six months, or the couple will be in conflict and live badly, with the wife mistreating her husband. It is also said that this mansion is bad for buying slaves, who will do ill to their master, or run away, or be irksome or bad. If captured, a captive will soon gain freedom. Abenragel also writes that the Indians, who called this mansion Sahaddadebe, or Al Sa'd al Dhabih, say it would be good for medicine and journeys, except for last third of the day. It is also thought to be good for putting on new clothes.

According to al-Biruni, the mansion helps the escape of servants and captives and the curing of diseases. With the Moon here, one should take medicine, travel, but should not lend money or marry.

The Arab Picatrix tells us to make talismans to treat ill people and to recover from illness. Also to make talismans to separate lovers and married couples, to instigate an affair with a woman one longs for. It is also used for the escape of slaves and for their escape from their homeland. One should make talismans to separate comrades and to free prisoners, as well as locked up people.

In the Latin Picatrix we are told to make under this mansion, which is called Caadaldeba, talismans to heal infirmities, to set discord between two men, to make slaves and prisoners flee, to cause good will between associates, and to cause captives to escape.

According to Pliny, Sadahaca is for binding the tongues of men so they will not curse you. Make an iron ring on which the shape of a man with winged feet, wearing a helmet, is sculpted. Suffumigate with quicksilver, seal white wax with the ring when you use it for the safety of those who intend to be fleeing, and say:

> "You, O Geliel, bind the tongue of (name) lest they curse me, and make that they (name) may escape safely from their enemies."

Manazil

Wear this ring when you are fleeing, and seal black wax with the ring when binding tongues.

Ibn al-Hatim uses the image of a lion between whose paws are those of a fox. Its tail is turned in place of its head and its head is in place of its tail. Suffumigate with the hair of a lion. It should be engraved out of wax and buried in the name of the wazir whom you wish to harm. Also pray in the name of its lord. Destruction and misery will turn to the wazir. Its speciality is the separation between kings and their wazir. Giordano Bruno's description of the image is that of a man with a winged helmet and winged feet, fleeing to safe refuge.

Ibn-Arabi's attribution for this mansion, which he calls Al Sa'd al Dhabih, s Minerals and Metals. The Divine Attribute is the Precious.

Bonatti and Jafar note that this mansion is temperate, lucky, and fortunate
From a natal perspective, Brenner writes in his 1559 edition:

> Who is born during Zaddadena's rise will be of fierce temper and a man of blood, killing and bludgeoning people who are in desperate straits. Therefore, he will die in sin. He will be boisterous in his youth but wise in old age, sometimes happy, but still an angry man. And harmful as much as possible, therefore he will be rumoured to use magical cunning. When he will be fifteen years old, he will bet ill. If he recovers, he will reach 36 years. Thereafter he will be ill again. If he recovers again, he will live 60 years. Thereafter he must die, be it man or woman.

Peter Stockinger

23rd Lunar Mansion Sa'd al Bula, The Fortune of the Swallower

The 23rd lunar mansion is called Sa'd al Bula, the Fortune of the Swallower Agrippa calls it Swallowing. Sometimes the name is shortened to al-Bula, and Ibn al-Hatim calls it Sa'd bal. In the West, this mansion is known by the names of Zobrach, or Sabadola, to name only a few of its transliterations. Al-Biruni writes that the mansion consists of two stars with a third and hardly visible one between them, which looks as if one of them had devoured it, so that it glided down from the throat to the breast. According to others, it was called so because Sa'd is considered as he who devoured the middle star, robbed it of its light and concealed it. Ideler writes that the brighter star [epsilon Aquari] was called Bali, the Devourer, because he swallows the darker one, taking its light. Ideler also writes that, given the mansion's name, it would be difficult to find a justification for it containing three stars, as some sources do. He suggests that the addition of a point above the mansion's name's last letter (Sa'd balg) could change its name to "faustum sides boni exitus propositi" (a lucky star for the good outcome of a project).

The tropical boundaries for the 23rd lunar mansion are 12*51'26" Capricorn and 25*42'52" Capricorn. The sidereal boundaries, given in tropical Zodiac longitude, precessed for 2024, are 11* Aquarius and 23* Aquarius. The determinant stars are mu Aquarii, nu Aquarii, and epsilon Aquarii (Albali). The modern longitude (2024) of fixed star Albali is 11*44' Aquarius. Albali, meaning 'the swallower' is thought to have a generally positive, enthusiastic influence. There is a warning though, that too much enthusiasm and too little discernment can lead to situations that are hard to control.

There are different names for the lord or angel of this mansion. Ibn al-Hatim calls him Sani sanahin; in the Picatrix we find the name to be Zequebin, and Agrippa gives the name as Requiel.

According to Abenragel, Dorotheus said that this mansion was good for partnerships. It is bad for marriage, since a wife will mistreat her husband and they will not be together much. It is good for entering a ship, if a short voyage is wanted, and for buying slaves. If captured, the captive will soon regain liberty. Abenragel also writes that the Indians, who called this mansion Zadebolal, or Al Sa'd al Bula, say that it would be good for taking medicine, for putting on new jewellery and clothes, and for a journey in the middle third of the day. It is bad to entrust something to someone. According to al-Biruni, the mansion can cause divorces, the liberty of captives, and it can heal the sick. With the Moon here, marry, sow, take medicine and lead an army.

The Arab Picatrix tells us to make talismans to treat the ill, and to recover from illness. Also make talismans to destroy goods, to separate couples, and to free or dismiss prisoners.

In the Latin Picatrix we find that this mansion, named Caaddebolach, is used to make talismans to heal infirmities. Also to make talismans to unite friends, or to divide a man from his wife. Lastly, make talismans to make prisoners escape from their cells.

According to Pliny, Zaadebola is for destruction and devastation. Make an iron sigil in the image of a cat with a dog's head. Suffumigate with dog hair and say:

"You, O Zequebin, desolate (name of place), destroy and devastate it."

Show this sigil to the stars when this mansion is rising. On the subsequent night bury the sigil in the place you wish to destroy.

Ibn al-Hatim writes that the image is that of a lion from the fore part; the lion's head is that of a dog and its body that of an ape. He also writes that the talisman should be shaped out of potter's clay. He recommends to suffumigate the talisman with the hair of a dog or a wolf. Its speciality is to ruin and to bring disease upon whoever one wishes. Giordano Bruno's description of the image is that of a cat grabbing a dog by the head, the dog having the cat by the back, the ground shaking, with a man falling to the ground.

Ibn-Arabi's attribution for this mansion, which he calls Al Sa'd al Bula, is Plants. The Divine Attribute is the Nourisher.

Bonatti and Jafar note that this mansion is wet, lucky, and fortunate.

From a natal perspective, Brenner writes in his 1559 edition:

> Who is born under Sabadola is clean, unjust, and sometimes nasty to father and mother. He is always covering up his shameful behaviour and his end is better than his beginning. He will love his wife and he will overcome a malady brought on by a sorceress. It can be said that he is

useless with women and a great drunkard. Belly ache will dry him and eat him up. If he can overcome it, he will live 21 years. Thereafter he will get ill. If he recovers, he will live for 68 years, then he will die.

24th Lunar Mansion Sa'd al Su'ud, The Fortunate of the Fortunate

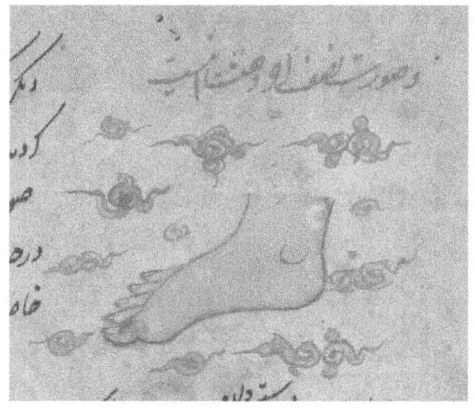

The name of the 24th lunar mansion is Sa'd al Su'ud, the Fortunate of the Fortunate. Agrippa calls it the Star of Fortune. In the West, this mansion was also known as Sadabath, Sadahad, or Zaadescod, to name only a few of the many transliterations. Al-Biruni writes that this mansion consists of three stars, one of which is brighter than the other two. It is called Sa'd al Su'ud because people consider its rising as a lucky omen. It may also be because the mansion rises when the cold decreases, when the winter is past and the season of the continuous rain sets in. Two of these stars stand on the left shoulder of Aquarius; the third one stands on the tail of Capricorn. Al-Qazwini calls this mansion the Highest Lucky Star, adding that its rising takes place on 12. s'ebât (February), and its setting on

14. Âb (August). Determinant fixed stars are beta Aquarius (Sadalsuud) and xi Aquarius.

The tropical boundaries for the 24th lunar mansion are 25*42'52" Capricorn and 8*34'18" Aquarius. The sidereal boundaries, given in tropical Zodiac longitude, precessed for 2024, are 23* Aquarius and 7* Pisces. The modern longitude (2024) of the determinant fixed star is 23*44' Aquarius (Sadalsuud). According to Ptolemy this fixed star is of the nature of Saturn and Mercury, which is said to cause trouble and disgrace.

There are different names for the lord or angel of this mansion. Ibn al-Hatim calls him Afratim abriyas; in the Picatrix we find the name to be Abrine, and Agrippa gives the name as Abrinael.

According to Abenragel, Dorotheus said that this mansion was good to buy a slave who will be strong, loyal, and good. It is bad for partnerships, which will end in great harm and conflict, and also good for entering a ship. Marriage begun during this mansion will only last a while. If somebody is captured, they will soon be free. Abenragel also writes that the Indians, who called this mansion Zaadescod, or Al Sa'd al Su'ud, say that it would be good for medicine, and for sending out armies and soldiers. It is indifferent for journeys, and bad for merchandise and jewellery. Putting on new clothes or marriage is also bad during this mansion. According to al-Biruni, the mansion gives marital happiness, victory of soldiers but prevents the execution of government. With the Moon here, it is fortuitous to build, marry, make friends and travel.

The Arab Picatrix tells us to make talismans for the blossoming of the trade business, and for harmony between married couples. Also make talismans for victory of troops, to separate comrades, and to free bound people. Who undertakes an alchemical operation during this mansion will not succeed and will not accomplish what they set out to do.

The Latin Picatrix tells us that in this mansion, named Caadacohot, you should make talismans to improve commerce and its profits. It is also good to bring good will to a husband and his wife. Also useful to make talismans to give soldiers victory over enemies. Lastly, use this mansion to make talismans to ruin the riches of friends, and to disrupt enterprises such that they might not come to fruition.

According to Pliny, this mansion called Caadazod is used to make talismans to increase herds. Take a well cleaned and most suitable horn of a castrated ram. On it draw a figure of a woman who is nursing her son in her arms. Suffumigate with the bits you have taken off the horn while cleaning it, and say:

"You, O Abrine, improve and guide the herd of (name)."

Then tie this image on the neck of a ram in that herd. If you have done this for a herd of cows, make those things from a bovine horn and tie it on a bull's neck. These herds will increase and mortality will not overcome them.

Agrippa writes to seal it in [the horn] burning with an iron seal the image above [woman nursing her son], and hang it on the neck of the cattle who is leader of the flock, or seal it in its horn.

Ibn al-Hatim agrees with the image given in the Picatrix, adding that it should be made out of fat and flour, or engraved on a ram's horn. You should say the name and bury the talisman in the house, so that no suffering will reach the cattle and inhabitants of the house. The talisman's speciality is the improvement of cattle and driving away of reptiles, as well was infectious and other diseases. Giordano Bruno has a fuller description of the image. According to him it shows a woman suckling a child that holds a ram's horn in its hands, followed by a multitude [?].

Ibn-Arabi's attribution for this mansion, which he calls the Fortune of the Fortunate, is animals; the Divine Attribute is the Humbler.

Bonatti and Jafar note that this mansion is temperate, lucky, and fortunate.

From a natal perspective, Brenner writes in his 1559 edition:

> Who is born under Sadahad will live well and full of virtues. He will lose many positions through an accident, will experience anxiety and sorrow. He will have many children and wives, and will eat much. But who is born during the second hour of the day will be a proud man. He will live 24 years, then he will get ill. If he recovers, he will receive honour and worthiness. The devil will fight him but can only do little damage. He will be weak of heart and courage. But who is born in the fourth hour will live fifty years. Then he will be dead, killed by as word, which is true.

25th Lunar Mansion Sa'd al Ahbiyah, The Fortune of the Hidden

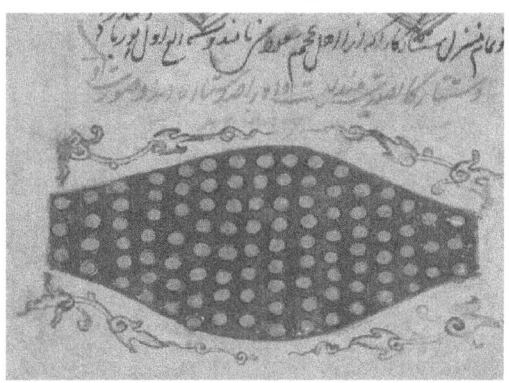

The name of the 25th lunar mansion is Sa'd al Ahbiyah, the Fortune of the Hidden. Agrippa calls it the Butterfly, or Unfolding. It is also known as the Good Luck Star of the Tents. In the West, this mansion was also known as Sadalabra, Caalda, or Sadalbachia, to name only a few transliterations. According to Ideler, *achbija* is the plural of *chiba*, the Arabic name for a nomad's tent, quoting the Orientalist Jacob Golius, "lana et pilis camelinis constans duobus vel tribus palis innitens" [consisting of wool and camel hair, resting on two or three poles]. His source for this was probably the 15th century Tartar astronomer Ulug Beg, who put zeta Aquarius in the centre, making this the top of one tent. Al-Biruni writes that this mansion consists of four stars, three forming an acute-angled trigone, and one standing in the middle, as it were the centre of a circumscribed circle. The central star is Sa'd, and the three surrounding stars are his tents. According to others, this Station was called so because at the time when it rises all reptiles that had been hidden in the earth come forth. Al-Qazwini generally agrees with al-Biruni, adding that the mansion's rising takes place on 25. s'eba.t (February), and its setting on 27. âb (August). Having read al-Qazwini, Ideler seems convinced that this mansion was named thus, because its name referred to the happy times when the nomads, after a winter of starvation, once again returned to their grazing places in the Arabian desert.

The tropical boundaries for the 25th lunar mansion are 8*34'18" Aquarius and 21*25'44" Aquarius. The sidereal boundaries, given in tropical Zodiac longitude, precessed for 2024, are 7* Pisces and 23* Pisces. The modern longitude (2024) of determinant fixed star gamma Aquarius (Sadalachbia) is 07*03' Pisces. The other determinant stars are zeta Aquarius, eta Aquarius, and pi Aquarius. To my knowledge there is no astrological star lore recorded.

There are different names for the lord or angel of this mansion. Ibn al-Hatim calls him Asyal; in the Picatrix we find the name to be Aziel, and Agrippa gives the name as Aziel, too.

According to Abenragel, Dorotheus said that this mansion was good for buying slaves, who will be strong, loyal, and good. It is also good for erecting a building, which will be solid and durable, and for voyages, though there will be delays. He writes that marriage will only last for a while. It is bad for partnerships, which will end badly and harmfully. During this mansion, a slave could escape. Abenragel also writes that the Indians, who called this mansion Sadalabbia, or Al Sa'd al Ahbiyah, say that it would be good for besieging towns and encampments. It is also good for going into a quarrel, for pursuing enemies and doing them harm. Furthermore, it is good for sending messengers and favours journeys southwards. It is bad for marriage, for sowing, for merchandise, and for buying livestock.

According to al-Biruni, the mansion is favourable for besieging and revenge. It destroys enemies, causes divorce, helps prisons and buildings, hastens messengers, hinders childbirth, and hinders the action of the body. With the Moon here, it is unfortunate for everything except taking medicine.

In the Arab Picatrix we are told to make talismans to besiege cities, to harm enemies, to gain victory over them, and to achieve that evil and nasty things will come upon them. Also, to make talismans to send messengers and spies and their success. Furthermore, make talismans to separate married couples. It is also used for the destruction of crops, and for the binding of genitals and all limbs. Also to bind prisoners and to lay, with the help of talismans made during this Mansion, basements to buildings which will secure their steadfastness.

The Latin Picatrix tells us in this mansion, which is named Caadalhacbia, to make talismans to position armies around cities and villages, to take vengeance upon enemies and to inflict evil upon them as you please. Also, make talismans to hasten envoys to deliver their messages and return quickly. Make talismans to separate a wife from her husband, to wither harvests, and to bind a man and his wife, or woman and her man in such a way that they cannot have sex. Also, make talismans to bind any limb of the human body you wish so as to render it useless. Make talismans to further reinforce the prisons of captives. It is good for making buildings.

According to Pliny, Zaadalahbria is for protection of vegetation, and harvests from unfortunate circumstances. Make a sigil out of fig wood and on it carve the image of a man planting trees. Agrippa Suffumigate with the flowers of these trees, and say:

> "You, O Aziel, guard my harvests and my trees, so that they may not be damaged or suffer any unfortunate circumstances."

Place this image with a tree in the place you want protected. If the image remains there, no harm will occur there.

Ibn al-Hatim writes that the talisman should be made of white fig wood. The image should be that of two men. One of them is treating an illness, the other one is helping a plant whose fruit is between his hands. Wherever it is buried, it will improve fruit and arable land. It also protects from blights and calamities of the heavens after it has been fumigated with the flowers of the fruit trees. Giordano Bruno's image is that of a man planting a tree, another sowing grain.

Ibn-Arabi's attribution for this mansion, which he called The Fortune of the Hidden, is the Angel. The Divine Attribute is the Strong.

Bonatti and Jafar note that this mansion is dry, lucky, and fortunate.

From a natal perspective, Brenner writes in his 1559 edition:

> Who is born under Sadalachia will always have plenty to eat. He will be gentle, but suffer from all the negative that will happen to him. He will win great riches, but he will lose it all and it will disappear. He will be healthy but suffer from back pain which he will recover from. He loves women, and will outlive father and mother. He will be talkative and will gain property in his old age. No bad luck will harm him. He will get rid of his enemies which will make him suffer much sorrow and pain. A cat or another animal will bite him so much that he will hardly recover. He will receive a head wound and will have a mark on his shin, on his leg, his genitals, on his arm, and a fifth on his heart. He will live 24 years, then he will get ill. And if he recovers, he will live 40 years. Thereafter he will be ill again. If he recovers, he will live 70 years, but a sword will

cause his last day. But who will be born in the second hour will die from the wheel and no other way.

26th Lunar Mansion Al-Fargh Al-Mukdim, The First Spout

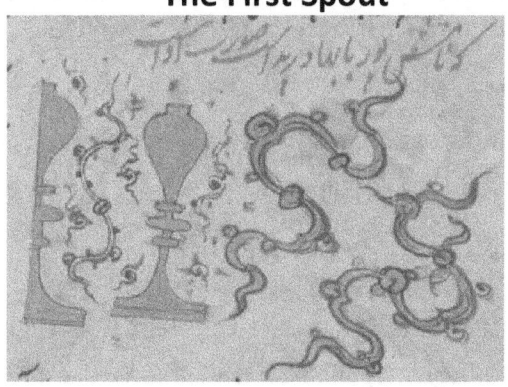

The name of the 26th lunar mansion is al-Fargh al-Mukdim, also known as al-Fargh al-muqaddam, al-Fargh al-awwal, or Faragh al-dalw al-muqaddam. In the West, this mansion was also known as Alm, Aporaboyl, or Phragal, to name only a few of the many transliterations. Some sources call the mansion the First Spout of the Bucket. Agrippa calls it the First Drawing, or Draining. Al-Biruni calls this mansion Alfargh Al'awwal, also known as the Upper Handle (of the bucket), and the First Two who move the Bucket in the Well (in order to fill it). It consists of two bright stars, alpha Pegasi, and beta Pegasi. Separated from each other, these are standing on the spine and shoulders of Pegasus. Al-Qazwini writes that the water bucket, eddelw, consists of four stars forming a spacious square. Two of them are the front and two the back ferg', which should be understood as the spout where the water runs out of the bucket, between the two crossbars. The rising of the first ferg' takes place on 9. ad'ar (March) and its setting on 9. Ailûl (September). Ideler takes a more practical approach, thinking that the square (al-nadim) was a wooden construct, consisting of two posts which were positioned above four posts building a square, whereupon a wheel was fixed, used to lower down a bucket into a well. He thinks it possible that the nomads carried one of those constructs with them on their travels. The four stars in the square are the determinant stars of the 26th and 27th lunar mansion.

The tropical boundaries for the 26th lunar mansion are 21*25'44'' Aquarius and 4*17'10'' Pisces. The sidereal boundaries, given in tropical Zodiac longitude, precessed for 2024, are 23* Pisces and 9* Aries. The modern longitude (2024) of determinant fixed star alpha Pegasi (Markab) is 23* 49' Pisces. Beta Pegasi's (Scheat) longitude is 29*43' Pisces. Alpha and beta Pegasi are known as the Flying Horse's shoulder, and its saddle Markab is the Arabs' word for a saddle, ship, or any vehicle. According to Ptolemy, Markab is of the nature of Mars and Mercury. It promises honour, riches, and fortune. On the downside, there is also the suggestion of danger from fevers, cuts, blows, or stabs.

The second determinant star is Scheat, derived either from al Sa'id, the Upper Part of the Arm, from Sa'd, appearing in the subsequent three pairs of stars. According to Ptolemy Scheat is of the nature of Mars and Mercury. It suggests extreme misfortune, murder, suicide, and drowning. Elsbeth Ebertin agrees, pointing out that a conjunction with the a malefic could lead the native to lose his life in catastrophes, such as floods, shipwreck, or other accidents.

There are different names for the lord or angel of this mansion. Ibn al-Hatim calls him Nafsiyal; in the Picatrix we find the name to be Tagriel, and Agrippa gives the name as Tagriel, too.

According to Abenragel, Dorotheus said that this mansion was good to build houses which will be solid and durable. It is also good for buying a slave, who will

Manazil

be loyal and good, as well for entering a ship, though there will be delays. It is bad for partnerships. Marriage will not last. If captured, the captive will be in prison for a long time. Abenragel also writes that the Indians, who called this mansion Fargalmocaden, or Al Fargh al Mukdim, say that it would be good for making a journey in the first third of the day, but the rest would be neither good for journeys nor any other beginning.

According to al-Biruni, the mansion causes union, health of captives, and destroys buildings and prisons. With the Moon here, plant, sow, bargain, marry but do not navigate.

The Arab Picatrix tells us to make all kinds of talismans for good purposes, as well as for the combining of souls in love. It is also that one who is planning a journey, will have his wishes granted. Make talismans for the safe journey of seafarers, to separate comrades, and to bind prisoners.

The Latin Picatrix indicates that in this mansion, which is named Almiquedam, it is good to make talismans to unite men in mutual esteem, to protect those travelling by carriage, to reinforce the prisons and cells of captives, and to inflict evil upon them.

According to Pliny, the first Alfarg is for generating love. Take white wax and mastic gum, and melt them together. From this make an image of a woman with her hair untied, holding before her a container (as if she wanted to put her hair in into it). Suffumigate with odorous things and say:

"You, O Tagriel, draw me to the love and friendship of (name)."

Place the image in a small container, combine it with nice smelling things and carry it with you.

Peter Stockinger

Ibn al-Hatim writes that the image for the talisman should be that of a woman whose hair hangs down. She is wearing a variety of coloured cloths. Between her hands is a pot of perfume she perfumes herself with. Write on her chest the name of the man overcoming her love for herself. Giordano Bruno has a different description of the image. According to him it shows a woman washing and combing her hair in front of a winged boy.

Ibn-Arabi's attribution for this mansion, which he called the First Spout, is the Jinn, the Divine Attribute is the Subtle.

Bonatti and Jafar note that this mansion is wet, lucky, and fortunate.

From a natal perspective, Brenner writes in his 1559 edition:

> Who will be born when Aporaboyl is rising will receive many goods. He will lose it all but will be lucky and, although he does not have enough goods, will be handsome and healthy. But who will be born during the second hour of its rise will be full life and handsome. Who will be born during the third hour will be black. He will have enough children, although some of them will die. He will like wine, be proud and angry, and will die alone in poverty. He will walk around with good salb [?] and he will receive a mark form wood or iron. He will live healthily 22 years, thereafter he will get ill. If he recovers, he will live 52 years. Then he will get ill. If he recovers, he will live 72 years, but not an hour longer.

27ᵗʰ Lunar Mansion Al-Fargh al Thani, The Second Spout

The name of the 27ᵗʰ lunar mansion is al-Fargh al Thani, the Second Spout, Lower Handle, or the Later Two. Agrippa calls it the Second Drawing, or Draining. It is also known as al-Far al-mu'ahhar, Alfargamahar, or Faragh al-dalw al-mu'akhkhir. In the West, it was known as Alcharya, Ahhalgalmoad, or Algarfermuth, to name only a few of the transliterations. Al-Biruni calls it the Lower Handle (of the bucket), and the Later Two, who move the Bucket in the Well (in order to fill it). It consists of two stars similar to Alfargh Al'awwal (see the 26ᵗʰ lunar mansion). Al-Qazwini calls the mansion elferg' et't'âni, the Second Spout. It rises on 22. ad'âr (March) and sets on 22. Ailûl (September).

The tropical boundaries for the 27ᵗʰ lunar mansion are 4*17'10'' Pisces and 17*08'34'' Pisces. The sidereal boundaries, given in tropical Zodiac longitude, precessed for 2024, are 9* Aries and 00* Taurus. The modern longitude (2024) of determinant fixed star gamma Pegasi (Algenib) is 9*29' Aries. The other determinant star is alpha Andromedae (Alpheratz) at 14*39' Aries. Algenib, is a star marking the tip of Pegasus' wing. The star is said to be of the nature of Mars and Mercury. It suggests misfortune, notoriety, and dishonour. Elsbeth Ebertin mentions a penetrating mind and strong-willed determination, as well as a gift for oratory.

The name of the second determinant star, Alpheratz, derives from the Arabians' Al Surrat al Faras, translated as the Horse's Navel. The star was once associated with Pegasus. Later, it was transferred to the head of the Chained Woman, Andromeda. According to Ideler, it was Ulug Bekh who called the star Ras al-Mar'a al-Musalsala (head of the chained). According to Ptolemy, the star is of the nature of Jupiter and Venus It suggests freedom, honour, and a sharp intellect.

There are different names for the lord or angel of this mansion. Ibn al-Hatim calls him Amriyal lamiyal; in the Picatrix we find the name to be Abliemel, and Agrippa gives the name as Alheniel.

According to Abenragel, Dorotheus said that if starting a partnership during this mansion, it will begin well but end in harm and conflict. Entering a ship will bring damage, dangers, and travails. A slave bought will be bad. If captured, he will not leave prison. Abenragel also writes that the Indians, who called this mansion Alfargamahar, or Al Fargh al Thani, say that it would be good for sowing, and useful for trading. It is also good for marriage. The mansion is indifferent for journeys, except for middle third of night when it is very bad. It is also bad for entrusting something to someone, or lending anything.

According to al-Biruni, the mansion increases harvests, revenues, gain, heals infirmities, hinders buildings, upholds prisons, causes danger to seamen and destruction of enemies. With the Moon here, marry, take medicine, pursue business but do not travel or lend money.

Manazil

The Arab Picatrix tells us to make talismans for trade to prosper, for blessed yield of crops, for swift recovery from illnesses, to destroy somebody's estate, to sow disharmony between a married couple, to prolong the time of imprisonment for prisoners, and to spoil slaves.

In the Latin Picatrix we find that in this mansion, which is named Algarf almuehar, it is good to make talismans to improve commerce and its profits, to unite associates, to increase harvests, to heal infirmities, and to ruin someone's riches. Also make talismans to impede the construction of buildings, to hinder those sailing, to prolong the incarceration of prisoners, and to inflict harm on whomever you wish.

According to Pliny, the latter Alfarg, is for destroying a bath. Take red soil from which you should make the image of a man with wings, holding an empty, pierced vessel in his hands, raising it up to his mouth. Place it all over a fire until it is cooked. Then put into this vessel asafoetida and liquid storax, and say:

> "You, O Abliemel, destroy (name) bath of (name) man. Bury the image in the same bath."

Ibn al-Hatim agrees with the Picatrix, adding that the talisman should be fumigated with wax and naphtha. The name should be engraved on the head of the image so that no one should pass by this region. Giordano Bruno has a different description of the image. According to him it shows a man casting a bottle into the hole of a well.

Ibn-Arabi's attribution for this mansion, which he called the Second Spout, is humanity. The Divine Attribute is the Uniter.

Bonatti and Jafar note that this mansion is temperate, unlucky, and unfortunate.

Peter Stockinger

From a natal perspective, Brenner writes in his 1559 edition:

> Who will be conceived when Alcharga is rising during the first hour of the day will be clever and win many goods. He will be white, fair, true, and healthy. But at some point, he will get into terrible trouble, so much that he will lose all his possessions. He will be working for a master and will continue so that many people will want to cause him harm. But they will not achieve this as much as they try. But who will be born during the second hour of the day will receive great honours. He will survive his parents, have many children, and will be cured of all pains. And he will be lucky in 'Ostland' in the sea. He will have long eyes, his faith [?] is ill. He will win many things, but lose much also. He will live healthily 27 years. Thereafter he will get ill. If he recovers, he will get to 54 years. Thereafter he will get ill. If he survives, he will live 70 years. Then his last day will approach and he will have to die.

28th Lunar Mansion Batn al Hut,
The Belly of the Fish, The Ribbon

The name of the 28th lunar mansion is Batn al Hut, The Belly of the Fish. This mansion is also known as al-Risha, the Ribbon. Agrippa calls it the Fishes or Pisces (see al-Biruni, below). In the West it was known as Albotham, Alchalh, or Beualhot, to name only a few of its transliterations. Ideler writes that Ulug Bekh knew that this lunar mansion was called Batn al-hhut, consisting of many stars in the shape of a fish. It is also called al-rascha (the Ribbon). The tail lies in the south, the head towards the north. There seems to have been some confusion, because at times some of the determinant stars have also been part of Andromeda. Ulug Bekh included beta Andromeda, which he called Dscheinb al-musalsela, the side of the Chained Woman. Al-Biruni writes that the mansion is also called Kalb-Alhut. It is a bright star in the one half of the womb of a fish (a star) called Ribbon, which must not be confused with the Two Fishes, one (the 12th) of the zodiacal signs. These stars stand above Libra and belong to Andromeda (lit. The chained wife who had not seen a husband). Al-Qazwini writes that its rise takes place on 4. nîs'ân (April) and its setting on 5. tis'-rîn elawwal (October).

The tropical boundaries for the 28th lunar mansion are 17*08'34'' Pisces and 00* Aries. The sidereal boundaries, given in tropical Zodiac longitude, precessed for 2024, are 00* Taurus and 3* Taurus. The modern longitude (2024) of the determinant fixed star beta Andromedae (Mirach) is 00*44' Taurus. According to Ptolemy, Mirach is of the nature of Venus. This fixed star promises personal beauty, a brilliant mind, and a successful marriage. Inspired artistry is also supported. Assistance in life can come from others, and friends are made easily.

There are different names for the lord or angel of this mansion. Ibn al-Hatim calls him Anush; in the Picatrix we find the name to be Anuxi, and Agrippa gives the name as Amnixiel.

According to Abenragel, Dorotheus said that this mansion was good in the way that a partnership started will begin well but end badly. A slave bought will be bad, irascible, and very proud. If captured, he will not leave prison. Abenragel also writes that the Indians, who called this mansion Bathnealoth, or Al Batn al Hut, say that it would be good for trade, sowing and medicines. It is also good for marriage, but indifferent for journeys, except for middle third of night when it is bad. It is also bad for entrusting something to someone, or lending anything.

According to al-Biruni, the mansion increases harvest and merchandise, and helps travellers through danger. It strengthens prisons and causes marital happiness and loss of treasure. With the Moon here, travel and take purgatives.

The Arab Picatrix tells us to make talismans for the flowering of trade, and the prosperity of crops. Also make talismans for the recovery from illnesses, for the loss of deposits, for safe journey of travellers, to reconcile married couples, to bind and tie up prisoners, to do seafarers any kind of harm.

Manazil

The Latin Picatrix suggests that in this mansion, which is named Arrexhe, it is good to make talismans to improve commerce, to besiege cities, to increase harvests, to balance things, to ruin jokes, to cause someone to lose treasure, to protect those travelling by carriage and ensure their return in good health. Also make talismans to instils peace and harmony between husband and wife. Furthermore, to reinforce prison cells of captives, and to inflict harm upon those who sail by ship.

According to Pliny, Arrexe is for gathering fish in one place. One should make a sigil out of zinc on which should be sculpted the image of a fish with a coloured spine. On its side write the name of this mansion. Suffumigate with the skin of a sea fish, then bind it with string and throw it into the water (namely in the place where you want the fish to gather).

Ibn al-Hatim agrees with the Picatrix, adding a fish, whose back is striped with colours, carries a small fish in its mouth. He writes that the talisman should be made of silver, and advises to suffumigate with the skin of a goat. The talisman should be tied in a place where you wish to seize fish to yourself by means of a strong string. Giordano Bruno has a different description of the image. According to him it shows a fish leaping through the air above water in which swim many more.

Ibn-Arabi's attribution for this mansion, which he calls the Belly of the Fish, is the Hierarchy of the Degrees of Existence, not their Manifestation. The Divine Attribute is the One Who Elevates by Degrees.

Bonatti and Jafar note that this mansion is wet, lucky, and fortunate.

From a natal perspective, Brenner writes in his 1559 edition:

Who will be born if Beualhot is rising in the first hour of the day will be white, strange, and very rich. He will be ingenious, not too small, and not too tall either.

He will be avoiding many illnesses and will be healthy. His goods will be enjoyed more by strangers than by his friends. He will have many children. He will have marks on his neck and near his eyes and two on one foot. But who will be born in the second hour will have marks on his finger or somewhere else on his body. He will break a bone. If he recovers it will not happen again. He will be left with all honours and goods of two women. He will be mean, which is why he has not got enough. He is longing for goods on water and on land. He will have a brave son and will be an honourable father. He will experience an adventure, fall into water, and get out again. And a master will be angry with him, which will lose him money. But he will still have enough. He will live healthily for 28 years. Thereafter he will get ill. If he recovers, he will live 56 years. Thereafter he will be ill again. If he recovers, he will get to 80 years. Then it will be finished.

Part 3

Source Material

For they made images against disease and hatred and for a prosperous journey when the Moon was positioned anywhere from the seventeenth degree of Virgo to its end.

(Masilio Ficino, Three Books on Life)

Book of Instructions in the Elements of the Art of Astrology, by Abu'l-Rayhan Muhammad Ibn Ahmad Al-Biruni, written in Ghaznah, 1029A.D. Reproduced from Brit. Mus. MS.Or.8349, Translation by R. Ramsey Wright, London, Luzac & Co, 1934

Mansions of the Moon

164. Fa ma manazil al-qamar. As the zodiac, the course of the sun in a year, is divided into twelve equal signs, so also the path of the moon among the fixed stars is divided into daily stations, the mansions of the moon. Of these there are twenty-seven according to the Hindus and twenty-eight according to the Arabs. Just as the signs are called after the constellations, so the mansions are called after the fixed stars in which the moon is stationed for the night. They begin as in the case of the sun at the vernal equinox.

1. al-sharatain, (two signals), the first mansion, is marked by two bright stars on the horns, sarugahp, of Aries; they are disposed in a north and south line, the apparent distance between them, about a fathom, being the same as that between the southern one and a third smaller star. Also called butters, natha.

2. al-butain, three stars from the tail of Aries disposed in a triangle. Diminutive of batn, belly, because smaller than batn al-hut, No. 28.

3. al-thuraiya, parvinp, six stars from the shoulder of Taurus, grouped like a bunch of grapes. Generally, and especially by poets, the number is supposed to be seven, but this is a mistake. Although the term najm is applicable to every star, thuraiya alone is specially distinguished as 'al-najm'.

4. Al-dabaran is a large shining red star in the easterly eye of Taurus. The head of Taurus is shaped like a bowl with its mouth to the north, (while the muffle of the bull (mouth and lips) are directed south). Aldebaran, the 'follower' of the Pleiades is also called tabi' al-najm.

5. Al-haq'a, is formed by three small stars from the head of Orion arranged like a trivet, so close together that they look like one. On this account Ptolemy regarded them as a single nebula.

6. Al-han'a, two small stars from the feet of Gemini, the one smaller, the other somewhat brighter.

7. Al-dhira', the extended foreleg of the Arab lion, for the contracted one is formed by Procyon and its mirzam (a mirzam is a small star, coupled to another bright one). Al-dhira' is formed by two bright stars from the heads of Gemini, distant from each other as much as the distance between Al-sharatain.

8. Al-nathrah, the nose of the lion, formed of two small stars of Cancer, which are interpreted as the nostrils. Between them is a nebula which some call the lion's uvula, lahat, malazah, but the Greeks call the stars the two asses, himarain and the nebula, the manger, ma'laf, (Praesepe).

9. Al-tarf, the eyes of the lion; these are two bright stars, one from Leo, the other from outside it, apparently about a cubit from each other.

Manazil

10. Al-jabhah, or jabhat al-asad, the lion's forehead, is formed by four bright stars, not in a straight line from north to south. The largest and brightest and most southerly is the heart of Leo. qalb al-asad, or al-malaki (Regulus).

11. Al-zubrah, the mane of the Arab lion, formed by two stars from the hind-quarters of Leo, distant more than a cubit. Also known as al-kharatan.

12. Al-sarfah is a bright star at the tip of the tail of Leo, but according to the Arabs on the tail itself, (and regarded by them and the astrologers as the scrotum). Al-dafirah (Coma Berenices) is the group of small stars like the Pleiades forming the tuft of hair, hulbah, at the tip of the tail.

13. Al-'awwa, four stars running (from north to south) and curving at last like the letter lam; they are from the breast and wings of Virgo, and the Arabs speak of them as dogs barking behind the lion.

14. Al-simak, the unarmed one of the two considered by the Arabs to be the hind legs of their lion, but according to the Greeks al-'azal is an ear of corn, craxus, in the hand of Virgo, which the translations have rendered by sunbulah)Spica). It is sunbulah by which the sixth sign is so well-known. It occupies a similar position to that of al-dafirah (in its relation to Leo.)

15. Al-ghafr is formed by two small stars on the train, dhail, of Virgo, quite inconspicuous; the name is derived from their concealment.

16. Al-zubana, the claws of the scorpion, two stars from the scales of Libra, which are at the spear's length from each other.

17. Al-iklil or the crown, three bright stars from the forehead of Scorpius, arranged in a slightly curved line from north to south.

18. Al-qualb, i.e. qualm al-'aqrab, the heart of Scorpius, Antares, is a red and trembling star which astrologers describe as having the nature of Mars; in front of it is another star, and behind it a third, the three being disposed in a curve.

19. Al-shaulah, the sting of Scorpius, which is turned forwards over the joints of the tail; two stars bright, but not large, separated by about a span from each other.

20. Al-na'a 'im, the ostriches, four bright stars from the bow, arrow, and foreleg of the horse of Sagittarius forming a quadrangle. The Arabs compare the milky way to a river, and these stars to ostriches going to the river, na'am waridah al-nahr, while there are four others which they speak of as na'am sadiron, returning from watering.

21. Al-baldah, an area of the heavens behind Sagittarius, devoid of stars, and compared to a desert or a gap (between the eyebrows). These stars which border it (on the west) from the tresses of Sagittarius are called al-qiladah, the necklace.

22. Sa'd al-dhabih, the sacrificer; here are two stars, not bright, disposed horizontally with more than a cubit between them; both are on the horn of Capricorn. Near them is a third star which the Arabs call a sheep about to be sacrificed.

23. Sa'd bula', the glutton, marked by two stars on the left hand of Aquarius, between them is a third about to be devoured by the glutton.

24. Sa'd al-su'ud, three stars in a row from north to south from the tail of Capricornus and the shoulder of Aquarius.

25. Sa'd al-akhbiyah is marked by four stars on the right hand of Aquarius; the outline of the group resembles a duck's foot; three of the stars form a triangle which conceals in its interior the fourth, the lucky one. According to the Arabs these are not the only fortunate stars, for there are many outside the mansions of the moon which are.

26 and 27. Al-fargh al-ewwal and al-thani or muqaddam and mu'akhkhar, are each marked by two stars, situated a spear's length from each other, and all from Pegasus. The Arabs compare the four stars to a bucket dalw, but the eleventh sign

of the zodiac is so known; fargh really means the place for pouring out the water, but these are often interpreted as the upper and lower handles, 'arquwatan.

28. Batn al-hut is marked by two bright stars from the head of Andromeda, near to which is a group of small stars in a curved line, out of which the Arabs make a fish, and these stars are falling into the wide-open mouth of the fish, whence the name belly. Others call this mansion risha, comparing the fish to a rope, so that the bucket in Pegasus should not lack a rope.

The Chronology of Ancient Nations, Al-Biruni

The Arabs divided the celestial globe into 28 parts, so that each Station occupies nearly 12 5/6 degrees of the ecliptic, and each zodiacal sign contains 2 ⅓ Stations. Some poet says:

"Their number is, if you want to count them,

Twenty stars, and a number 8 after them.

In each of the zodiacal signs there are

Two Stations and one complete third of a Station.

A peculiar system of computation belongs to them, and they have

Their heliacal risings and settings,

Which are the reason that winter and summer revolve."

The Arabs used the Lunar Stations in another way then the Hindus, as it was their object to learn thereby all meteorological changes in the seasons of the year. But the Arabs, being illiterate people, could not recognise the Lunar Stations, except by certain marks, visible to the eye. Therefore, they marked the Stations by those fixed stars which lie within them. And the rising of the fixed stars in the east early after the rise of dawn they considered as a sign of the sun's entering some of the Stations, and so they could do, since the stars do not recede from their places except after the lapse of long spaces of time, and, besides, the Arabs were not educated enough to notice such a variation. Further, they composed verses and rhymed poetry, so that these things could easily be remembered by illiterate people, and recorded therein the annual physical influences which, according to their observation and experience, coincided with the rising of each particular Station. These sayings and verses they use to indicate certain circumstances of theirs, e.g.:

Manazil

"When the moon joins (I.e. stands in conjunction with) the Pleiades, In
a third night (of a month), then the winter is gone."

For the Pleiades occupy the place from 10* of *Taurus* till about 15* of Taurus. When, therefore, the moon joins the Pleiades in the 3rd night of a month, the distance between sun and moon is about 40 degrees. Then the sun stands in the first part of *Aries*. Further:

"When the full-moon is complete and stands with the Pleiades, Then
you get the beginning of the cold season, the winter."

For when the moon stands in opposition to the Pleiades, the sun stands in the middle of Scorpio, and that time is the beginning of the cold season. Further:

"When full-moon joins Aldabaran,
In the 14th night of a month,
Then winter encircles the whole earth.
Being like riders who ride about, telling people to warm themselves,
And full-moon rises in heaven high overhead, so that
The shadow of the tent-poles disappears,
When the night has reached its middle
And the air is free from dark clouds."

For at that time the sun stands in Scorpio close to *Alkalb* (the 18th Lunar Station); it is the time of cold and of morning frosts. The moon stands in some degree of northern declination, and frequently she stands in such a latitude from the ecliptic towards the the direction of the declination that she culminates (stands right) over the heads of the Arabs. In consequence, the shadows of all bodies disappear at the time when she reaches the middle of heaven, i.e. at the time of midnight. Further:

Peter Stockinger

"When the new moon of a month first appears

To the eyes of people at the beginning of a night, standing in *Alna'a'im*,

Then you get cold winds from every side,

And you find it agreeable a little before dawn to wrap a turban round your head."

For at that time the sun stands in the first part of Sagittarius. Further:

"The complete night, with all that belongs to it, has become cold,

And the sun stands in the Station of *Al'awwa*."

For the stars of Al'awwa (the 13th Lunar Station) lie around the vernal equinox, as the table of Lunar Stations will show. However, if I were to communicate to the reader all the verses and sayings in rhymed prose which relate to the rising of each Lunar Station, I should also have to interpret their meanings, and to explain the rare words that occur in them. This, however, we may omit since it has been sufficiently done by the authors of the books of 'Anwa', who we mentioned above.

Since the Arabs attribute all meteorological changes to the influence of the rising and setting of the stars, in consequence of their ignorance of physical sciences, thinking that all changes of the kind depend upon the bodies of the stars and their rising, not upon certain parts of the celestial globe and the sun's marching therein, they believe a great many things similar to that which we have mentioned of the *Sirius Jemenicus*, during the rising of which Hippocrates in his time forbade taking hot drugs and phlebotomizing.

Manazil

And this subject reminds me of an occurrence in my life which serves to confirm the verses of Ahmad b. Faris:

"A wise man of bye-gone times has said:
'The importance of a man lies in his two smallest things.'
I on my part also speak like a wise man, saying:
'The importance of a man lies only in his two dirhams.'
If he has not his two dirhams with him,
His bride does not care for him.
In consequence of his poverty he is despised,
So that people's cats piss at him."

For when I was separated from the court of His Highness, and was bereft of the happiness of the royal service, I met a man in Rai (Rhagae) who was counted among the learned astronomers. He had studied the conjunctions of the stars which form the Lunar Stations, and he had commenced to collect them in order to derive certain sentences (astrologoumena) from the Stations and their single parts, and thereby to pronosticate all changes of the air. Now, I told him that the truth is the very reverse of his theory, that the nature and peculiarities which are attributed to the first Station, and all that which the Hindus relate of the connection of this Station with others, are peculiar to the first part of Aries,. And never leave this place, although the star (or stars which form the Lunar Station) may leave it. In a similar way, all that is peculiar to Aries does not move away. But then the man became very haughty, and treated me slightingly, though he was inferior to me in all his knowledge. He told me my theory was a lie, and behaved very rudely to me, being very lengthy about the difference between us in wealth and poverty, which changes subjects for glory into subjects for blame. For at that time I was in a miserable condition, tried (troubled) on all sides; afterwards, however, when my troubles had subsided (ceased) to some extent, he chose to behave in a friendly way towards me.

It is evident that, if the science of meteorology were to depend upon the rising of the bodies of the stars, as observed by eye-sight, the times and seasons of the Meteora would differ in the same proportion as the stars change their places; besides, they would be different in different countries, and we should require for them as well as for the appearing and disappearing of the planets various kinds of tiresome methods of calculations.

In reality the rising of the Lunar Stations means that the sun on entering one of them covers it and the preceding one too, whilst the third one, according to the inverted order of the zodiacal signs, rises between the rise of dawn and that of the sun, at that time which Ibn Alrakka' describes in the following verses:

"The observers saw Sirius distinctly,
As he turned away, when the morning prayer approached.
I recognise Sirius shining red, whilst the morning is becoming white.
The night, fading away, has risen and left him.
The night is not afraid to lose him, since he follows her,
But the night is not willing to acknowledge that he belongs to the night."

The rising of a Lunar Station they called its *Nau'*, i.e. rising. The influence of the rising they called *Barih*, the influence of the setting they called again *Nau'*. The interval between the risings of two consecutive Lunar Stations is 13 days, except the interval between the rising of *Aljabha* (the 10th Station) and the following Station, which is 14 days. So the following verses:

"All time, you must know, consists of fourths,
And each fourth consists of sevenths.
A complete seventh belongs to the rising of a star,
And to the influence (*Nau'*) of a star setting in the west.

Manazil

> Between the rising of each star
> And that of the following star there are *four* nights
> And *nine* nights more."

There is a difference of opinion regarding the *'Anwa*. Some maintain that each influence (of a Lunar Station) is brought about between the risings of the two consecutive Stations, that therefore the influence is attributed to the former of these two Stations. According to others, a certain space of time is peculiar to the rising and setting of each Lunar Station, and everything that occurs in this time is attributed to the Station in question; occurrences which fall after the end of this space of time are no longer attributed to it. The last view is the generally adopted one.

Besides, there are differences about the length of these spaces of time, which we shall afterwards describe.

When the influence of some Station has been found out and is known, and nothing happens at its time, people say: the star was *empty*; or: the Station was *empty*, i.e. the time of its *Nau'* has gone by without there being any rain, or heat, or cold, or wind.

(On the Winds.) - Regarding the direction of the winds, the planes over which they blow, and their number, there are different opinions. Some maintain that the directions of the wind are six, as Ibn Kunasa relates, on the authority of 'Abu-Muhammad Ja'far b. Sa'd b. Samura b. Jundub Alfazari, whilst, according to most others, there are noble four, as Khalid b. Safwan realties; the latter is the opinion of most nations, although they differ regarding the planes of the blowing of the winds. Both these opinions of the Arabs are comprised in the following two circles; the former view is represented in the inner circle, the latter in the outer circle.

There you also find the names of the winds and the directions of their planes. Here follows the circle:

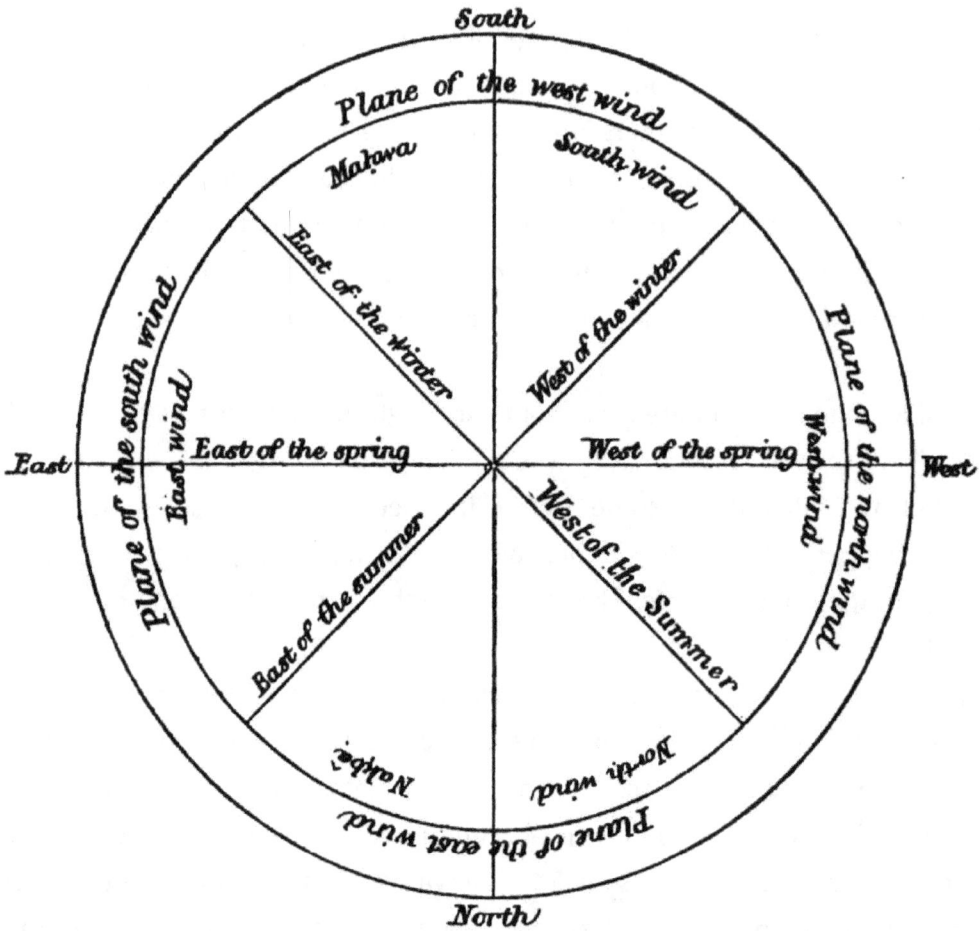

In the first theory the author (Ibn Kunasa) places the wind *Mahwa* near the south wind, whilst it is well known that *Mahwa* is the north, wind, because it extinguishes (destroys) the clouds when they are empty, after the south wind has

Manazil

driven them on, full of rain. In the same theory he assigns a separate plane to the wind *Nakbu*, whilst it is well known that Nakba is every wind, the plane of which lies between the planes of any two other winds of the four cardinal winds. Dhu-alrumma mentions the winds, *Nabka* (sic) included, in this way:

> "Heavy rain-showers of some Anwa and the two Half (south wind and west wind),
> Which drove the sand-masses of the dusty-coloured mountains away over the house.
> And a third wind, blowing from the side of Syria, a cold one,
> Blowing with whirlwinds along its road over the sand.
> And a fourth wind coming from the rising-place of the sun, driving
> The fine dust of Almi'a and of Kurakir over the house.
> The side winds, carrying along the dust, excited it (the east wind) to still greater   vehemence,
> So that it frequently roared like the she-camels in the tenth month of their pregnancy, when the throes are near."

The two *Haif* are the south wind and west wind; the wind blowing from Syria is the north wind; the wind coming from the rising-place of the sun is the east wind.

The planes of the winds with the Persians are the same as with the ancient Greeks, and all physical scholars; their centres correspond to the four directions. They are represented by the following circle:

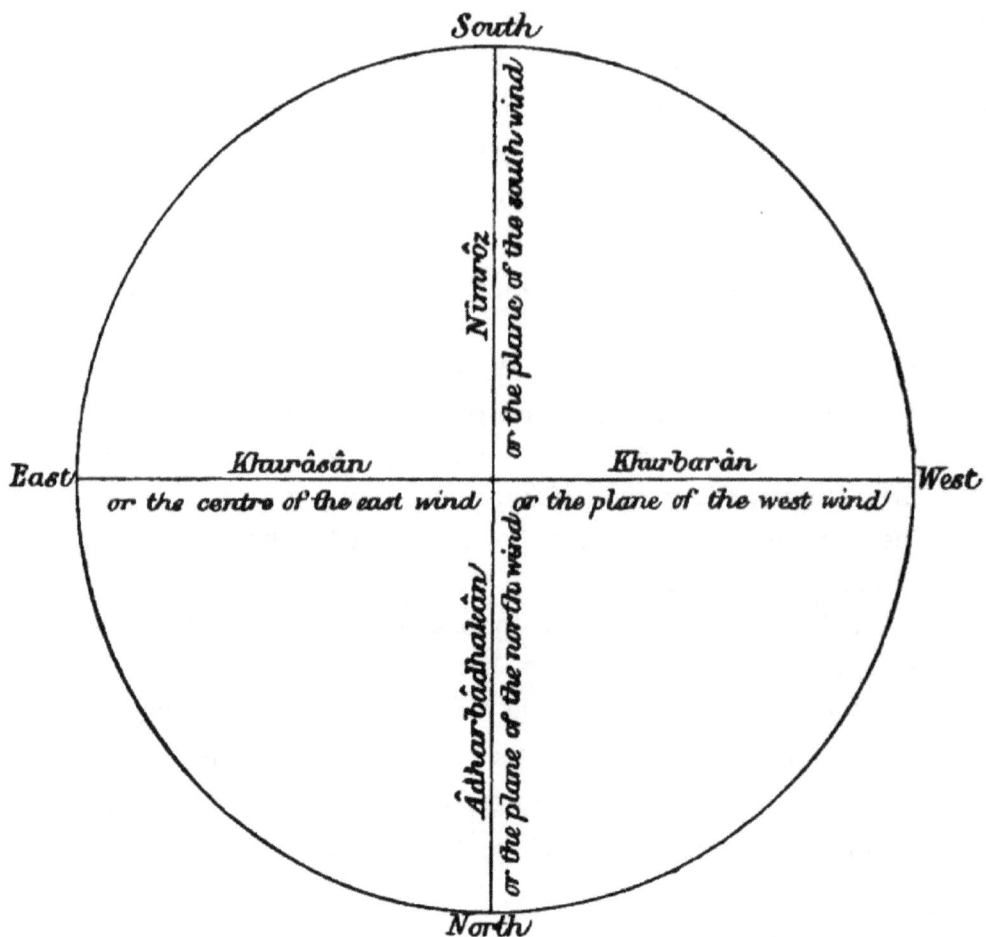

Any wind that lies between the centres of the planes of two other winds is referred to that centre which is the nearest (and receives its name therefrom). Other people refer an intermediate wind to the rising and setting places of the sun at the time of the solstices, and call it by a Greek name.

Manazil

(Method for finding the time of the Nau' and Barih of a Lunar Station.) –

The following is a good method to find the times of the influences (greek word) of the rising and the setting Lunar Stations: Take the time from the 1st of Ilul till that day the nature of which you want to find out, and divide the sum of days by 13. If there is no remainder, proceed in this way: If the moon stands opposite the sun or in one of her quadratures, you get rain, if it is the season for rain, or some change of the air in consequence of wind, or heat, or cold. For if there is no remainder (as in this case), it is the time of the rising of one Lunar Station and the setting of the opposite Station. On the 1st of Ilul falls the Barih (influence of the rising) of *Alsarfa* (the 12th Station) and the *Nau'* (influence of the setting) of *Sa'd-al'akhbiya* (the 25th Station). From this date you begin counting, for this special reason, that it is the first of a month and the beginning of autumn. If, besides, the moon happens to be in one of the *Foundations*, the influence (of the Lunar Station) will come out very strong.

Abu-Ma'shar says:

> "We have tried this method A. H. 279 in Shawwal at the time of the full moon. They were 130 days; dividing them by 13 you get no remainder, and the *Ascendens* of the full moon (or opposition) was *Amphora*. So we got rain on that day, and when the moon stood in her right quadrature, also on that day we had rain."

Further, he says:

> "We tried it also in the following year. We counted the days from the 1st Ilul till Thursday the 13th of Kanun. I.; the sum of days we divided by 13, and there was no remainder; the distance between sun and moon

was as much as half a zodiacal sign (i.e. 15 degrees), the moon had turned away from the hexagon of Mars and stood in conjunction with Venus. At that time we got rain."

Now, this is a testimony of Abu-Ma'shar, showing that trough this method you obtain correct results. If, besides, you take to help the mansions (the places of the Lunar Stations) of the Hindus and their single parts, you are pretty sure in your calculation to come near the truth.

People relate that among the Arabs the Banu-Mariya b. Kalb and the Banu-Murra b. Hammam b. Shaiban had the most accurate knowledge of the configuration of the stars.

In enumerating the *Nujum-al'akhdh*, i.e. the Lunar Stations, the Arabs commenced with *Alsharatan*, since in their time they stood in the first part of *Aries*. Other nations begin with the Pleiades. I do not know whether they do this because the Pleiades are more easily and clearly visible without any study or research than other Stations, or because, as I have found in some books of Hermes, the vernal equinox coincides with the rising of the Pleiades. This statement must have been made about three thousand years before Alexander. God knows best what they intended!

We shall adopt the Arabian system in enumerating the Lunar Stations, and shall begin, as they do, with

1. *Alsharatan (beta, gamma Arietis),*

i.e. the two *signs*. They are called so for the same reason that the soldiers of the body- guard of a prince are called *Shurat*, since they mark themselves by some *sign*, by the black colour, or something else. It consists of two stars belonging to

Aries (beta and gamma). Sometimes, also, a third star near them is added, and then this Station is called *Al'sharat* (plural instead of the dual Sharatan). Between the two stars, when standing in the middle of heaven, there is an interval of two yards according to eye-sight; one of them belongs to the northern half, the other to the southern.

All measures of distances between the stars, according to eye-sight are to be understood only for that time when they stand in the middle of heaven, for these distances appear greater near the horizon in consequence of the intense refraction of the ray of light in the watery vapours that surround the earth. This has been explained in the books on the geometrical configurations (of the stars). Further, the distance between two stars increases in the direction from north towards the south; frequently, too, when the stars march towards the horizon, it increases in the direction from east to west, or pretty nearly in the direction of one of the cycles of altitude. The reason of this is that the spheres decline from the perpendicular direction which they have on the equator.

The station *Al'sharat* is also called *Alnath* (i.e. horn), because the two *Sharat* are placed on the root of the two *horns* of Aries. The meteorological influences of this station are peculiar to the first (i.e. original) position of Aries, and in no way depend upon the stars from which the Station has got its name. The stars have migrated from their original place (in consequence of the precession of the equinoxes) and have in our time come to occupy a second position (different from the former).

2. *Albutain* (epsilon, delta, pi Arietis).

It consists of three stars at the end of the womb of Aries, forming an isosceles triangle. The word is the diminutive of *Batn*, so as to mean the *little womb*, so called in comparison with Batn-alhut (the womb of the fish), which is the 28th Station.

3. *Althurayya* (Pleiades)

Consists of six stars close to each other, very similar to a cluster of grapes. According to the Arabs they form the *clunis* of Aries, but that is wrong, because they stand on the hump of Taurus.

The word is a diminutive of *Tharwâ*, which is originally identical with *Tharwa*, i.e. a collection and great number of something. Some people maintain they were called so because the rain, which is brought by their *Nau'*, produces *Tharwa*, i.e. abundance. They are also called *Alnajm* (i.e. *The Star*).

Ptolemy mentions only four stars of the Pleiades, since he had not observed more of them, because to eye-sight they seem to lie quite close together.

The forty days during which this Station disappears under the rays of the sun, are, according to the Arabs, the worst and most unhealthy of the whole year. Al'asadi says:

"Althurayya never rises nor sets unless bringing some harm."

And one of their medical men says:

"Warrant me the time between the disappearing and the rising of Althurayya, and I shall warrant you all the remainder of the year." The Prophet is related to have said: "When the Star rises, all harm (mishap) rises from the earth;" and according to another tradition: "When the Star rises, all mishap is raised from every place."

Manazil

4. *Aldabaran* (alpha Tauri),

A bright red star, so called because it *follows* after the Pleiades, standing over the southern eye of Taurus. It is also called *Alfanik*, i.e. a great camel-stallion (not serving for riding), because they call the stars around it *Kilas*, i.e. young she-camels (serving for riding). Other names of it are *"The follower of the Star"*, because in rising and setting it follows immediately after the Pleiades, and *Almukhdij* (i.e. a she-camel giving birth to a young one of imperfect formation).

5. *Alhak'a* (lambda, phi', phi'' Orionis)

Consists of three small stars close to each other, looking like so many dots impressed upon the earth by the thumb, the fore-finger, and the middle-finger, the fingers being closely pressed together. They were so called because they were compared with a circle of hairs on the side of the horse at the joint of the foot; such a horse is called *Mahku'*. They are also called *Altaha'i*, (or *Altahayi*). Ptolemy considers them as one cloudy star, and calls them the nebula on the head of Aljabbar, i.e. Aljauza (Orion).

6. *Alhan'a* (gamma, xi Geminorum)

Consists of two bright stars in the Milky Way between Orion and the head of Gemini, distant from each other as far as the length of a whip. The one is called *Zirr* (button), the other *Maisan* (walking along proudly); they stand on the foot of the second twin. According to Alzajjaj, *Han'a* is derived from the verb *Hana'a*, i.e. to wind and twine one thing round the other, as if each of them were winding and twining around the other. According to others, this name is to be understood of a third star, stranding behind their middle, which gives them the appearance of an *inclined neck*. The Arabs consider Alhan'a and six other stars as the bow of Orion, with which he shoots at the Lion.

7. *Aldhira'* (alpha, beta Geminorum)

Consists of two stars, one yard distant from each other. The one is the blear-eyed Sirius or Sirius Syracus, according to the Arabs, the outstretched arm of Leo; the other is Sirius *'Abar* or Sirius Yemeniens, the arm of Leo which is not stretched out. According to the astronomers, the outstretched arm is the head of Gemini, and the other arm belongs to the stars of *Alkalb Almutakaddim* (Procyon). But people differ greatly regarding these stars and produce various futile traditions and stories in support of the names which they give them. The rising of *Ghu??isa* (the blear-eyed Sirius) in the year 1300 of Alexander took place on the 10th Tammuz, and that of Sirius Yemenicus on the 23rd Tammuz.

8. *Alnathra* (Praesepe) (epsilon) et duo Aselli (gamma, delta) Cancri)

Is the place between the mouth and the nostrils of the Lion. It is also called *Allaha* (the uvula), and consists of two stars, between which there is a nebula, the whole belonging to the figure of Cancer.

9. *Altarf*,

The eye of Leo, two stars close to each other, one belonging to Leo, the other to the stars outside the figure of Cancer. In front of them there are stars called *Al'ashfar*, i.e. the eyebrows of Leo.

Manazil

10. *Aljabha* (zeta, gamma, eta, alpha Leonis),

The front of Leo, for stars, each star distant from the other by the length of a whip, lying athwart from north to south in a curve, not in a straight line. According to astronomers, they stand on the mane of Leo. The most southern star of them they call the *Heart of the Royal Lion*; it rises when Suhail rises in Alhijaz. Suhail is the 44th star of Argo Navis, standing over its oar. Its latitude is 75 degrees in the southern half. Therefore, it does not rise very high above the horizon, in consequence of which it has something unsteady for the eye. People say that a man, if his eye falls on this star, dies, as they also relate that on the island of Ramin, belonging to Ceylon, there is an animal the sight of which kills a man within forty days afterwards. The most curious instance of the connection between animal life and its material influence is the fish called *Silurus Electricus*. For the hand of the fisherman who has caught it takes care not touch it as long as it is in the net still living. If you take a reed and touch the living fish with one end and keep the other end in your hand, the hand becomes feeble and drops the reed.

Further, the worms in Raghad, one of the districts of eastern Jurjan. For there you find in certain places small worms; if a man carrying water treads upon them, the water becomes bad and foul; if he does not tread upon them, the water remains good and keeps its nice odour and sweet taste.

The death of a man bitten by a panther, when a field-mouse pisses at him -

[Lacuna]

11. *Alzubra* (delta, theta Leonis),

I.e. the shoulder of the Lion, the place where the neck begins. According to Alzajjaj, it is the place of the mane on his neck, because the mane *bristles up* when he is in wrath. According to Alna'ib Alamuli, Zubra is a piece of iron by which the two shoulder-blades of a lion are imitated.

This station consists of two stars, distant from each other by the length of a whip. They are also called the *Two Khurt*, i.e. holes, as if each of them were penetrating into the interior of the Lion, one of them on the root of the tail. When they rise, Suhail is seen in Al'irak.

12. Alsarfa (beta Leonis),

A bright star near to some very dim ones, called the *Claw of the Lion*. It stands on the end of the Lion's tale, and is called so because the heat *turns away* when it rises, and the cold *turns away* when it disappears.

13. Al'awwa (beta, eta, gamma, delta, epsilon Virginis)

Consists of five stars in a line, the end of which is turned. And therefore, the Station is called so because the verb 'Awa means to turn. Alzajjaj says: "I do not know of anybody else besides me who has explained the word this way. Those who say that these stars are dogs running behind the Lion and *barking* are wrong." They stand on the breast and wing of Virgo.

14. Alsimak Al'a'zal (Spica)

It is also called the *Calf of the Lion*, and *Alsimak Alramih* is his other calf.

This Simak is called *'A'zal* (i.e. bare), because whilst the other Simak Alramih (the shooter) is accompanied by a star, said to be his lance, this one has no such accessory, and is therefore said to be bare of weapons.

Manazil

According to Sibawaihi, Simak is called so on account of it rising high, or, according to others, because the moon does not enter this Station. But if that were the case, *Alsimak Al'a'zal* would not deserve the name of a Lunar Station, for, of course, the moon enters and frequently covers it (so as to make it disappear).

It is a brilliant star on the left palm of Virgo, which some people call *Sunbula* (the ear). But this is wrong, because the Ear (Spica) is *Alhulba*, (i.e. hog's bristle), which Ptolemy calls *Aldafira*, i.e. *Crines plexi*. This is a number of small stars behind the tail of the Great Bear, very much like the leaf of *Lublab*, i.e. helxine. The whole zodiac sign is also called so (i.e. Spica).

According to the Arabs, *Alhulba* (the hog's bristle) stands on the end of the Lion's tail, being the small hairs on the end of the tail.

15. *Alghafr* (iota, kappa, lambda Virginis)

Consists of three not very brilliant stars on the rain and the left foot of Virgo. According to the Arabs, it is the best of the Lunar Stations, because it stands behind Leo and before Scorpio. The evil of the Lion lies in his teeth and claws, the evil of the Scorpion lies in its venom and the sting of its tail. A Rajaz poet says:

"The best night for ever

Lies between Alzubana and Al'asad (Leo)."

People say that the horoscopes of all the prophets lie in this Station; but this does not seem to be true, except in the case of the Messiah, the Prophet who keeps off all mishap. The birth of Moses - according to the reports of the Jews - must have coincided with the rising of the tooth of Leo and the moon's entering the claws of Leo.

It is called *Ghafr*, because the light of its stars is imperfect, from the verb *Ghafara*, i.e. to cover a thing, or, because it rises above the claws of Scorpio and becomes to it like a *Mighfar* (i.e. coat of mail). According to Alzajjaj, the name is derived from *Ghafar*, i.e. the hair on the end of the Lion's tail.

16. *Alzubana* (alpha, beta Librae)

Consists of two brilliant stars, separated from each other as far as five yards, and standing in a place where the two claws of *Scorpio* might be; they belong, however, to *Libra*. The word is also derived from *zabana* (i.e. to *push*), as if the one of them were being *pushed* away from the other, not united with it.

17. *Al'iklil* (beta, delta, pi Scorpii)

Is the head of Scorpio, consisting of three stars which form one line. Ibn-Alsufi declares this to be impossible, and maintains that it consists of the 8th star of *Libra* and the 6th one of the stars outside Libra, as also Ptolemy has it in his Almagest. According to Ibn-Alsufi, those who consider the three bright stars in one line as *Al'iklil* are mistaken, for he says that the Crown, (i.e. Al'iklil) could not be anywhere but upon the head. However, the general view of the Arabs - in opposition to that of Ibn-Alsufi - is this, that the three stars in one line are *Al'iklil*. The Arabs have a proverb applicable to this subject, saying:

"The two contending parties were content, but the judge declined to give a judgment."

18. *Alkalb* (alpha Scorpii)

Is a red star behind Al'iklil and between two stars called Alniyat (praecordia).]

Manazil

19. *Alshaula* (lambda, nu Scorpii)

Is the sting of *Scorpio*, so called because it is always mushala, i.e. raised. It consists of two bright stars near each other on the top of the tail of Scorpio.

20. *Alna'a'im* (lambda, delta, epsilon, eta, omicron, phi, zeta Sagittarii)

Consists of eight stars, four of them lying in the Milky Way in a square, which are the *Descending Ostriches*, descending to the water, which is the *Milky Way*; and four of them lying outside the *Milky Way*, also in a square, which are the *Ascending Ostriches*, ascending and returning from the water.

Alzajjaj reads the word *Alnu'a'im*, i.e. the beams placed above the mouth of a well, where the sheaves of the pulley and the buckets are fixed (attached).

The stars were compared to ostriches, as if four of them were descending, four ascending. The *Descending Ostriches* stand on the bow and arrow of Sagittarius, and the *Ascending Ostriches* stand on his shoulder and breast.

21. *Albalda*

Is a desert district of heaven without any stars, at the side of the Horse, belonging to Sagittarius. According to Alzajjaj, this station was compared to the interstice between the two eyebrows, which are not connected with each other. You say a man *'ablad*, which means that his eyebrows do not run into each other.

22. *Sa'd-Aldhabih* (alpha, beta Capricornii)

Consists of two stars, the one to the north, the other to the south, distant from each other about one yard. Close to the northern one there is a small star, considered as the sheep which he (Sa'd) slaughters. The two stars stand on the horn of *Capricorn*.

23. *Sa'd-Bula'* (mu, nu, epsilon Aquari)

Consists of two stars with a third and hardly visible one between them, which looks as if one of them had *devoured* it, so that it glided down from the throat to the breast. According to others, it was called so because Sa'd is considered as he who *devoured* the middle star, robbed it of its light and concealed it. According to Abu-Yahya b. Kunasa, this *Station* was called so because it rose at the time when God said: "O earth, *devour* thy water" (Sura xi.46). This is a rather subtle derivation. These stars stand on the left end of Aquarius or Amphora.

24. *Sa'd Alsu'ud* (beta, xi Aquarii)

Consists of three stars, one of which is more bright than the two others. It is called so because people consider its rising as a *lucky* omen, because it rises when the cold decreases, when the winter is past and the season of the continuous rain sets in. Two of these stars stand on the left shoulder Aquarius; the third one stands on the tail of Capricorn.

25. *Sa'd-Al'akhbiya* (gamma, zeta, pi, eta Aquarii)

Consists of four stars, three forming an acute-angled trigone, and one standing in the middle, as it were the centre of a circumscribed circle. The central star is *Sa'd*, and the three surrounding stars are his *tents*. According to others, this Station was called so because at the time when it rises all reptiles that had been *hidden* in the earth come forth. These stars stand on the right hand of Aquarius. God is all-wise!

26 *Alfargh Al'awwal* (alpha, beta Pegasi)

Also called the *Upper Handle* (of the bucket), and the *First Two who move the Bucket in the Well* (in order to fill it). It consists of two bright stars, separated from each other, standing on the spine and shoulders of Pegasus.

27. Alfargh Althani (gamma Pegasi and alpha Andromedae),

Also called the *Lower Handle* (of the bucket), and the *Later Two who move the Bucket in the Well* (in order to fill it). It consists of two stars similar to *Alfargh Al'awwal*. According to the Arabs *Amphora* consists of these four stars.

28. Batn-Alhut (beta Andromedae),

Also called *Kalb-Alhut*, is a bright star in the one half of the womb of a fish (a star) called *Ribbon*, which must not be confused with the *Two Fishes*, one (the 12th) of the zodiacal signs. These stars stand above Libra and belong to Andromeda (*lit.* The chained wife who had not seen a husband).

———————————————————————

The preceding notes we have condensed and have added thereto other notes relating to Lunar Stations; this we have arranged in the form of a table, showing the nature of the Lunar Stations according to the different theories. We have also noted the rising of the stars of the Stations for the year 1300 of Alexander according to mean calculation; this we have also deposited in a table of the conditions of the stars of the Lunar Stations. If you look into these two tables you will find that the superscriptions at the top of each column render it superfluous to consult anybody beforehand as to their use. Here follow the two tables.

Lunar Mansions, from: El-Qazwini's Wonders of Creation

The Lunar Mansions

These are 28 stations, and the Moon ingresses into one of them each night, from the beginning of his first phase until the 28th of the month. Thereafter, it hides, and this being hidden is the so called ma.hâ.k, the (seemingly) complete disappearance of the Moon, so that none of it can be seen. If the month has 29 days, the ma.hâ.k falls onto the night of the 28th, if it has 30, on the night of the 29th, during which he crosses a whole station. Of these 28 lunar mansions, there are always only 14 visible above the earth during the night, and 14 disappear underneath the earth. Every time one of them is setting, the one opposed is rising. The Arabs call 14 of these stations Syriac and the other 14 Yemeni. The first of the Syriac is es's'ara.tain, the two signs (β and γ on the head of Aries) and the last one is essimak el azal, the unarmed Simak (in Virgo). The first of the Yemeni is elg'afr, the covering (φ, ι, $\varkappa$ in Virgo) and the last erris'â, the band (in the constellation of northern Pisces). The Arabs call the heliacal setting of a star in the west at dawn nun and the heliacal rising of the opposing one nau. The setting of each star occurs after 13 days, except g'ebha (the 10th lunar mansion in Leo). Thereafter one has to add 14 days, so that the end of the setting of the 28 [lunar mansions] coincides with the end of the solar year. Then the matter returns to the first state [Zustand] at the beginning of the following year. There are many different views concerning the degree of the nau's length. Some have come to the conclusion that everything that lies between the setting of a star and the setting of the following star would be nau and this would be a period of 13 days. Therefore, what happens concerning rain, wind, heat or cold, during theses 13 days, would fall into the nau of this setting star. And the natural philosophers have provided long discussions about the assessment of the ingress time of the luminaries (Sun and Moon) in these mansions, and also [about the] rise of nativities. And the ancient Arabs also had many sayings concerning their rises and settings, their pictures, names and nau's, the rain showers, winds, heat and cold which occurred in them. They also had rhymed sayings about the rising of each star and emblems for the fruitful and barren times of the year. Because the sayings of the Arabs are closer to the truth, I have left the sayings of the natural philosophers to one side and only submitted what the Arabs say about each of these mansions, by calling onto God for support; and he is sympathetic and a splendid advocate.

Concerning the Syrian mansions, the first one is:

1. es's'ara.tain, the two Signs.

They are the two horns of the Ram, which are also called ennâ.ti.h, the pusher. According to a visual estimate both are separated by approximately two arc lengths (two astronomical ells [astronomische Elle] or 4°) and their shape is thus:

++

When they are appearing in Midheaven (culminate), one of the two is located in the northern and the other in the southern cardinal direction. When the Sun is there, the equinox occurs (Spring Equinox) and the temperature is moderate. The versifier says:

"When the two Signs are rising, day and night are equal. All the people make their way home; friends and acquaintances give gifts to each other."

Their rising takes place on 16. nîsân (April) their setting on 18. tis'rîn ellawal (October). The Sun ingresses into them on 20. ad'âr (March) and every time this happens one year has passed in the world. They are only called s'ara.tain, Signs,

Manazil

because they mark the beginning of the year. This is why it is also said, in an overall fashion, elas'rât, which means the Signs reduce [the amount] of water in the well. What was meant was the reduction of water, found in hidden wells during the month of nîsân. In the nau of the two Signs the time of year gets pleasant, the waters are plentiful, fruits and roses begin to grow and the barley is cut. - The opposite lunar mansion is elg'afr.

2. elbo.tain, the Belly

What is meant by that is the belly of the Ram, consisting of three dark stars (ε, δ, and 3 ρ) which have the triangular shape of hearthstones. They are located between es's'ara.tain and the Pleiades. Their shape is thus:

+

++

The rising of Bo.tain takes place on 29. nîsân (April) and its setting on 31. tis'rîn elawwal (October). When it is setting, the sea is getting so rough that no ship can sail on it, harriers, vultures and swallows retreat to lower regions and the ants hide in their anthill. The versifier says:

"When Bo.tain is rising, one collects debts, chasing after the smith and the drug pedlar."

This means that, after the people returned to their homes during the rising of s'ara.tain, whose nau has now come to an end, and elbo.tain is rising, everybody who is owed something is demanding it now. Also, people are longing for delicacies and visit the blacksmith to get their tools and appliances in good working order. - Ibn-ela'râbi recorded that the old Arabs said:

"Never will Bo.tain and Debarân, or one of them, rise in a way that its nau will bring rain, it had to be that the nearly all of this year would be barren and dry".

A chronicler says:

"This is the worst of all lunar mansions, and the one that brings least rain, an often, if it hits people with bad luck, the nau of the Pleiades also deceives their hopes (like being infected by it), whilst their nau is usually the one that is the best and brings the most rain of them all. In the nau of Bo.tain the feed is drying, the barley will be cut in its entirety, and the cutting of the wheat will begin"

- The lunar mansion opposite Bo.tain is ezzubânâ.

3. et't'urajja, the Pleiades

It is said that they form the Ram's buttocks. They are the most famous of all lunar mansions and consist of six stars, in the middle of which stand a lot of dark ones, shaped thus:

+ + + +
   + +

They are also simply called ennag'm, the Star[s] and are compared to a bunch of grapes when they are setting. The poet says:

"They are hanging (from the sky) like a bunch of grapes".

The Arabs say:

"If the Pleiades are rising in the morning, the shepherd is looking for the water tube."

They want to express that a drink is needed, due to the high level of heat. - The versifier says:

Manazil

"The heat is in highest glow when the seven star rises, the feed is parched, the donkeys like to bite."

The rising of the Pleiades takes place on 13. ajâr (May) and they are setting on 13. tis'rîn elâhar (November). They will be visible in the east at the beginning of the night, when the cold begins, then they climb higher every night until they reach Midheaven at sunset. At this time the cold is strongest. Thereafter they begin to decrease from Midheaven and get closer towards the western each night until the new moon appears together with them. Then they move away for a while and are invisible for approximately 50 nights, this invisibility is called their istisrâr (their hiding); thereafter they appear at dawn in the east with great heat. - The Arabs have many verses and rhymes about the proceedings mentioned above, for example:

"If the Pleiades rise in the evening, the shepherd is looking for warm clothes."

The prophet says: At the Pleiades' heliacal rising, all damage comes to an end, particularly all damage of fruits, because this happens in Hig'âz, when grapes [Herlinge: grapes grown on side shoots only] begin to redden. The Pleiades' nau is generally a laudable and plentiful one and they are the best of all stars connected with spring rain, because their rain falls at a time when the earth suffers from a lack of water. Suleimân ben Kerîma says: When the Pleiades are rising, the sea begins to move in an undulated way, the winds blow here and there and God appoints the G'innen [?] as rulers over the waters; and one of the prophet's proverbs reads:

"Who is sailing the seas after the Pleiades' rising, against him the duties of the cliental have ceased."

- During the Pleiades' nau the winds are in violent motion, the heat increases, pears and apricots are ripening, and the feed dries. At their end, the Nile swells, and the milk is flowing more abundantly. - The lunar mansion opposite the Pleiades is el iklîl (the crown on the Scorpion's head).

4. eddebarân (α in the Bull, usually together with the Hyades)

This is a reddish glowing star, following the Pleiades, and this is why it is called tâbi' -nnag'm (that which follows the Pleiades). It has the name Debarân because it follows the Pleiades. Its shape is as follows:

+ + + +

  +

    +

Its nau is not laudable and the Arabs think of it as a bad omen. Its rise takes place on 26. ajâr (May), and its setting on 26. tis'rin elâhar (November). The Arab's versifier says:

"When Debarân is rising, hard rocks are glowing, the fires get awkward, the barrels are barren and the ponds dry up."

Several stars are standing before Debarân, amongst them two little ones who are so close together that they nearly touch each other. The Arabs call these two his helbain or dogs, and the others his k.ilâs or little camels. The bright, reddish star is also known as elfa.hl, the stallion or .hâdi-'nag's, the driver of the Pleiades. In his nau, the heat increases, and evil winds begin with him, hot desert winds are blowing and the grapes take on a dark colour. - The mansion opposite Debarân is el.kalb.

Manazil

5. elhe.k'a, the Stars on Orion's Head

These are three little stars, looking very similar to a triangle built of hearth stones. It is recorded that a man wanted to divorce his wife as many times as there are stars in the sky. Ibn- 'Abbâs said: Concerning her (his wife), Orion's he.k'a should be enough! She is called he.k'a because she is similar to the white tuft of hair on the horse, known as he.k'a, and her shape is this:

   *

* *

She is rising on 9. .hazîrân (June) and setting on 9 kânûn ellawal (December). Her nau is almost always called nat of Orion, which brings plenty of rain. The versifier says:

"When the He.k'a rises, people are rising to leave, are on the way back home from the search for fodder."

In her nau, melons and the other fruits will ripen, the heat is getting stronger and plenty of simooms are blowing. - The mansion opposite he.k'a is es's'aula.

6. elhen'a (Υ and ξ in the Twins)

These are two whitish glimmering stars in the milky way, approximately one whip length apart from each other (that is two ells). One of them is called ezzirr, the button, the other one elmaisân, he who struts proudly. Three others are surrounding them, so that there are five altogether (four are following each other in one direction, one deviates to one side) in the shape of an upturned Kufic (shaped like a square) alif. Her shape is as follows:

* * * *

*

Adhem el'abdi says: elhen'a is the bow of g'auzâ, which he uses to shoot the lion's paw with. She comprises eight stars in the shape of a bow and the grip are the two (above mentioned) stars ezzirr and elmaisân. The rising of hen'a occurs on 22. hazîrân (June), its setting on 22. kânûn elawwal (December). Its nau belongs to the ones of g'auzâ. Huntsmen and fishermen are going hunting and fishing from the rising of the Pleiades until the rising of hen'a. After that date, it will be impossible because of leanness (obviously referring to the leanness of the animals to be hunted and fished). The versifier says:

"When the g'auzâ rises, (here a combination of elhe'ka and elhen'a) the gazelles flee into their hideouts and cells (because of the mighty heat, so that they grze by night during this time); the neck is dripping with sweat and everybody enjoys (because of the heat) the protecting tent."

- In the nau of hen'a are falling the mightiest heat, the ripening of fresh dates and figs, and the detirioration of the waters. The mansion opposite hen'a is enna'âim.

7. ed'd'irâ (α and β in the Twins, Castor and Pollux)

This is the retracted paw of the lion d'irâ"lassad elma.kbû.da. The lion has two paws, the retracted one, ma.kbû.da, and one stretched out, mabsû.ta. The latter is directed towards Jemeny (to the south), the former towards Syria (to the north), and the Moon moves into the former. It consists of two stars, two whip-lenghts apart from each other, as well as the stretched out paw. The retracted one has is shaped thus:

    *

 *

Manazil

It rises on 4. tamûz (July) and sets on 4. kânun elâhar (January). Its nau is laudable and only rarely dashes expectations. The Arabs claim, even if there is no rain all year, ed'd'irâ does not dash expectations, even if it only brings a small rain shower. D'urrumma says: "ed'd'irâ followed after it, with a nau rich in water and it burst out in full flow". The versifier says:

"The full disc of the sun is exposed when d'irâ rises, the horizon is set alight by her [the sun's] rays, and flickering mirages are seen everywhere".

In this nau, the heat and blaze of evil summer winds increases, pomegranates ripen, grapes [Herlinge] turn red, and the Nabatean Rohr [reed grass?] is cut. - The mansion opposite ed'd'irâ is elbelda.

8. Ennet'ra, the brattice [Nasenscharte], which is the Crib in the Crab.

It consists of three stars next to each other. One of them looks as if it would be a little cloud and this is the nose of the Lion, anf-elasad. The shape of it is thus:

*

   *

*

The Lion's nau's bring plenty of rain and are highly laudable. For this reason, D'urrumma said about the amount of rain: "the nau of the Pleiades or the Lion's brattice shows itself in it". Their rise is on 7. Tamûz (July), their setting on 17. kânun elâhar (January). The Arabs said:

"If ennet'ra is rising, the grapes are turning brown (and it is the time the dates are ripening), dates are harvested at dawn (because at this time of day it is still cool), the animals are herded into the stables to be milked. No drop of milk is allowed to stay in the udder (because there is need of milk and they drain everything in the udders because they want to wean off the calves. If there would be anything left in the udders, they [the calves] would be longing for their mothers and not want to graze)."

- When this station is setting, sap moves into the woody stem and the young palm plants are easy to replant. In its nau, the amount of heat reaches its uppermost target and a destructive Samûm is blowing, so that it is said: in its nau, there will be some damage each day, spoiling some of the grains or fruits. - The opposing station is ed'd'âbi.h.

9. e.t.arf (ξ in the Crab and λ in the Lion)

Which is .tarf-elesad, the eye of the Lion. They are two little stars in front of el-g'ebha (the Lion's forehead), similar to the far.kadain (the two calfs in Ursa major), but they are of less brilliance than the latter, in a somewhat crooked line. They look like this:

    *

*

Rise on 1. âb (August) and set on 30. kânûn elâhar (January). The versifier says:
"When e.t.arfa is rising, trade and sales are slowing down; plenty of fresh fruit is arriving (because at this time people from Egypt are travelling) and the landlord has no problems with his business".

- In its nau, evil winds and hot desert winds are blowing, in it [the nau] fresh dates are eaten and grapes are harvested. - The station opposite e.t.tarf is sa'd bula'.

Manazil

10. Elg'ebha, which is g'ebhat-elasad, the Lion's forehead ($\zeta, \gamma, \eta, \alpha$ in the Lion)

It consists of four stars in a crooked line, of which each couple is approximately one whip length apart and they are positioned in oblique direction from south to north. The astrologers call the southerly [star] .kalb-elasad, heart of the Lion. The shape of those is:

```
     *

 *       *
     *
```

They rise on 14. âb (August), together with the ones of the Suhail [a number of stars typically seen near the southern horizon from Arabia], and their setting takes place on 12. s'ebâ.t (February). At the time of their setting, winter comes to an end, truffles can be found in Neg'd, the trees grow leaves, and fruitful winds are blowing; this is also the time for deliveries and births. The Arabs say:

"If the rise of the g'ebha would not be, the Arabs would not know what comfort means".

- Its nau is laudable and it is said: every time a Wâdi fills up with water after the g'ebha has risen, it will certainly be filled with animal feed also. - Suhail rises in Hig'âz together with g'ebha, and when both are rising the grapes [Herlinge] are beginning to ripe and they make a drink called fâ.dich, out of (crushed) unripe white Regina grapes [Datteltraube] which spoils at the time Suhail rises. It is said that Suhail urinated into the drink. In the nau of g'ebha the cold comes to an end, fresh dates are plentiful and dew begins to fall. - Opposite g'ebha stands sa'd-essu'ûd.

Peter Stockinger

11. Ezzubra which is zebra-elasad, the back hair, the mane of the Lion (δ and θ in the Lion, also called kâhil-elasad, interscapilium leonis.

These are two bright stars, one whip length apart. They are called elhurtân, the two eyes of needles. Zubra is called the Lion's hair, which stands up when he is angry. One of these two stars is brighter than the other and both of them are standing in a crooked line. Their shape is this:

*

*

Their rising takes place on 24. âb (August) and their setting on 25. s'ebâ.t (February). During its nau, strong rain is falling and if this does not happen it is getting cold. When Zubra rises, the Suhail is visible in 'Jrâ.k and the night is cool. During the day the Samûm blows. - The station opposite zubra is sa'd-elahbija.

12. e.s.sarfa (the Changer, β in the Lion)

A single star, following zubra, glowing white and very bright; next to it there are multiple, blurred stars of which one could think that they are the same as .kumb-elasad (see above). The shape of it is *. It is called .sarfa because heat and cold are changing during his rising and setting. Its rise takes place on 9. ailûl (September) and its setting on 9. ad'âr (March). During the rising of this star, the Nile begins to swell and the last days of winter fall in its nau. The Arabs say that if a child is weaned in the nau of .sarfa, it will only rarely ask for milk. The versifier says:

"When e.s.sarfa rises, everybody is busy with their trade, but the stallion abstains from mating (the stallion abstains because the mare will be noticeably pregnant)."

Manazil

In its nau, rain showers, wind, low temperature by night, including many different storms occur, and the first spring rain falls. - The station opposite s.arfa is ferg'-eddelv elmu.kaddam.

13. el'awwâ, the Barker (β, γ, δ, η and ε in the Virgin)

These are four stars, following .sarfa, similar to an aleph, whose bottom end is bent a little backwards, just like the Kufic way of writing, in this shape:

*

*

   *

    *

They are seen as dogs, following the Lion, and some say that they would be warakâ'lasad, the Lion's hips. Their rising takes place on 22. ailûl (September), and their setting on 22. ad'âr (March), and their nau is depleted of rain. The versifier says:

"When the 'awwâ rises, the climate is pleasant, but it is awkward to sleep on the open field (because of the low temperature); the tube is dry (because it has rarely been soaked in water) and the tent is pitched up."

The equinox occurs in their nau, the nights are getting longer and the days shorter, it is the beginning of autumn. Opposite the 'awwâ lies ferg'-eddelw elmuahhar.

14. essimâ.k, Spica

This is essimâk el'azal, the unarmed Simâk, because essimâk errâmi.h, the Simak with a lance, or Arcturus, is not a lunar mansion. The Simâk consists of one whiteish glowing star, which is called unarmed only because next to the lance-bearing [Simak] there is a star called râjet-essimâk, the Flag of Simak, which is missing in the unarmed one. - The Arabs saw the two simâk as the two sâ.k-elasad, the Lion's Shinbones. The unarmed Simâk is the division line between the Jemeni and the Syrian stars. All stars below his place of rising belong to the Jemeni, because this hemisphere is orientated to the south, which is the direction of Jemen, - all others, positioned above simâk belong to the Syrian, because this is the hemisphere in northerly direction, where Syria lies. Also, simâk was only used as the border because of its close proximity to the equinoctial line. The rising of simâk el'azal occurs on 5. tis'rîn elawwal (October), and its setting on 4. nîsân (April). Its nau brings plenty of rain, and it is very rare that it fails to rain. Its rain hits the so-called hat.âi.t, which are the regions between two areas of land, watered by the rain, that have stayed dry. There may be only one negative remark to be made, namely that it encourages the nes'r to grow. This is a herb that grows on the roots of already dried animal feed and makes camels who feed on it ill. - The archaic Arab poet says:

"oh, if only the simâk and its nau would not fail to arrive!"

The versifier says:

"When the simâk appears, the strong heat ceases and the camels don't cue up at the watering place." (Because they don't drink much during this season).

In its nau falls the ripening of the dates, the cutting of the green animal feed, and the first after-rain (after the Spring rain) appears. Opposite simâk lies ba.tn-el.hut.

Manazil

This is the last of the Syrian lunar mansions. Following are Jemen, of which the first one is:

15. elg'afr, the Covering ($\varphi, \iota, \varkappa$, in the Virgin)

These are three dark stars, shaped thus:

```
    *
*       *
```

They are only called the Covering because at the time of their rising, the Earth's gleam and array (i.e. the summer clothes) are concealed. Their rising takes place on 18. tis'rîn elawwal (October), and their setting on 18. nîsân (April). The Arab's versifier says:

> "When elg'afr appears, the chill breath makes the traveller shudder.
> The bright, fresh glow of summer disappears from earth, tree, and bush".

It is also said: Worst is a birth after elg'afr's setting, because the warm season ends and winter comes rushing in. In their nau, dates are cut, Persian reed [Persisches Rohr] is cut and their rain brings forth truffles. - The station opposing elg'afr is es's'ara.tain.

16. ezzubânâ, which is zubâna-'l'a.krab, the two claws of the Scorpion (α and β in the Scales).

These are two separate stars, approximately five ells apart, shaped like thus:
**

They rise on 31. tis'rîn elawwal (October) and set on 29. nîsân (April). The Arabs accredit bad winds to their nau, particularly the strongest north wind, which is hot in the summer. The Arab's versifier says:

"When ezzubânâ rises, make sure that your whole house is quickly brought in order".

He wants to say that suddenly cold weather has appeared and now the father of the family has to set to work, repairing tools and making sure that all necessaries against the cold are prepared. Some also say: The rising of ezzubânâ depresses him who has a lot of draught cattle, and he always says:

"such and such has happened to me",

which means he is sacrificing himself to guarantee the prosperity of his draught cattle and he recounts and talks much (to his friends about his misfortunes). - In the nau of this star, citizens of the region around Babel move into their houses, the cold increases, and the rain falling in it produces truffles. - The station opposite ezzubânâ is elbo.tain.

17. eliklîl, the Crown

This is the head of the Scorpion (β, δ, π in the Scorpion). It consists of three whiteish glowing stars, lined up in an oblique line, shaped thus:

```
        *
    *
*
```

The Crown's rising takes place on 13. tis'rîn (November), and their setting on 13. ajâr (May). The Arabs' versifier says:

" When the Crown appears, the stallion is madly in love, the clothes are girded up, and the rivers burst their banks".

Manazil

When the Crown sets, all the waters of the earth are sinking continuously until the setting of ba.tn-el.hût, which takes place on 5. (October). In this nau, numerous rain showers and thick clouds appear. Opposing the Crown are the Pleiades.

18. el.kalb, which is kalb-el'a.krab, the Heart of the Scorpion (Antares)

This is the reddish star behind the Crown between two stars called ennijat (praecordia), which are not as reddish as he [Antares] is. Together they create the following shape:

* ☉ *

In the desert, the time of birth giving begins when el.kalb and ennesr elwâ.ki (Vulture Cadens in the Lion) are rising. Both of them rise at the same time during the cold [weather], on 26. tis'rîn elâhar (November). The setting of el.kalb takes place on 26. Ajâr (May). - Everything that is born during this time is hard to nourish, because of the cold and the lack of milk and green plants. The versifier of the Arabs says:

" When the Herat of the Scorpion has risen, winter comes, gnarling like a dog, and one can see the bedouins in need and trepidation."

The Arabs call el.kalb and ennesr elwâ.ki' together elharrârain, the two creaking ones, because at the time of the rising of these stars, the frost is creaking. The nau of k.alb is not laudable at all, and the Arabs think of it as a bad omen. They also avoid to travel once the Moon enters the Scorpion. The poet says:

"Begin your journey with Antares, it doesn't matter to you it promises misfortune or blessing."

During its nau, the cold increases, cold winds blow, and the water resides in the roots of the trees. Opposite Antares stands Eddebarân.

19. es's'aula, the Lifted Tail
or Sting of the Scorpion (λ and υ in the Scorpion)

These two stars are close, nearly touching each other; they are the tail of the Scorpion. They are called s'aula, similar to the lifted part of the tail, because of their elevation, and in Arabic, one says: s'âla bid'anabihi, it has lifted its tail. Behind it is the real Scorpion's Sting, looking like a little cloud. They rise on 9. kânûn elawwal (December) and set on 9. .hazîran (June). The Arab's versifier says:

"The whole house begins to wail and to lament when s'aula is rising."

In their nau, the leaves begin to fall, rain showers become more frequent, and the Beduins who settled near watering places, distribute into all directions. - Opposing s'aula is elhe.k'a.

20. enna'âim, the Ostriches

(after Schier to be taken as deliciae, γ, δ, ε, η, σ, φ, τ, ζ in the Archer).

They are eight stars, following s'aula; four in the Milky Way, namely enna'aim elwârida, the ostriches heading for a drink. This is because they walk into the Milky Way as if they would go and have a drink. And four outside the Milky Way, namely enna'âim sârida, the ostriches returning from having a drink. This is because they are located outside the Milky Way, as if they had a drink and climbed up from the water. Their shape is similar to two squares:

```
* *  * *
* *  * *
```

Their rising takes place on 22. kânûn elawwal (December), and their setting on 22. .hazîrân (June). - The versifier says: "Are the na'âim rising, the animals lose their coats, the herdsmen meet up and share their tattle." This means that the herdsmen have less work to do and meet up, gossiping about what happens to other people. Their nau has nothing worth mentioning, in it falls the begin of winter and the autumn equinox. - Opposite the na'âim stands elven'a.

21. Elbelda (the City in the Archer)

A place devoid of stars, between the na'âim and sand-ed'd'âbi.h (in the Seagoat). In this place there is only one single, nearly extinguished and hardly visible star. It is also called bedlam-et't'a'lab, the home of the fox, comparing it to a corner, a fox has retreated to. Now it is banging its tail, separating the other stars from him. Sometimes the Moon also avoids this space and moves into el.kilâda, the neck jewellery [necklace?] instead. They are a circle of six small, dark stars, similar to a bow, and therefore some Arabs call them el.kaus, the bow, others elude.hî, the nest. Opposite the bow is a star, called sahm-errâmi, the archer's arrow. El.hu.sain mentions it when he says:

"An archer is in front of them, releasing the arrow."

These stars are located in front of the sa'd-ed d'âbi.h. The figure of the bow is thus:

```
        *              *
           *        *
             *    *
               *
```

Belda's rising takes place on 4. kânûn elâhâr (January) and their setting on 4. tamûz (July). The Arab's versifier says:

"when elbelda has risen, the ground is embellished with g'a'da plants [?] and everybody longs for fresh butter." - In their nau, freezes the water and the heavy cold of the winter is increasing. The gardens are free of bushy weeds and the wines are cut. Opposite belda stands ed"d'irâ'.

22. sa'd-ed'dâbi.h,
the Lucky Star of the Slaughterer in the Sea Goat, α and β

These are two not glowing stars, approximately one Elle apart from each other. One of them is elevating towards the north, the other one is descending towards the south. Close to the upper one is a smaller, closely connected star. The Arabs say that this would be the sheep to be slaughtered by him. The figure of this star is like this:

```
*
*
```

Its rising takes place on 17. kânûn elâhâr (January), and its setting on 17. Tamûz (July). The versifier says:

"When the Lucky Star of the Slaughterer is rising, the dog protects its master (i.e. it is not separating from him because of the cold) and the animals are making loud noises, moving onto the field early in the morning (because of the shortness of the day). In its nau, the sap rises up into the trees' branches; nuts and almonds are ground up and everybody asks for rain."

- Opposite sa'd-ed'dâbi.h lies ennet'ra.

23. sa'd bula', the Lucky Star of the Devourer, μ and ν in the Water bearer

These are two parallel stars of which one is darker. The larger one is called bâli', the devourer, as if he would have swallowed the other, darker one, and taken his light. Their shape is thus:

   *

*

Their rising takes place on 30. kânûn elâhâr (January), and their setting on 1. Ab (August). The versifier says:

"When the happy star of bula' rises, the camel's first- and second born is strong and fast (without being able to be held), the hazel hen [Haselhuhn] (mur', a species of bird, found in Arabia at this time) is hunted, and on the ground the herbs are getting parched. During its nau, al lot of rain is falling, the frogs begin to croak, the sparrows are copulating, the hoopoe is laying eggs, a southerly wind is blowing, and the milk is flowing sparsely.

- Opposite sa'd bula' stands e.t.arf.

24. sa'd-essu'ûd, the Highest Lucky Star, β and ξ in the Water bearer

It consists of three stars, of which one is brighter and the other two are less bright, shaped thus:

```
  *
*   *
```

The Arabs see this as a lucky omen, which explains the name. Its rising takes place on 12. s'ebât (February), and its setting on 14. Âb (August). The versifier says:

"When the lucky star is rising, the trunk's wood is filled with liquid, it is annoying to sit in the sunshine, and the body's skin gets soft and smooth" (because the dryness of the winter's cold has ceased). - Its nau is praiseworthy and this is why an old Persian poet said: "Sa'd essu'ûd, through your celestial body you have brought down abundant rain onto my homeland."

In its nau, the first green feed crops are beginning to appear, the birds are singing, and the cats come into heat, Leaves begin to appear on the trees, the swallows are approaching, camels and cows find their fodder, and the roses, as well as the other fragrant flowers begin to bloom. - Opposite sa'd-essu'ûd stands elg'ebha.

25. sa'd-elahbija (or elahbia), the Lucky Star of the Tents or Hidden Places, γ, ζ, π, η in the Water Bearer.

It consists of four stars which are close to each other, and one is in the middle of the others. They are similar to the foot of a duck. Two are aligned lengthwise and two widths wise, and the shape is thus:

```
*   *
  *
  *
```

It is said that the sa'd or lucky star is the brightest one, and the three others are his ahbija. Others say that it would be called sa'd-elahbia, because it is rising before it gets warmer and all the reptiles that were hidden in their holes would come forward. This interpretation is a miraculous one, and the poet's verse gives a clue:

"Now sa'd has appeared with bad threats, because its retinue of warriors announces the heat."

Retinue of warriors (g'unûd, lit. Demons of the Stars) are here all the reptiles. Its rising takes place on 25. s'eba.t (February), and its setting on 27. âb (August). The versifier says:

"When sa'd-elahbija has appeared, the Schlauche are greased (because they have dried out during winter and are worn, but are needed now). Everything is moving out of the winter quarters and the houses collapse."

Its nau is not laudable, it produces numerous rain showers and the wine is pruned. -Opposite says-elahbija stands ezzubra.

26. elferg' elawwal

Which is ferg' eddelw-elmu.kaddam, the Front Spout of the Bucket, α and β in Pegasus. The water bucket, eddelw, consists of four stars forming a spacious square. Two of them are the front and two the back ferg', which should be understood as the spout where the water runs out of the bucket, between the two crossbars. Their shape is thus:

* *.

The rising of the first ferg' takes place on 9. ad'ar (March) and its setting on 9. Ailûl (September). The versifier says:

"When eddelw appears in the sky, fresh green cabbage is cut, the donkey loses its body hair, and who is lonely and forsaken is going to marry a woman (actually, seeks deliciousness ellahw, which can either mean coitus or the woman herself, after the dictum of the almighty God; if we were planning to seek deliciousness, which means after some people's explanations, to take a wife, and so forth. The lonely man seeks marriage, by the way, especially at this time, because he has escaped the tight grip of winter, can move freely, arrange matters, and is able to choose his occupation)."

- The nau of this ferg' is a very praiseworthy one, in it the third g'amra disappears, almonds, pears and apricots tend to fruit in hot countries, but its cold destroys the fruits. - es.s.arfa stands opposite.

27. elferg' et't'âni

the Second Spout, γ in Pegasus and α in Andromeda, as already described above. It rises on 22. ad'âr (March) and sets on 22. Ailûl (September). Its nau is very praiseworthy and brings lots of rain. The rising and setting of both ferg' mark the approach and retreat of the cold. At the time of the back ferg's setting, dates are cut and honey is collected in Hig'âz, Tehâma, and all of G'aur. Its shape is thus:

**

The end of winter falls in its nau, green herbs for feeding are plenty, Lote tree fruits [Lotesfrucht] and beans are ripening, and the Spring Equinox takes place. - Opposite the second ferg lies el'awwâ.

28. ba.tn-el.hut, the Belly of the Fish

These are numerous stars in the shape of a fish. They are also called erris'â, the Band. The tail of these stars is pointed oblique towards Jemen, and the head towards Syria. The consist of two rows, a leading one towards west, and a rear one looking towards east. The leading row includes one star which is the brightest of them all, and in the middle of the rear row is another, big, bright star. This is the one where the settlement will take place on Judgment day. Their shape is thus:

[missing]

Its rise takes place on 4. nîs'ân (April) and its setting on 5. tis'-rîn elawwal (October). When it sets, the lowering of the water level comes to its end. After its rise, the s'ara.tain are rising and everything will revert back to how it was the year before. The versifier says:

> "When the constellation of the Fish has risen, one can move freely, but the thorn of the sa'dan plant sticks easily to one's clothes (because it sticks easiest and hardest to fabric); the bird nets are erected (because birds will be caught in them) and the season feels pleasant to the poor pilgrims (because they are not harassed by heat or cold).

- Opposite ba.tn el.hut lies simak. In its nau, rain is pouring down and seldom fails to appear. This is the time to cut rye in the hot countries.

Abû is.ha.k ezzag'âg'i says:

> "Each year has four parts and each of these parts seven lunar mansions or nau's, and each nau consists of 13 days. Add one day so that the year has 365 days, and this is the approximate time of the Sun's movement through the zodiacal sphere. A nau is, as already explained, the rising of a star in the east at dawn and at the same time the setting of the opposite [star] in the west."

Brenner: Das Gross Planeten-Buch, Strassburg, 1559

Of the Twelve Heavenly Signs

There are twelve roads in the sky / these are the twelve signs / Aries, Taurus, Gemini, Cancer, Leo, Virgo, Libra, Scorpius, Sagittarius, Capricornus, Aquarius, Piscis. Ram / Bull / Twins / Crab / Lion / Virgin / Scales / Scorpion / Archer / Sea Goat / Waterbearer / and the Fishes. Each of them is xxx degrees wide / that is as much as the Sun moves in thirty-one days / but sometimes she can do this in xxx. Days / and even in fewer days which happens in February in some years in Hornung [February]. And if a planet is located under one of these signs / it is said he is living therein / and is therefore rightly called a living space.

These twelve living spaces have lots of meanings and power / three [are] dry and hot / Aries / Leo / Sagittarius / these are similar to fire. Three [are] moist and hot / they are similar to air / Aquarius / Gemini / Libra. Three [are] moist and cold / they are similar to water / Cancer / Scorpius / Piscis. And the last three [are] dry and cold / similar to the earth / Taurus / Capricornus / Virgo.

Amongst these twelve signs are four which push people towards love / Aries / Taurus / Leo / and Capricornus / therefore who is born hereunder / will undoubtedly be a lover / but if it should happen / that Venus would come between them / he would be of such morals / namely so fiery from courting / that he could not look out for commendation / appraisal and hounour / so much deluded are men and women. Now I will continue to write about the stars which stand above the twelve signs.

Manazil

Of the Stars Above the Twelve Signs

The stars above the twelve signs are uncountable / and many of them have no names / but wise men named them by comparison / for example one can see seven stars in a row / similar to a chariot / therefore one says / it would be a chariot / with four wheels and three horses / People also know St Martin's Staff / Three Maries / and the Grave / the Seven Stars and the Leitting / etc / There are also some names in Latin / which are connected to important things / and I will describe part of it / because they are showing to us much luck/ and possible bad luck / to take on the former / and avoid evil / And there are xxviii named as follows / Alnacha / Albocain / Alcoreia / Aldabaran / Almusin / Alkaia / Aldira / Abiatra / Alcharph / Algebla / Alcoraten / Alserfa / Algane / Alchimecht / Algapahr / Alsibinin / Alactil / Alcabin / Alsebra / Alnagain / Alneda / Zaddadena / Sabadola / Sadahab / Sadalachia / Alparaboil / Alcharga / and Beualhot.

Of the Order of the Twelve Signs with the Stars including their Influence

Each of the twelve roads / which is / each sign is divided into three parts / beginning / middle and the end / so that one of the mentioned stars is therein / which is called its living space. Therefore the star Alnacha is in the first part of the Ram / Albocain in the middle and the end thereafter.

In the beginning of the Bull there shall stand Alcoreia / Aldaboran in the middle / and at last Almusin at the end two parts. At the beginning of the Twins is the third part of Almusin / Alkaia in the middle / and Aldira stands in the third part. In the first part of the Crab stands Abiatra / Alcharph in the middle / Algebla in the third part.

Thereafter the other two parts of Algebla are standing in the first part of the Lion/ Alcoraten stands in the middle on the right side / two parts of Alsarfa at the end.

The third part of Alsarfa is in the beginning of the Virgin / Algane is in the middle / Alchimecht at the end.

In the first part of the Scales stands Algaphar / Alzibinin stands in the middle / and Alactil at the end of the third part / which has luck and health.

The other two parts of Alactil are standing in the first part of the Scorpion / Alkabin in the middle / two parts of Alsebra at the end thereafter.

At the beginning of the Archer is the third part of Alsebra / Alnagaim in the middle / but Alneda in the end.

At the beginning of the Sea Goat stands Zaddadena / Sabadola in the middle / Sadahad at the end of the third part.

Thereafter is the Waterbearer / he stands in the eleventh house / and has two parts of Sadahad at its beginning / Sadalachia stands in the middle / Alparaboil at the end of the third part / bringing great health.

Thereafter is the twelfth part / the Fishes / the last part of Alparaboil is therein / and Alcharga stands in the middle / Beualhot at the end. Of these stars / what good or evil will happen to people / who are born there under / I will tell you right until the end of the first part of the Planeten Buch.

Of the Star Alnacha / and its Effect

A child / male or female born when Alnacha is rising in the first hour of the day / will have a mark near its mouth / and as well near the eyes / will have a beautiful nose / will come into possession of property but will be of cloudy mood / whatever he wishes for or wants will happen / [he] will have a frightful face / and will do bad things everywhere / so that he will be feared / He will also be judging over country and people / tall and ill in his heart / bad tempered / hard to get friends / nobody loves him / But if he should have a wife / he will have two children by her / both of them will be male / all because of this star / rising at the time / He will also be black / [and] have long teeth / he shall protect himself from being burnt by fire / and from being struck by iron / He is said to use the art of magic / or an evil spirit would be inside him / he has a mark on his upper thigh between his legs / or another was on both shoulders close to the sides he is big and [schwanck ?] / pretty feet / dignified he will be in whichever land he will travel / and will rise higher from one to the other / he will have a good voice / rough [?] and not uncovered [?] / He will get to the age of xxiii years. These are the attributes of a child / which is born when Alnacha rises early with the Sun of the first hour.

If the star rises in the second hour / and a child will be born / be it female or male / it will be poor throughout its life / and without property / [and] shall have misery and no sympathy [?] / shall have many children / would like to own and wear pretty clothes / like to eat spices / intelligent / well brought up / [and] is of soft predisposition / his enemies and master will give him a lot of trouble / he will not escape this. rc.

If a child is born at a different hour than this one / be it day or night / it will be beaten to death by the might of the star / god may prevent us from that.

Of the star Albokain / and its effect

If a child / man or woman / is born during Albokain rising / it will be happy and good / God is making him happy through riches / anybody who sees him or knows him will come to love him / he is are black beautiful (?) [schwartz schön] / And has a round [scheibelecht] face.

Who is born during the night / will be different / he is rough / with a huge beard that is strong and hard / his friends he will be preferred (?) [bevorgahn] / talkative /

he will have watery eyes and a beautiful nose / large eyebrows / white teeth / and pretty cheeks.

Who is born in the evening / when the cattle is taken off the fields / will like to fence and argue / hate and envy his innocent neighbours / he will love other men's wife / and other men [will love] his wife / he will be secretly molested [geschaendet] / he will use up his estate / and will nourish himself in a sinful way / he will not amass riches / but he will have to work hard to strife towards it / and he will live his life with a lot of pain / he will take on a profession / will give up on it due to an accident / and will therefore not save enough money during his lifetime / to pass anything on to his children / it will cause him to take what he hasn't put there / Proud and red he will come to no harm [kumers not] / his days will be miserable / or he will be dead due to magic trickery [zauberlist] / His enemies will besiege him (?) and send him away (?) [werden ihn bemühen und fahen] / honour and virtue makes him sick / His face shall be marked with two signs / one is above the eyes / he will be bitten by dogs / and be wounded by iron / ill in back and lumbar region.

But if one would be born in the early hours of the morning when the star is rising / then this child will be blind due to the power of Albokaim / or white spots will cover the eyes / so he will only be able to see a little bit / He will have intercourse with many women / will have a mark on his mouth / will inherit property / and will have a temper / he will have three marks / one on the neck / the other one on the head / the third one on the ? [duennen]. He will live healthily xl. Years / then he will be weak / if he recovers / he will live lxxx. years / or thereabouts. I tell you this because of this star's effects [nach des sternes art].

Manazil

Of the star Alcoreia / and its effect

If Alcoreia is rising at the birth of a child / it will be a great thinker / much loved / with grey hair / and dog eyes. But if the star is rising with the Sun / and in the seventh hour the planet Mars is also rising / who is tempting some to do evil / and a child is born / be it man or woman / they will experience much in their youth and will have much work to do / they will be poor in old age / will have four wives / many children / and he will be a fine fellow when it comes to play and companionship.

But if this star is rising in the evening when it gets dark / and a child will be born / it will have enough on its table throughout its entire life / has a small head / a big nose / what he purchases in foreign lands / will not last long / liiii years he will live and nourish himself / thereafter he will get seriously ill if he will recover /he will live 80 years.

Of the star Albdaboran / and its effect

A child that is born during Aldaboran rising / likes to laugh / and is red / rich and he will be angry with his parents / he shall have many duties / and make a living from them / he will bequeath everything to one of his friends / only few thoughts shall confuse him throughout his life / [he] shall love his wife like his own body / [he] shall not like to eat and drink / [he] shall beckon to two wives / and find goods beneath the earth. But if it rises during the night / and child will be born / it will be as quiet as a lazy woman / [it] will live under its own roof / [and] will not travel anywhere / where he is allowed to travel.

And if Aldaboran is rising in any hour / and somebody will be born / he shall be poor / an animal will bite him / many coughs come out of his chest / [he] is angry and frightened [freydt] / [he] will be wounded by iron / rarely or not at all shall he be happy / and he will never be lucky / a sone will hurt him / he will break a bone / he will die in a foreign country / and nobody will be there to bury him. When he is 40 years old, he will become ill / if he recovers, he will be xx years old / thereafter he will be ill again / if he recovers / he will live xlviii years / then he will be ill again / and if he survives he will get to the age of 88.

Of the star Almusin / and its effect

A child being born during Almusin rising / will have / a big forehead / bald and without hair / [and] will have lots of strange thoughts. But if he is born during the night / he will have to live with a lack of power / in misery [and] toilsomeness / many women will surround him / he will have a sign on one arm / and as well on the penis (?) [dien] / he will be wounded by a stone / hurt by iron / and a dog will bite him / women will love him and find him and he will get two more signs / one on his heart / and one on his arm / he will break a bone / or fire will burn him / [he] shall luck with women and beasts' / but it will take time to give his wife a child. He will live healthily [for] xxxv years / thereafter he will become ill / if he recovers / he will get to 60 years.

Of the star Alkaia / and its effect

A child born during Alkaia's rise / will be rich / honest / keep his own / and do well with it / have grey hair / thick eyebrows / and a cleft (furrow?) above the nose / his adornment will be red / and [he will] suffer [from] illness in his back / an evil spirit will haunt him / and women will love him very much.

Manazil

But if the star rises in the second hour after sunrise / and a child will be born / it will have spots in its eyes / will lose many teeth / and will have grey hair.

But if it rises in the third hour / who will be born / will be of high rank / and will achieve deeds of wonder / of which an equivalent is hardly found in any kingdom.

And who will be born / if it rises in the fourth hour / shall be healthy / and if Mars rules / has to sell meat / and [he will] let blood / his livelihood shall be made through buying / he will live healthily for ten years /then he will be ill / if he recovers, [he] will live xliiii years / thereafter he will be ill again / if he recovers / he will reach the age of ninety.

Of the star Aldira / and its effect

Who is born during the rise of Aldira / shall teach and know a lot / [he will] drink a lot / his heart will be very mild / he will find treasure beneath the earth / [he will be] very angry / and if he cannot get revenge / he will not believe his eyes / his first wife will be ugly and dark / nature will provide him with two or slightly more children / very often he will be annoyed with his father and mother / which he and his brothers will outlive / He shall be in a way / that no man shall outdo him / if he was not of high rank / He will be wounded on his head / on his arm [shall be] a mark / [and] one in his groin / and two on his genitals between his legs / and another one on his mouth / He will live naturally for xliiii years / thereafter he will die from an illness on his neck.

Of the star Abiatra / and its effect

A child born during Abiatra rising / will learn to fence and fight / and he will reject all the teachings of his elders / [he] does not love his friends / often gets angry / which often shows his foolish immodesty / He will become a drinker and a glutton / a rouge / reveal secrets / [be] very angry / he will have a mark on his face etc. Similar will happen to the one born during the day.

Who is born during the night / has to live a diabolical life / [he] will mercilessly punish the ones to be chastised / he will arrive in the country of a lord / which will bring him little piety / his end will be hard and bitter / he will better his life during old age / His head will become ill / and he will suffer from pressure on his heart / and in his back. Otherwise he will stay healthy for xxx years / thereafter he will get ill / if he recovers / he will become an old man / and will reach ninety years.

Of the star Alkarffes / and its effect

A child born / when Alkarphes [sic] is rising / will be sad / and cry / many children will come from it / but they will not live long / many will commit unchastity / (?) [viel leuten zu tage sthan] / and most lovely to their masters / much ill / innocent and shapely / a wound on the head / and a mark on the back / the bite of an animal on one leg / and two marks between the legs on the genitals / one caused by fire. He will have enough property / both land and plough / And if he escapes / which he will not want / he will return / which is of great benefit to him / and the time he was away / will lead to his ruin / He is tough enough / to live fresh and healthily xliiii years / thereafter he will get ill / if he recovers / he will be well until he reaches ninety years / than he will die in a foreign land.

Of the star Algebla / and its effect

If Algebla is rising when a child is born / it will be pale / most lovely / proud and boisterous / [he] will think of himself as mighty / that he would be a king's companion / therefore many will try / to kill him / but no harm will come to him / because due to his wisdom he will escape / and [he] will come from one virtue to the next / through which he will win a lot / but lose it all soon after. Iron will wound him / his head [will be] unhealthy / he will suffer from smallpox / which will make him recognisable / [he] will be a well-repeated man / [and] a great illness will befall his head / and if his anger will lead him / he will be raging and mad / [he] will have a big nose / his shoulders will be high / his loin will be well formed / When he is ten years old / he will be at the mercy of a master / thereafter he will get ill / if he recovers / he will live xl years / thereafter he will have to deal with a great illness / if he recovers / he will live lxviii years / but he will die from a great illness at last.

Of the star Alkoraten / and its effect

If a child is born during Alkoraten's rise / it will have a long face / its speech will be soft and ill / uncourtly and nefarious / bad things will happen [to the child] / very often it will be angry / there will be a mark on his loins / but if there is no mark / it will come to much chagrin.

If the star rises during the night / who is born / does not care what he does / will be a good orator / [there will be] a mark on his legs / [and he will] also have marks on face and neck.

But if it rises in the second hour of the day / who will be born / will have many children by two wives / but nearly all of them will die / The first child will be a girl / the other one a boy. He will be ill in his eleventh year / if he recovers / he will live healthily for xxiiii years / thereafter he will suffer from illness and will have to work hard / if he survives / he will live lviii years.

Of the star Alsarpha / and its effect

If a child is born during Alsarpha's rise / it will be of placid nature / and [have] much honour and property / [he] will be well established with great masters / who will give him much / [he] will be lucky / if he chooses / [he] will be a farmer and winemaker / but he will not be lucky [and] move from one town to another / After he will find a wife / he will get some property / and he will be busier than he ever was before / and will neither be concerned with riches / nor with unrighteous indulgence / nobody can catch him out in his wisdom / he will suffer from a serious illness / which he will endure with patience / very modest / talkative / to be a merchant will only serve him during wintertime / [He] will rule over much land / be modest in the amount of food he eats / his hair is beautiful and curly / he will have a son / who will be a thief / and run away from his master / [He] will break a bone / and have many marks on his body / one from iron / one from fire / on the belly / or the leg / or one each of his legs / on the neck / and on [his] hands / [he] will die in a foreign land. When he is xliiii years of age / he will be ill and weak / if he recovers / he will live ninety-seven years / Thereafter nobody can prevent it / be it man / or woman / they must die.

Of the star Algane / and its effect

If a child is born when Algane is rising / it will collect many goods and treasures / but he will not keep them / he will have many children / but few will survive / [he] will be of pleasant appearance / and when he will be xxxvi years of age / he will be honoured / and everybody will be pleased for him / much honour and many good things will be the result / if he decides to be a merchant instead / he will make more money / if he nurtures it / but he will have a great sorrow / and there will be a mark on his elbow. He will have a mark on his belly or his genitals / which is caused by fire etc. He will live xxxvi years.

But if a child is born / if the star is rising in the second hour of the day / he will be ruler over his dynasty / tersely nothing will be to his detriment / [he] will not fail or falter.

But if it happens in the third hour / it will be the child of a king / and if he is from a lineage in the Holy Roman Empire he will be emperor. Should he be a poor man / who will not have such dignity / he will still be the ruler of his line / and will rise above his peers / with honour / with riches / with property / and with respectability etc.

If he is born with Algane in the fourth hour / he will die from all illnesses.

And if a child is born with the star in the fifth hour / it will be rich / ever unhealthy / but will live forty years longer than the others / due to this star's power.

Of the star Alchimech / and its effect

Who is born during Alchimech's rise / shall benefit much from women / all of whom will die / [but] all his affairs shall continue / [he has] beautiful hair / white / and his advice will be good / a dog will bite him / his beard will be long / his face broad and not thin. Nature will give him children / who will not live long / he will not get old / rather die than reach a proper age. On the upper lip near the nose / he will have a mark. He will live xlii years / and that would be the longest / he will live naturally.

But if he is born during the night / he will pass on much property to his children / legally he shall have two wives / affable / a burn mark on his belly / he will travel to a master's land / buy many things / and will die / and other people will own / what he inherited / will keep his property / they were of little bravery [die es hetten kleinen mut]. He will get ill in his xiiii year / if he recovers / he will live xxx years / and will get liii years old / thereafter will be his end / nobody can prevent that.

Of the star Algaphar / and its effect

Who is born during Algaphar's rise / all his children will die / he will be handsome and affable / have burning eyes / charming / and will be captured due to the envy of a lord / a dog will bite him / or he will get burned / he will have a mark on his face / his head / his heart and [his] gallbladder will be unhealthy.

But if the same hour is on a Monday / as may well occur / who will be born then / will be master of his house / but it will not be of any use to him. When he reaches xv years / and will get ill and shapeless / if he recovers / he will get xxxviii years old / thereafter he will get ill again / if he escapes / he will live ninety years / than he will suffer from death.

Of the star Alzibinin / and its effect

[Who will be] born when Alzibinin rises / will be proud and shining (?) [scheinber] / a king's chancellor / or scribe / he will judge people / a wealthy man / he will be a useless and a burden for many / but useful and good for himself. His heart shall be diseased / [he will] get burnt / break a bone / [and] will have a mark on his face / he will have a wise wife / will inherit much from his father and mother / In his youth he will be devilish / but in his old age he will be good / When he is sixteen years of age he will get ill / if he recovers / he will get to the age of xxxvi years / thereafter he will have to die from a great illness / or be killed by iron.

Manazil

Of the star Alactil / and its effect

If Alactil rises / and a child will be born / it will be hairy / always an ill man / he will have a mark / on his hand / or elsewhere / and he will never get rid of his illness / he will be poisoned / travelling (?) [ein herr faben] / or worry him greatly / his tongue will be loose / he will talk much / to be both serious and badmouthing / his eyebrows will be growing together / [he will be] full of hate and envy / not arguing quickly / [he will be of] good complexion / recover from a great illness / will become wealthy / and defer one after the other / he shall be indebted to many / being very honourable / [he will] inherit his father's estate / and have a good time with his wife of whom he will have four. When he's is xiiii years / he will get ill / thereafter he will be healthy until his xvii year / thereafter he will get ill / if he recovers he will get to the age of lxv / thereafter he will die on the bed in his house.

Of the star Alcab / and its effect

Who is born when Alcab is rising / will do many bad things / he is handsome / imposing / angry / reddish brown / experiences hardship / sorrow / [has] evil urges / is quick to seek revenge like a fool / his back and his head are always unhealthy.

If somebody is born / when the star is rising in the first hour of the day / he will have much to cry and hardship / which will continue / [he will have] heart problems / pain in one lag / which will never be healed / he will be accused of magical cunning.

Who will be born in the second hour of the day / will receive sorrow and hardship / [he] will become a wealthy man through building and working / his heart and his bravery is based on a small amount of property due to his success as a merchant / other people will become merchants also due to his wares / his property will increase and grow / and get more and more all the time / [he] will have pain in his belly / at the age of sixteen / he will get ill and heavy [und schwer] / and if he recovers / he will live xxx years / thereafter he will get unwell / unhealthy and weak / if he recovers / he lives xlviii years / then he will die / and get killed by iron suffering death of unforeseeable misery.

Of the star Alsebra / and its effect

[Who is] born under the star Alsebra / he will be a fake and a liar who likes to spin new tales / his intention is evil in hidden and open ways / he likes to insult his neighbours / a fraud / if he can bring about confusion and hostility amongst people / he will do so all the time / [he] has small and bright eyes / handsome eyebrows / well-formed / quite a pretty man / with a slim body / [he] will be going to war on horseback / will have four wives / and the fourth will be the prettiest / [he will] have two marks on his neck / and two on the shoulders / [he is] optimistic and evil / does not care what he is doing / a dog or another animal will bite him.

And if he will be born in winter / he will be black / In summer [he will be] white perry and clear / [he will] have curly hair / nearly red complexion / [will] win many treasures / [he] will wound and kill many people / which will cause much hardship / He shall have two children with his wife and will be their enemy / he will receive a spot on his eye and another mark on one of his fingers. When he is seventeen years of age / he will get ill / if he recovers / he will live healthily until xxxvi years / then he will get ill again / if he recovers / he will live lvi years / thereafter he will receive bad things / and iron will kill him / [and] he will have different problems [es wenn dann solchs ein ander not] / which rarely happens.

Manazil

Of the star Alkanaim / and its effect

[Who is] born under the star Alkanaim will be black / have a big nose / [will be] quick and have a small head / will inherit his father's estate after his death / will fall into water / will have short teeth / and an ill heart / [he will] lose his best friend / will have an evil tongue / [he will] have an evil tongue to gossip and slander / will have two wives / but it happens / that he will not like to be with women / which happens due to an impediment of his nature / but he will have enough children / which may also apply at times to women / who are born under this star. He will receive many goods / will lose some of them at times / but luck will have it that they will increase day by day / [he] will have a heavy heart due to fright / be slim / and because of a women / or something else he will be at the mercy of an enemy / [he] will have five marks on him / and when he reaches xx years / he will fall ill / if he escapes / he will get to the age of li years / thereafter he will get ill again / if he recovers / he will become an old man / of lxxx years / thereafter it will not continue / he has to perish / and die miserably.

Of the star Alneda / and its effect

[Who is] born under the star Alneda will have much grief / will ride much / and will be a strong sword fighter / an archer / who is useful to himself / with his weapons and his piety he will win much / he will burn himself on iron / being careless / be it good or bad / and will be wealthy.

And if Saturn joins also / this star is not beneficial to humans / and all path he rides or walks on will be / dull [?] / [he] will cough / and his head will be numbed by an illness / which is unlikely to cease.

But if a person / is born / when the star is rising in the second hour of the day / their forehead will be big and bold / will have two children / [he] is lusting after women in an evil way / will have a handsome body / all over / and will recover from great illness / his possessions will be increasing and decreasing as luck will have it. He will fall into poverty / and die a strange death / killed by a bite. If he gets to the age of twenty-one years / he will get weak / then he will be ill for four years / if he recovers / he will get to the age of lxx / then he will die from the bite of a poisonous animal.

Of the star Zaddadena / and its effect

Who is born during Zaddadena's rise / will be of fierce temper / and a man of blood / killing and bludgeoning people who are in desperate straits / therefore he will die in sin. He will be boisterous in his youth but wise in old age / sometimes happy / but still an angry man / and harmful as much as possible / therefore he will be rumoured to use magical cunning. When he will be fifteen years old / he will bet ill / if he recovers / he will reach xxxvi years / thereafter he will be ill again / if he recovers again / he will live lx years / Thereafter he has to die / be it man or woman.

Of the star Sabadola / and its effect

[Who is] born under Sabadola is clean (?) [von speis sauber] / unjust / sometimes nasty to father and mother / always covering up his shameful behaviour / his end is better than his beginning / [He] will love his wife / will overcome a malady brought on by a sorceress / that he is useless with women and a great drunkard / belly ache will dry him and eat him up / if he can overcome it /

he will live xxi years / thereafter he will get ill / if he recovers / he will live for xlviii years / then he will die.

Of the star Sadahad / and its effect

[Who is] born under Sadahad / will live well and full of virtue / lose many positions through an accident / will experience anxiety and sorrow / will have many children and wives / and will eat much.

But who is born during the second hour of the day / will be a proud man / [he] will live xxiiii years / then he will get ill / if he recovers / he will receive honour and worthiness / the devil will fight him / but only do little damage / [he] will be weak of heart and courage.

But who is born in the fourth hour / will live fifty years / than he will be dead / killed by as word / which is true.

Of the star Sadalachia / and its effect

Who [is] born under Sadalachia / will always have plenty to eat / [be] gentle / but suffer from all the negative that will happen to him / [he] will win great riches / but he will lose it all and it will disappear / [He] will be healthy / but suffer from back pain / which he will recover from / loves women / will outlive father and mother / talkative / will gain property in his old age / no bad luck will harm him / he will get rid of his enemies / which will make him suffer much sorrow and pain / A cat or another animal will bite him so much that he will hardly recover / [he] will receive a head wound / [have] a mark on his shin / on his leg / his genitals / on his arm / and a fifth on his heart. He will live xxiiii years / then he will get ill / and if he recovers / he will live xl years / thereafter he will be ill again / if he recovers / he will live lxx years / but a sword will cause his last day.

But who will be born in the second hour / will die from the wheel / and no other way.

Of the star Aporaboyl / and its effect

[Who will be] born when Aporaboyl is rising / will receive many goods / will lose it all / but will be lucky / and although he does not have enough goods / he will be handsome and healthy.

But who will be born / during the second hour of its rise / will be full life and handsome.

Who will be born during the third hour / will be black / [will] have enough children / although some of them will die / [he] will like wine / proud / and angry / [and] will die alone in poverty / will walk around with good (?) [salb] / [he] will receive a mark form wood or iron / [He] will live healthily xxii years / thereafter he will get ill / if he recovers / he will live lii years / then he will get ill / if he recovers / lxxii years / but not an hour longer.

Of the star Alcharga / and its effect

[Who will be] conceived when Alcharga is rising during the first hour of the day / will be clever and win many goods / white / fair and true / and healthy / but at some point he will get into terrible trouble / so much that he will lose all his possessions / [he] will be working for a master / and will continue so that many people will want to cause him harm / but they will not achieve this as much as they try.

Manazil

But who will be born during the second hour of the day / will receive great honours / he will survive his parents / have many children / will be cured of all pains / and will be lucky in 'Ostland' in the sea / [he] will have long eyes / his faithful (?) is ill / [he will] win many things / give away (?) [vleuert] much also / He will live healthily xxvii years / thereafter he will get ill / if he recovers / he will get to liiii years / thereafter he will get ill / if he survives / he will live lxx years / then his last day will approach / and he will have to die.

Of the star Beualhot / and its effect

[Who will be] born if Beualhot is rising in the first hour of the day / will be white strange / and very rich / ingenious / not too small / not too tall / avoiding many illnesses / healthy / his goods will be enjoyed more by strangers than by his friends / he will have many children / he will have marks on his neck and near his eyes / and two on one foot.

But who will be born in the second hour / will have on his finger / or somewhere else on his body have marks / [he] will break a bone / if he recovers / it will not happen again / He will be left with all honours and goods of two women / [he] will be mean / which is why he has not got enough / he is longing for goods on water and on land / will have a brave son / and will be an honourable father / He will experience an adventure / fall into water / and get out again / and a master will be angry with him / which will lose him money / but he will still have enough / He will live healthily for xxviii years / thereafter he will get ill / if he recovers / he will live lvi years / thereafter he will be ill again / if he recovers / he will get to lxxx years / then it will be finished.

Peter Stockinger

Key:

Alnacha: 1st part of the Ram -> 1st Mansion al-Saratan
Albocain: 2nd and 3rd part of the Ram -> 2nd Mansion al-Butain
Alcoreia: 1st part of the Bull -> 3rd Mansion al-Turaija
Aldabaran: 2nd part of the Bull -> 4th Mansion al-Dabaran
Almusin: 3rd part of the Bull / 1st part of the Twins 5th Mansion al-Haq'a
Alkaia: 2nd part of the Twins -> 6th Mansion al-Han'a
Aldira: 3rd part of the Twins -> 7th Mansion al-Dira
Abiatra: 1st part of the Crab -> 8th Mansion al-Natra
Alcharph: 2nd part of the Crab -> 9th Mansion al-Tarfa
Algebla: 3rd part of the Crab / 1st part of the Lion -> 10th Mansion al-Gabha
Alcoraten: 2nd part to the right side of the Lion -> 11th Mansion al-Zubra
Alserfa/Alsarfa: two parts of Alserfa in the 3rd part of the Lion /
1st part of the Virgin -> 12th Mansion al-Sarfa
Algane 2nd part of the Virgin -> 13th Mansion al-Auwa
Alchimecht; 3rd part of the Virgin -> 14th Mansion al-Simak
Algapahr: 1st part of the Scales -> 15th Mansion al-Gafr
Alsibinin/Alzibinin: 2nd part of the Scales -> 16th Mansion al-Zubana
Alactil: 3rd part of the Scales / 1st part of the Scorpion ->
17th Mansion al-Iklik
Alcabin: 2nd part of the Scorpion -> 18th Mansion al-Qualb
Alsebra: two parts of Alsebra in the 3rd part of the Scorpion/
third part of Alsebra in the 1st part of the Archer -> 19th Mansion al-Saula
Alnagain/Alnagaim: 2nd part of the Archer -> 20th Mansion al-Na'a'im
Alneda: 3rd part of the Archer -> 21st Mansion al-Balda
Zaddadena: 1st part of the Sea Goat -> 22nd Mansion Sa'd al-Dabih

Manazil

Sabadola: 2nd part of the Sea Goat -> 23rd Mansion Sa'd Bula'
Sadahab/Sadahad: 3rd part of the Sea Goat /
two parts of Sadahad at the beginning of the Water Bearer -
> 24th Mansion Sa'd al-su'ud
Sadalachia: 2nd part of the Water Bearer -> 25th Mansion Sa'd al-ahbija
Alparaboil: 3rd part of the Water Bearer /
1st part of the Fishes -> 26th Mansion al-Farg al-muqaddam
Alcharga: 2nd part of the Fishes -> 27th Mansion al-Far al-mu'ahhar
Beualhot: 3rd part of the Fishes -> 28th Mansion Batn al-Hut

Brenner, Sebastian: Das Grosse Planeten Buch, Frankfurt am Main, 1789

[Chapter 20] Of the Twelve Heavenly Signs

There are twelve roads in the sky, these are the twelve signs, Aries, Taurus, Gemini, Cancer, Leo, Virgo, Libra, Scorpius, Sagittarius, Capricornus, Aquarius, Piscis. In German: [Widder] Ram, [Stier] Bull, [Zwillinge], Twins, [Krebs] Crab, [Löw] Lion, [Jungfrau] Virgin, [Waag] Scales, [Scorpion] Scorpion, [Schütz] Archer, [Steinbock] Sea Goat, [Wasserman] Waterbearer, and the Fishes [Fische]. Each of them is 30 degrees long, that is as much as the Sun moves in thirty-one days, but sometimes she can do this in 30 days, and in even fewer days which happens in February in some years in February [Hornung]. And if a planet is located under one of these [signs], it is said that he is living therein, and is therefore rightly called a house.

These twelve houses have lots of meanings and power. Three are dry and hot, Aries, Leo, Sagittarius, these are like fire. Three are moist and hot, they are like air, Aquarius, Gemini, Libra. Three [are] moist and cold, they are like water, Cancer, Scorpio, Piscis. And the last three [are] dry and cold, are like earth,Taurus, Capricornus, Virgo.

Amongst these twelve signs are four which push people towards love, Aries, Taurus, Leo and Capricorn. Therefore, who is born hereunder will undoubtedly be a lover. But if it should so happen, that Venus would come between them, he would be of such morals, namely so fiery from courting, that he could not look out for commendation, appraisal and hounour, so much deluded are men and women. Now I will continue to write about the stars which stand above the twelve signs.

Manazil

[Chapter 21] Of the Stars Above the Twelve Signs

The stars above the twelve signs are uncountable, and many of them have no names, but wise men named them by comparison. For example, one can see seven stars in a row, similar to a chariot, therefore one says it would be a chariot with four wheels and three horses. People also know St Martin's Staff, Three Maries, and the Grave, the Seven Stars, and the Leitung [?], etc. There are also some names in Latin which are connected to important things and I will describe some of them, because they are showing to us much luck and possible bad luck to take on the former and avoid evil, and there are 28 named as follows / Alnacha / Albocain / Alcoreia / Aldobaran / Almusin / Alkaia / Aldira / Albiatra / Alcharph / Algebla / Alkraten / Alserpha / Algant / Alchimechi / Algaphahr / Alsibinin / Alactil / Alcabin / Alsebra / Alnagain / Alneda / Zaddatena / Sabadola / Saddahab / Sadolachia / Albaraboil / Alcharga / and Beualhot.

[Chapter 22] Of the Order of the Twelve Signs with the Stars, including their Influence

Each of the twelve roads, which means each sign, is divided into three parts, beginning, middle, and end, and if one of the listed stars is therein, it is called its house. Therefore, the star Alnacha is in the first part of Aries, Albocain in the middle and the end thereafter.

In the beginning of Taurus, there shall stand Alkoreia, then Aldaboran in the middle, and at last at the end two thirds of Almusin.

At the beginning of Gemini is the last third of Almusin, then Alkaia in the middle, and in the third part stands Aldira.

In the first part of Cancer stands Albiatra, Alcharph in the middle, one third of Algebla.

Thereafter the other two thirds of Algebla are standing in the first part of the Lion, Alcoraten stands in the middle to the right hand side, two thirds of Alserpha [stand] at the end.

The last third of Alsarfa is in the beginning of Virgo, Algant is in the middle and Alchimechi at the end.

In the first part of Libra stands Algaphar, Alzibini stands in the middle, and Alactil at the end one third of Alactil, which has luck and health.

The other two thirds of Alactil stand in the first part of Scorpio, Alkabin in the middle, and two thirds of Alsebra at the end thereafter.

At the beginning of Sagittarius is the last third of Alsebra, Alnagaim in the middle, and Alneda in the end.

At the beginning of Capricorn stands Zaddatena, Sabadola in the middle, and one third of Saddahad at the end.

Thereafter comes Aquarius, he stands in the eleventh house, and has two thirds of Sadahad at its beginning, Sadalachia stands in the middle, and one third of Albaraboil is at the end, which brings great health.

Thereafter is the twelfth sign, Pisces, and the remaining part of Albaraboil is therein, and Alcharga stands in the middle, Beualhot at the end. Of these stars, what good or evil they will convey to people who are born under them will I tell you right until the end of the first part of the Planeten Buch.

[Chapter 23] Of the Star Alnacha, and its Effect

This star begins in 28 degrees and 54 minutes of Aries, and reaches with its nature up to 11 degrees and 45minutes of Taurus, and is of temperate nature regarding the weather, and brings bad luck to people's possessions.

A child, male or female, born when Alnacha is rising in the first hour of the day will have a mark near its mouth, and as well near the eyes, will have a beautiful nose, will come into possession of property, but will still be unhappy whatever they ask for or desire will happen, they will have a frightful face, and will do bad things

Manazil

everywhere so that they will be feared. They will also be judging over country and people, ill in their heart, bad tempered, worrisome to their friends, nobody loves them, and if he shall have a wife, he will have two children with her, both of them will be male, all because of this star rising at the time. He will also be black, have long teeth, he shall protect himself from being burnt by fire, from being struck by iron and being bitten by animals. He will fall victim to cunning magic, or he will be possessed by an evil spirit, his hair will turn grey. He will have a mark on his upper thigh between his legs, or elsewhere on the shoulders close to the sides, he is big and (?) [schwanck], has pretty feet, he will be dignified in whichever land he will travel and will rise higher from one to the other, he will have a good voice, rough [?] and not uncovered [?]. He will get to the age of 23 years. These are the attributes of a child which is born when Alnacha rises early with the Sun in the first hour.

If the star rises in the second hour and a child will be born, be it a man or a woman, it will be poor throughout its life and without property and shall have misery and no sympathy, shall have many children, would like to own and wear pretty clothes, like to eat spices, is intelligent and well brought up, is of soft predisposition, their enemies and masters will give them a lot of trouble from which they will not escape. rc.

If a child is born at a different hour than this one, be it day or night, it will be beaten to death because of the might of the star, God may prevent us from it. The colours of his clothes shall be reddish-brown, like his livestock. His best luck is in the morning [east] and at noon [south]. His main front door shall point into this direction, too. His bed's foot-end's feet and his big livestock's heads [also], because in such a house is his luck, wealth and health from the grace of god. The time of his bad luck, disgust and obstacles is the 10th, 13th, 14th, 15th, 20th, 25th, 27th 30th and 40th year, thereafter the 50th and 55th year, if he survives it, he will live until 78 years old. In these years, he shall be aware of quarrel and water [?]. He shall avoid Saturn, Moon, and Venus days in all good works, as well as white, green and black coloured clothes. He shall also be careful in August, October, February, as well when the Moon is in Virgo, Cancer and Pisces.

Chapter 24] Of the star Albokaim and its effect

This star begins in 11 degrees and 46 minutes of Taurus, reaches to 24 degrees and 37 minutes of Taurus, and is of dry nature and unhappy, [of the] nature of Saturn. It is also called Allothaim, Albothaim, Albechain, and under the government of Enedielis.

If a child, male or female, is born during the time of Albokaim rising, it will be happy and good, God provides him with wealth, a happy personality, anybody who sees him or knows him will come to love him. They are black beautiful and have a round face.

Who is born during the night will be different, he is rough with a huge beard that is strong and hard, he will be the leader of his friends (?) [vorgehen] is talkative, has watery eyes, and a beautiful nose, large eyebrows, white teeth, and pretty cheeks.

Who is born in the evening before the livestock is moving off the fields will like to fence and argue, hate, and envy his innocent neighbours. He will love other men's wives, and other men [will love] his wife, he will be secretly disgraced, he will use up his estate and will nourish himself in a sinful way. He will not amass riches but he will work hard to strife towards it and he will live his life with anguish, he will take on a profession, will give up on it due to an accident and will therefore not save enough money during his lifetime to pass anything on to his children it will cause him to take what he hasn't put there he will be proud, will hunger, his days will be miserable, or he will die due to magic trickery, his enemies will strife to see him, but honour and virtue will not be his. His face shall be marked with two signs, one is above the eyes, he will be bitten by dogs or be wounded by iron, [and] is ill in the back and lumbar region.

Manazil

But if one would be born in the second hour of the morning when the star is rising, then this child will be blind due to the power of Albokaim, or white spots will cover his eyes, that he will only be able to see a little bit, during his lifetime he will have intercourse with many women, will have a mark on his mouth, will inherit property, and will have a temper. He will have three marks, one on the neck, the other one on the head, the third one on the forehead.

The colours of his clothes will be green, white, metal-grey, honey-pale, yellow and horse-grey, grey, and white, mottled and yellow colours.

His luck is towards west [Niedergang] and south [Mittag]. His entrance door and the foot-end of his bed should be facing towards the countries which he is taught about, the same goes for the heads of his livestock.

He shall look at all good things in new light [Neumond], and especially what should be long-lasting, the lucky days are Moon, Venus, and Mercury.

The time of his bad luck and unpleasantness, obstacle, and death, are the 10th, 12th, 14th, 15th, 16th, 20th, 24th, 27th, 30th, 35th, [and] 60th year, if he survives these, with god's help, he will live until 70 or 85. His evil and unlucky days are Saturn and Mars.

His unlucky months are September, November, and March. Also, when the Moon is in Sagittarius, Libra, and Taurus.

[Chapter 25] Of the star Alkoreia and its effect

This star, also called Achoraye, Athoraye, or Achaomazone and is ruled by Amixiel, begins in 24 degrees and 37 minutes of Taurus, and reaches with its force unto 28 degrees and 10 minutes of Taurus, or the ox-eye, and is moist and more unlucky than lucky for humans. It is of Mercury and Moon nature. If Alkoreia is rising at the birth of a child, it will be a great thinker, much loved, with grey hair, and have dog eyes. But if the star is rising with the Sun and in the seventh hour the planet Mars is also rising (who is tempting some to do evil), and if a child is born, be it man or woman, they will experience much in their youth and will have much work to do [and] they will be poor in old age, [he] will have four wives, many children, [and] he will be a fine fellow when it comes to play and companionship.

But if this star is rising in the evening when it gets dark, and a child will be born, it will have enough on its table throughout its entire life, has a small head, a big nose, what he purchases in foreign lands will not last long.

His lucky days, colours, clothes, also love, housing, and what is necessary for him, will be listed under the other star, or Mansion, also about young or old light.

The time of his bad luck, sorrow, grief, and death is the 11th, 12th, 14th, 15th, 20th, 24th, 25th, 28th, 30th, 40th, 48th, 50th, 60th, 73rd, and 80th year.

[Chapter 26] Of the star Albdaboran / and its effect

This star, which is also called Aldebram, or Adelamen, and is ruled by Azariel, begins in the 7th degree and 28 minutes of Gemini, and reaches with its nature unto 20 degrees and 20 minutes of the same sign. It is of moist and venerial nature, and lucky for people in many ways.

A child that is born when Aldaboran is rising likes to laugh and is red, rich, and will be angry with their parents. It shall have many duties and make a living from them, he will bequeath everything to one of his friends, only few thoughts shall confuse him throughout his life, [he] shall love his wife like his own body, shall not like to eat and drink, shall beckon to two wives, and find goods beneath the earth. But if it rises during the night, and child is born, its body will be quiet, like a lazy wife, [he] will have his room under his own roof / [and] will not travel anywhere to find out about anything.

And if Aldaboran is rising during daytime at any hour, and somebody is born, he shall be poor, an animal will bite him, much coughing will come out of his chest, [he] will be angry, cheeky and blasphemous, [he] will be wounded by iron, shall rarely be happy or not at all, and he will never be lucky, a sone will hurt him, he will break a bone, he will die in a foreign country, and nobody will be there to bury him.

Manazil

The colours of his clothes shall be blue, a mixture of brown and grey, his best luck in his occupation is towards the occident, towards west [Niedergang] and Septentrion. His front door shall be directed towards this direction, as well as the foot-end of his bed, and the heads of his livestock, the lucky days are Mercury and Jupiter.

The time of his bad luck, misery, and death, and other unpleasantness, is the 9th, 11th, 18th, 22nd, 24th, 30th, 34th, 43rd, 49th and 69th year. Particularly in October, December, and April, and when the Moon is in Taurus, or in Cancer, or in Capricorn, he aisle not begin anything new. He shall particularly beware of these, and also of Sun-, Moon-, and Venus days.

He shall not live in a house that is looking towards the Orient or the South [Mittag]. All good and long-lasting things he shall be begin in young light, but evil things during the waning moon.

[Chapter 27] Of the star Almusin / and its effect

This star, which is also called Alchatya, Albabchaya, or Achaya, and who is ruled by Cabriel or Gabriel, is seen in 20 degrees and 12 minutes of Gemini, and reaches with its power unto the 3rd degree and 44 minutes of Cancer. [It] is of barren nature, and subjected to the Sun, bringing moderate luck.

A child being born during Almusin rising will have a big forehead, bald and without hair, [and] will have lots of strange thoughts. But if he is born during the night, he will have to live with a lack of power, in misery, [and] toilsomeness, many women will surround him, he will have a mark on one arm, and on the loins, he will be wounded by stones, hurt by iron and a dog will bite him, women will love him and loath him and he will get two more marks, one on his heart, and one on his arm, he will break a bone, or fire will burn him,[he] shall have luck with women and beasts, but it will take time to give his wife a child.

His lucky days and colours of clothes and beasts, and other things, necessary for him, are listed under the fourth star or Mansion.

The time of his bad luck, and misery is the 6th, 7th, 9th, 12th, 15th, 17th, 18th, 25th, 30th, 40th, 42nd, 49th, 80th and 85th year, in these years he should not change his circumstances and avoid to begin anything new, because otherwise these things would turn to bad luck.

[Chapter 28] Of the star Alkaia / and its effect

This star, also named Alhanno, or Alchaya and ruled by Dirachiel, begins his power in the 3rd degree and 43minutes of Cancer, extending it to the 15th degree and 54 minutes of the same sign. He is of temperate nature, brings people luck and is of Jupiter's nature.

A child born during Alkaia's rise will be rich, born in wedlock, keep his own and do well with it, have grey hair, thick eyebrows, and a cleft (furrow?) above the nose, his adornment will be red and [he will] suffer [from] illness in his back, an evil spirit will haunt him and women will love him very much.

But if the star rises in the second hour after sunrise and a child will be born, it will have spots in its eyes, will lose many teeth, and will have grey hair.

But if it rises in the third hour, who will be born will be an artist and will achieve deeds of wonder of which an equivalent will hardly be found in many kingdoms.

And who will be born if it rises in the fourth hour shall be healthy and if Mars rules has to sell meat and [he will] let blood, his livelihood shall be made through buying [and] he will live healthily for ten years, then he will be ill, if he recovers [he] will live for 13 years, thereafter he will be ill again, if he recovers, he will live 44 years, thereafter he will be ill again, if he recovers, he will get to the age of 90.

In October, November, December, and April, particularly when the Moon is in Sagittarius, Cancer, Capricorn, and Taurus, he shall not begin anything because these signs predict little luck.

The unlucky years are the 6th, 9th, 12th, 15th, 18th, 20th, 30th, 40th, 80th anything else is written under the fourth star.\

Manazil

It also must be stated that who is born under the first 6 degrees of Cancer shall look for the seventh star where he will find its meaning.

[Chapter 29] Of the star Aldira / and its effect

This star is also called Alarzach, Aldimiach, and Alazech, and whose ruler is Sekeliel, begins in the 15th degree and 55 minutes of Cancer and reaches with his power up to the 28th degree and 18 minutes of Cancer, is of moist nature, Venus, and Moon, means luck to people, if they apply to it and keep God fearing and pious.

Who is born during the rise of Aldira willll teach and know a lot, [he will] drink a lot, he will be a very mild master, he will find treasure beneath the earth, [he will be] very angry, and if he cannot get revenge he will not believe his eyes, his first wife will be ugly and dark, nature will provide him with two or slightly more children, very often he will be annoyed with his father and mother, which he and his brothers will outlive, he shall be in a way that no man shall outdo him if he wasn't of high rank. He will be wounded on his head [and] on his arm he will have a mark, [and] one in his groin, and two on his genitals between his legs, and another one on his mouth.

The days which are detrimental to him concerning his serious businesses are Saturn and Mars, the unlucky colours of this clothes are red, black, ashen, and mouse-grey, and all which is lovely and of such hair [?].

His unlucky months are November, December, January, and May, and especially when the Moon is in Gemini, Aries, Cancer, and Sagittarius, and impeded by Saturn, Mars, and Sun.

He should beware of the following years because his life will end in one of them. They are the 7th, 15th, 22nd, 25th, 26th, 30th, 31st, 34th, 37th, 40th, 44th, 49th, 68th, 75th, 80th, 89th year. But he who will look up to God, is pious and diminishes his evil ways, will have the evil effects of the stars and signs transformed into happy times. Everybody should notice this diligently, and direct his chattels and his doings and dealings according to God's commands. Then the aforementioned will assist him via his holy angels and protect him from all that is nasty and evil.

His luck is towards Septentrion [northern quarter of the sky] and towards the Orient with all his business, his front door should be pointing towards these countries, as well as the foot-end of his bed and the heads of his livestock.

His lucky days during the week are the Moon-, Jupiter-, and Venus day. The best months are June, July, March, and April. Also, when the Moon is in Leo, Cancer, Aries, or Capricorn.

Beneficial colours are green and white, pale-yellow, honey-colour, blue and brown, his livestock should be brown and reddish-brown, white, and spotted white.

[Chapter 30] Of the star Albiatra and its effect.

This star, also called Anatrarchia or Alnaza, which is ruled by Amnediel, begins in the 28th degree and 46 minutes of Cancer, and reaches with his power unto 11 degrees and 36 minutes of Leo, is of dark nature, lucky for people, and of the nature of Venus and the Moon.

A child born during Albiatra rising will learn to fence and fight and therefore he will reject all the teachings of his parents, [he] does not love his friends, often gets angry which often shows his foolish immodesty, he will become a drinker and a glutton, a joker, reveal secrets, [be] very angry in his words, he will have a mark on his face etc. Similar will happen to the one born during daytime.

Who is born during the night must live a diabolical life, [he] will be merciless, punishes when he must chastise, he will arrive in the country of a lord which will bring him little benefit, his end will be harsh and bitter, he will better his life during old age, his head will become ill, and he will suffer from pressure on his heart, and in his back.

Unlucky colours are listed in the seventh Mansion.

Manazil

His evil years, which will get him nasty illnesses and death, are the 4th, 6th, 8th, 12th, 15th, 20th, 22nd, 24th, 31st, 37th, 40th, 44th, 75th, and 80th. In these years his luck turns to bad luck.

[Chapter 31] Of the star Alcharphes and its effect

This star Alcharphes, also called Arschaam, ruled by Barbiel, begins in 11 degrees and 37 minutes of Leo and its nature reaches into 24 degrees and 29 minutes of Leo, is of dry nature, the Sun's nature, and brings people mediocre luck.

A child born / when Alcharphes is rising will be sad and cry, many children will come from it, but they will not live long, he will commit unchastity, will be repulsive to many, and most lovely to his master, [he will be] much ill, innocent and shapely, a wound on the head, and a mark on the back, the bite of an animal on one foot, and two marks between his legs on the genitals, also one caused by fire. He will have a lot of property, both land and plough, and if he travels, which he does not want, he will soon return which is of great benefit to him and if he would be away for a long time, it would lead to his ruin.

His luck is towards the Orient and south [Mittag] therefore his front door should be pointing towards sunrise or south [Mittag], and he should turn the foot-end of his bed towards these countries. The following days of the week are the best during which he can begin anything in a happy manner, they are Sunday and Jupiter day. The best colours of his clothes are yellow, red, yellow-golden, brown, and blue. Unlucky months are April, May, and August. Also, when the Moon is in Virgo, or Capricorn, or Gemini. All things that should last should be begun in early light, and especially when the Moon is in Capricorn, Leo, or Virgo.

The damaging and evil years which will bring damage to his body and his life and his food, are the 10th, 17th, 20th, 24th, 35th, 37th, 40th, 44th, 49th, 74th, 80th, and 89th. In these years he should not alter his standing, and be careful with his food and drink.

The evil months, which he should avoid, are December, January, [Hornung] and [Brachmonat], and particularly when the Moon is in Capricorn, Pisces, or Cancer, and when he will be hindered by Saturn, or Mars, or the Sun.

[Chapter 32] Of the star Algelba and its effect

This star, also known as Aglebb, Agdioche, or Alchelialche, and whose ruler is Ardesiel, begins in 25 degrees 29 minutes of Leo, and ends with its nature in 17 degrees and 59 minutes of Virgo. He is moister and of the nature of Venus and the Moon, luckier for people than unlucky.

If Algebla (sic) is rising when a child is born it will be wise, most lovely, proud and boisterous will think of itself as mighty, thinking that he would be the king's companion, therefore many will try to kill him, but no harm will come to him because due to his wisdom he will escape and [he] will come from one virtue to the next through which he will win a lot but lose it all soon after. Iron will wound him, his head [will be] unhealthy, he will suffer from smallpox, which will make him recognisable, [he] will be a well-repeated man [and] a great illness will befall his head, and if his anger will lead him, he will be raging and mad, [he] will have a big nose, his shoulders will be high, his loin will be well formed. When he is ten years old, he will be at the mercy of a master, thereafter he will get ill. His luck, evil and good days you can find noted in the ninth star.

[Chapter 33] Of the star Alkratea and its effect

This star, also known as Adarf, [and] whose ruler is Neziel, begins in 7 degrees and 20 minutes of Virgo, and reaches with his effect into the 20th degree and 24 minutes of the following signs, and is naturally well tempered, [of] Jupiter and Venus nature, [makes] people happy.

If a child is born during Alkratea's rise, it will have a long face, its speech will be soft and ill uncourtly and nefarious, bad things will happen [to the child], very often it will be angry, there will be a mark on his loins, but if there is no mark it will come to much chagrin.

Who is born when the star rises during the night does not care what he does, will be a good orator, has a mark on his legs [and he will] also have marks on face and neck.

But if it rises in the second hour of the day who will be born then will have many children by two wives, but nearly all of them will die. The first child will be a girl, the other one a boy. He will be ill in his eleventh year, if he recovers, he will live healthily for 24 years, thereafter he will suffer from illness and will have to work hard, if he survives, he will live 58 years.

His luck in buying and selling is towards the south [Mittag] and west [Niedergang], his front door and the foot-end of his bed and the heads of his livestock in the stable should point towards this country.

The time of his luck is September and June, also when the Moon is in the signs of Libra, Gemini, Cancer and Sagittarius, the best days of the week when he shall begin his deeds are Mercury and Venus.

The lucky colours of [his] clothes are ice-grey or mixed grey, blue, white, and green, horse-grey, dapple-grey [Apfelgraue] and brown.

The evil months are January, [Hornung], March, and July, also when the Moon is in Scorpio, Pisces, Leo, and Saturn [?]. The evil weekdays are Saturn and the Sun.

The unlucky years are the 5th, 11th, 20th, 22nd, 25th, 30th, 40th, 50th, 60th.

[Chapter 34] Of the star Alsarpha and its effect

This star also called Azorphe, Alzorpha or Alzarpha, which is under the rulership of Abdizuel, begins in 20 degrees and 25 minutes of Virgo, and lasts until 2 degrees and 22 minutes of Libra, is of moist nature, [of] the nature of Venus and of the Moon, mediocre luck.

When a child is born during Alsarpha's rise, it will be of placid nature and [have] much honour and property, will be well established with great masters who will give him much, [he] will be lucky if he chooses to be a farmer and winemaker, but he will be unlucky if he travels from one town to the other; after he will get married, he will get some property, and he will be busier than he ever was before and will neither be concerned with riches nor with unrighteous indulgence, nobody can catch him out in his wisdom, he will suffer from a serious illness which he will endure with patience, [he] is very modest, talkative, to be a merchant will not serve him well, during wintertime [he] will rule over much land, is modest in the amount of food he eats, his hair is beautiful and curly, he will have a son who will be a thief and run away from his master, [he] will break a bone and have many marks on his body, one from iron, one from fire on his belly, or the leg, or his foot, or on his neck and on [his] hands and will die in a foreign land. When he is 44 years of age, he will be ill and weak, if he recovers, he will live to be 84 years, if he gets ill thereafter but recovers, he will live 99 years. Thereafter nobody can prevent it, be it man or woman, they must die.

The good evil, and unlucky years and times, also which country, month, day, and sign which are bad or good for him, as well as other things, search for under the eleventh star.

[Chapter 35] Of the star Algayre and its effect

This star which is also called Alhayre, and is ruled by Jazariel, begins in the 2nd degree and 23 minutes of Pisces (sic) and reaches with his power up to the 15th degree and 54 minutes of Libra, is temperate of Jupiter and Venus nature, is more lucky then unlucky.

If a child is born when Algane is rising, it will collect many goods and treasures, but they will not help him, nature will give him many children but few will survive; will be of pleasant appearance, and when he will be 36 years of age, he will be honoured and everybody will be pleased for him, if he decides to be a merchant, he will make much money if he nurtures it, but he will have a great sorrow and

Manazil

there will be a mark on his elbow. He will have a mark on his belly or on his genitals, which is caused by fire, he may live naturally for 36 years.

But if a child is born when the star is rising in the second hour of the day, he will be ruler over his dynasty, tersely nothing will be to his detriment, [he] will not fail or falter.

But if it happens in the third hour, it will be the child of a king, and if he is from a lineage in the Holy Roman Empire, or another, he will be emperor. Should he be a poor man, who will not have such dignity, he will still be the ruler of his line and will rise above his peers with honour, riches, property and with respectability etc.

If he is born with Algayre in the fourth hour, he will die without any illness.

And if a child is born with the star in the fifth hour, it will be rich, ever unhealthy, but it will live forty years longer than the others, due to this star's power.

Also note that the power of this star reaches 6 degrees of Libra, and who is born under the 6th degree, search for his deeds under the 24th star.

His unlucky years are the 6th, 10th, 11th, 13th, 21st, 25th, 30th, 50th, 60th.

[Chapter 36] Of the star Alchimecht and its effect

This star begins in 15 degrees and 55 minutes of Libra, and reaches into the 28th degree and 45 minutes of Libra, is temperate, and of the nature of Satune and Venus, is unlucky for humans, but good to sow and plant. This star is the Virgin ear [Jungfer-Aehre] also by the Arabs and Indians called Azimech, Azimeth, Achureth, Atimot, Alcheymech, or Alhumech, and Ergediel rules over it.

Who is born during Alchimecht's rise will inherit many things from women all of whom will die, all his affairs shall turn out well, [he has] beautiful hair, is wise, and his advice will be good, a dog will bite him, his beard will be long, his face broad and not elongated. Nature will provide him with children who will not live long, he will not get old rather die than reach a proper age. On the upper lip near the nose, he will have a mark. He will live 43 years and that would be the longest [life] nature will grant him.

But if he is born during the night, then he will pass on much property to his children, legally he shall have two wives, is affable, a burn mark on his belly, he will travel to a master's land, buy many things, and will die and other people will own what he inherited [and] will keep his property, they who show little bravery. He will get ill in his 24th year, if he recovers, he will live 30 years and will get 53 years old, thereafter will be his end, nobody can prevent that.

His luck is towards the Occident with all his business, and towards Septentrion, his front door and the foot end of his bed shall be turned towards the Occident.

His lucky months are September, January, June, July, and when the Moon is in Libra, Scorpio, Cancer, and in Leo. The best days of the week are Saturn, Jupiter, and Venus. The best colours, which bring him luck, are black, ashen, brown, and green, also blue colours.

All long-lasting things, useful to him, shall be begun in young light, and when the Moon is in Cancer and Sagittarius.

Th unlucky months are February, March, April, and August, and when the Moon is in Pisces, Aries, Capricorn and in Virgo. The unlucky, evil days are Sun, Moon, and Mars.

The evil years are the 9th, 14th, 15th, 18th, 20th, 22nd, 23rd, 28th, 30th, 32nd, 36th, 38th, 40th, 44th, 66th, 73rd, 76th, 85th year.

[Chapter 37] Of the star Algaphar and its effect

The beginning of this star is in 28 degrees and 46 minutes of Libra, and ends in 11 degrees and 37 minutes of Scorpio, is of humid and of lunar nature, brings mediocre levels of luck in its nourishment. It is also called Alagarpha, Algaphar, or Agrapha, and his ruler is Ataliel.

Who is born during Algaphar's rise, all his children will die, he will be handsome and affable, have burning eyes, is charming, will be captured due to the envy of a lord, a dog will bite him or he will get burned, he will have a mark on his face, his head, heart, and gallbladder will be unhealthy.

But if the same hour is on a Monday, as may it well occur, who will be born then will be master of his house, but it will not be of any use to him. When he reaches 15 years, he will get ill and shapeless, if he recovers, he will live to be 38 years old, thereafter he will get ill again, if he escapes, he will live 90 years, then he will suffer from death.

What else is there to know can be found under the 14th star.

[Chapter 38] Of the star Alzibinin and its effect

This star begins in 11 degrees and 38 minutes of Scorpio, and ends in 24 degrees and 48 minutes of the same sign. [It] is humid, of the nature of Saturn and the Moon, and brings much evil to people. It is also called Ahubene, Azubene, and Azervelis rules over him.

Who will be born when Alzibinin rises will be proud and ostensive, apparently [scheinbar] like a king, etc, a chancellor, or a scribe, he will judge people, a wealthy man, he will be troublesome and a burden for many, but useful and good for himself, his heart will be diseased, [he will] get burnt, break a bone, will have a mark on his face, he will get bitten by poisonous animals, he will have a wise wife, will inherit much from his father and mother, n his youth he will be evil, wasting, squandering, and when drunk he will be bellicose, cantankerous, but in his old age he will be good and get comely nourishment, if he decides to do so. When he is 16 years of age, he will get ill, if he recovers, he will get to the age of 36 years, if he survives this illness, he will get to 43 years of age, thereafter he will have to die from a great illness / or be killed by iron.

His luck is towards Septentrion and Orient, his house shall [be directed] towards one of these lands, the foot-end of his bed, and the heads of his livestock in the stable shall be directed towards one of these lands.

The best months for his luck are November, February, July, and August, and when the Moon is in Sagittarius, Pisces, Leo and in Virgo. The good days are Mars and Jupiter, but Mars is the best [day] in the week.

Good colours to wear are fox-colour, green, brown, on his animals red, brown, fox-colour and grey.

All things useful and good should be begun in young light, particularly when the Moon is in Cancer, Leo, or Virgo, and is not debilitated by Saturn or Mars.

The evil times and places are towards South [Mittag] and West [Niedergang]. The evil months [are] March, April, May, and September, also when the Moon is in Aries, Capricorn, Gemini and Libra. The evil days the Moon and Venus. The unlucky years are the 10th, 14th, 17th, 20th, 21st, 24th, 28th, 30th, 33rd, 35th, 40th, 44th, 48th, 60th, 70th, 80th, 83rd, 88th.

[Chapter 39] Of the star Alactil and its effect

The beginning of this star is in 24 degrees and 49 minutes of Cancer, and reaches with his power up to 7 degrees and 28 minutes of Sagittarius, is moist, [of] Mercury and Moon nature, more lucky than evil for humans. It is also called Alchil, and its ruler is Adriel.

If Alactil rises and a child will be born, it will be hairy, always an ill man, he will have a mark on his hand or elsewhere and he will never get rid of his illness, he will be killed by poison, or it will make him gravely ill, his tongue will be loose, he will talk much, both serious and badmouthing, his eyebrows will be growing together, is full of hate and envy, not arguing quickly, of good complexion and shall recover from a great illness, will become wealthy and defer one after the other, he shall be indebted to many, be very honourable, [he will] inherit his father's estate and have a good time with his wives of whom he will have four. When he is 14 years old, he will get ill, thereafter he will be healthy until his 17th year when he will get ill, if he recovers he will get to the age of 65, thereafter he will die in bed in his house.

Manazil

If you would like to know more, look at the 16th star.

His unlucky years are the 6th, 12th, 13th, 15th, 17th, 20th, 26th, 45th and 89th year.

[Chapter 40] Of the star Alkab and its effect

This star, whose ruler is Egibiel, begins at 7 degrees and 28 minutes of Sagittarius, and extends with its nature and effect up to 20 degrees and 51 minutes of Aquarius, is of dry nature, of the nature of Mars and and the Sun, more lucky than evil to people.

Who is born when Alkab is rising will do many bad things, he is handsome, imposing, angry, reddish brown, experiences hardship, much sorrow, [has] evil urges, is quick to seek revenge like a fool, his back and his head are always unhealthy.

If somebody is born when the star is rising in the first hour of the day, he will have many scabs and hardship, which will continue, [he will have] heart problems, pain in one foot, which will never go away, he will be exposed to magical cunning.

Who will be born in the second hour of the day will receive sorrow and hardship, [he] will become a wealthy man through building and working, his heart and his bravery will be based on a small amount of property due to his success as a merchant, other people will become merchants also due to his wares, his property will increase and grow and get more and more all the time, [he] will have belly ache at the age of sixteen he will get ill and weak, if he recovers he will live 30 years, thereafter he will get unwell, unhealthy and weak, if he recovers he lives 48 years, then he has to die, and get killed by iron suffering death of unforeseen opinion.

His luck is towards the orient and south [Mittag], towards these countries should his trade be directed, his main door, the foot-end of his bed, and his livestock's heads in the stables should be directed towards this country.

The lucky months [are] November, December, August, and September, also when the Moon is in Sagittarius, Taurus, Scorpio, and Libra.

The best days of the week are Saturn, Jupiter, and the Sun.

The best colours of clothing are black, blue, brown and gold-coloured.

All long-lasting things should be begun in new light, especially when the Moon is Leo, Scorpio, Capricorn, and Sagittarius, but he must beware of bad things.

His bad luck is towards West [Niedergang] and North [Mitternacht], the evil months [are] April, May, June, and October. The evil days Moon, Mars, and Venus.

The evil years [are the] 7th, 14th, 15th, 23rd, 26th, 27th, 30th, 38th, 40th, 46th, 52nd, 55th, 77th, 80th.

[Chapter 41] Of the star Alsebra, or Axela, and its effect

This star, also named Alatha, Achala, Hycula, and Axala, which has Amutiel as his Lord, begins at 20 degrees and 11 minutes of Sagittarius, and extends with its influence up to 13 degrees and 43 minutes Capricorn. He is of moist nature and of the nature of Mercury and the Moon, bringing mediocre levels of luck to people.

[Who is] born under the star Alsebra, he will be a fake and a liar who likes to spin new tales, his intention is evil in hidden and open ways, he likes to insult the people surrounding him, a fraud, if he can bring about confusion and hostility amongst people he will do so all the time, [he] has small and bright eyes, handsome eyebrows, well formed, quite a pretty man, with a slim body, [he] will travel, will have four wives, and the fourth will be the prettiest, [he will] have two marks on his neck and two on the shoulders, [he is] optimistic and evil, does not care what he is doing, a dog or another animal will bite him.

And if he will be born in winter, he will be black, in summer [he will be] white pretty and clear, [he will] have curly hair, a nearly red complexion, [will] win many treasures, [he] will wound and kill many people, which will cause him much hardship, he shall have two children with his wife and will be their enemy, he will receive a spot on his eye and another mark on one of his fingers. When he is seventeen years of age, he will get ill, if he recovers, he will live healthily until he will be 36 years, then he will be ill again, if he recovers, he will live 56 years,

Manazil

thereafter he will die miserably, and iron will kill him / (?) [es wenn dann solchs ein ander not] / which rarely happens.

About the weather you will find at the 18th star. The bad and unlucky years are the 4th, 5th, 6th, 9th, 10th, 12th, 15th, 19th, 20th, 24th, 28th, 30th, 38th, 40th, 55th, 77th, and 80th.

[Chapter 42] Of the star Analkaim and its effect

This star is also known as Alkanaim, Alnahaya, and Tralos, and whose Lord is called Master Kyriel, rises in 3 degrees and 43 minutes of Capricorn, and extends until 15 degrees and 54 minutes of the same sign, and is moist, [of the] nature of Saturn and the Moon, bringing much bad luck to people.

[Who is] born under the mentioned hour [of] Alnakan will be black, have a big nose, [will be] quick with a small head, will inherit his father's estate after his death, will fall into water, will have short, pretty teeth, and an ill heart, [he will] lose his best friend, will have an evil tongue, too much gossip and slander, will have two wives, but it happens at times that he will not want to be with women, which happens due to an impediment of nature, but he will have enough children, which may also apply at times to women born under this star. He will receive many goods, will lose some of them at times, but luck will have it that they will increase day by day, [he] will have a heavy heart due to fright and because of a women or something else, he will be at the mercy of an enemy, [he] will have five marks on him and when he reaches 30 years, he will fall ill, if he escapes he will get to the age of 51 years, thereafter he will get ill again, if he recovers he will become an old man possibly of 80 years, thereafter nobody can fight it, he has to perish, and die miserably.

What else you need to know, seek it under the 18th star. This star covers the first 6 degrees, wherein one is born, then seek what you wish to know under the star that follows.

The evil and unlucky years are the 15th, 16th, 20th, 28th, 30th, 33rd, 40th, 43rd, 55th, 76th, and 87th.

[Chapter 43] Of the star Albeldach and its effect

The beginning of this star is in 15 degrees and 54 minutes of Capricorn, and ends in 28 degrees and 45 minutes of Capricorn, and is temperate, [of] Jupiter and Venus nature, brings more luck than bad luck to people. It is also called Abeda, Abelbach, and its Lord is Bethnael.

[Who is] born under the star Alneta will have much grief, will ride much and will be a strong man, an archer who is useful to himself, with his weapons and his piety he will win much, he will burn himself on iron, does not care what he does, be it good or bad, and will be wealthy.

And if Saturn joins it, this star will not be beneficial to humans, and all path he rides or walks on will be evil, [he] will cough and his head will be numbed by an illness which is unlikely to cease.

But if a person is born when the star is rising in the second hour of the day, their forehead will be big and bold, will have two children at once, [he] will be lusting after women in an evil way, will have a handsome body all over and will recover from a great illness, his possessions will be increasing and decreasing as luck will have it. He will fall into such poverty that he will die a strange death, killed by a bite. If he gets to the age of 21 years, he will get weak, then he will be ill for four years, if he recovers, he will get to the age of 70 years, then he will die from the bite of a poisonous animal.

His luck is towards south [Midday] and west [Niedergang], his main entrance, the foot-end of his bed, and his livestock in his stable, should point with their heads towards these countries.

The best and luckiest months are December, February, April, September, and October, and when the Moon is lucky in Capricorn, Sagittarius, Libra, and Scorpio, the lucky weekdays are Saturn and Mars.

Manazil

The lucky colours of clothes are black, ash-coloured, fiery red; on animals, black and mouse-coloured, red and fox-coloured: good and long-lasting things shall be begun in young light, in the days and months mentioned above, [he shall] travel in Capricorn, Taurus, and Scorpio.

The months of his bad luck are May, June, July, and November, also when the Moon is in Gemini, Cancer, Leo, and Virgo. The evil weekdays are Sun and Moon day. The evil years are the 10th, 12th, 14th, 18th, 20th, 21st, 24th, 25th, 35th, 36th, 40th, 43rd, 50th, 70th, 80th, and 88th.

[Chapter 44] Of the star Zaddadena and its effect

This star begins in 28 degrees and 46 minutes of Capricorn, and ends in 11 degrees and 37 minutes of Aquarius, and is of wet nature Saturn;s and the Moon's nature, more lucky for people than evil. It is also called Sadahacha, Sadacha, Zodeboluch, and Zendeldena, and its Lord is Geliel.

Who is born during Zaddadena's rise will be of fierce temper and a man of blood, killing and bludgeoning people, therefore he will die in sin. Before that, he will be boisterous in his youth but wise in old age, sometimes happy, but still an angry man and harmful as much as possible, therefore he will be hunted with magical cunning. If he will get to 15 years of age, he will get ill, if he recovers, he will reach 36 years, thereafter he may be ill again, if he recovers again, he will live 60 years, thereafter he must die, be they a man or a woman.

What else he needs to know can be searched for under the 21st star.

The evil years are the 10th, 12th, 17th, 20th, 25th, 33rd, 35th, 49th, 70th, and 79th.

[Chapter 45] Of the star Sadabadola and its effect

This star, also known as Zobrach, whose Lord is Requiel, rises in 11 degrees and 38 minutes of Aquarius, and ends in 24 degrees and 28 minutes of the imagined sign of Aquarius, and is [of] Saturn and Jupiter nature, themperate, bringing more good than evil to people.

[Who is] born under Sadabadola is of clean body, honest [aufrecht], sometimes bad-tempered to father and mother, always covering up his shameful behaviour, his end is better than his beginning, [he] will love his wife, will overcome a malady brought on by a sorceress that he is useless with women, he will be a great drunkard.

His luck will be in buying and selling, and agriculture, will barely receive great honours. He shall be righteous because he will be accused of evil deeds.

His luck is towards the Occident and Septentrion, his front door, the foot-end of his bed, and his livestock in the stable with their heads shall turn towards these lands.

The best days of the week are the Moon, Jupiter, and Mercury.

The best colours of his clothes and on hid cattle are black, and ash-colour, blue and grey mixed. On cattle, black and mouse-coloured, grey and brown.

The best months [are] January, Hornung, May, October, and November, also when the Moon is lucky in Aquarius, Pisces, Gemini, Scorpio, and Sagittarius.

All lucky things shall be begun in young light, when the Moon is lucky in Gemini, Scorpio and Taurus.

The evil years [are the] 6th, 13th, 15th, 20th, 30th, 36th, 38th, 40th, 42nd, 46th, 77th, 80th, 88th.

[Chapter 46] Of the star Sadahad and its effect

This star, also called Chadezoad, who has Abrinaeel as its Lord, begins in 24 degrees and 28 minutes of Aquarius, and ends in 17 degrees and 18 minutes of Pisces, and is Jupiter and Venus nature [and] temperate.

[Who is] born under Sadahad will live well and full of virtue, lose his belongings through an accident, will experience anxiety and sorrow, will have many children and wives, and will eat a lot. But who is born during the second hour of the day will be a proud man, if he lives 24 years, he will get ill, if he recovers, he will receive

Manazil

honour and worthiness, the devil will challenge him [anfechten], but will not do any damage, [he] will be weak of heart and courage.

What else he needs to know he can look for in the 23rd star.

The evil years are [the] 13th, 18th, 22nd, 26gth, 35th, 36th, 40th, 44th, 70th, 75th, 80th, and 87th.

[Chapter 47] Of the star Sadalachia / and its effect

The beginning of this star is in 7 degrees and 19 minutes of Pisces, the end is in 21 degrees and 11 minutes of Pisces, [it] is dry and of the nature of the Sun and Jupiter, [it] brings many good things to the people. It is also called Sadalabra and its Lord is Aziel.

Who [is] born under Sadalachia will always have plenty to eat, [is] gentle but suffers from all the negative things happening to him, [he] will win great riches but he will lose it all and it will disappear, [he] will be healthy but suffer from back pain which he will recover from, loves women, will outlive father and mother, [is] talkative, will gain property in his old age, no bad luck will harm him, he will get rid of his enemies who make him suffer much sorrow and pain, cat or another animal will bite him so much that he will hardly recover, [he] will receive a head wound, a mark on his shin, on his leg, his genitals, on his arm, and a fifth near his heart. He will live 24 years, then he will get ill and if he recovers, he will live 40 years, thereafter he will be ill again, if he recovers, he will live 70 years, but a sword will cause his last day.

But who will be born in the second hour will die from the wheel and in no other way.

His luck is towards Septentrion and Orient, his house wherein he lives and his front door, as well as his bed shall with the legs, and his livestock in the stable, with their heads, be turned towards these lands.

The best months are February, March, June, November, and December, also when the Moon is lucky in Pisces, Aries, Cancer, Sagittarius, Aries (sic), the best days are Jupiter and Venus.

The best colours are blue, brown and honey-coloured. In cattle, brown and white colours, also some red.

He shall begin long-lasting things in young light, when the Moon is in Capricorn and in Cancer.

The best years are the 6th, 7th, 10th, 12th, 14th, 15th, 20th, 24th, 38th, 30th, 40th, 80th, and 95th.

[Chapter 48] Of the star Alporabol and its effect

This star which is also called Alphorus and Phtahalmocaden, and has Tagriel as its Lord, can be found in 21 degrees and 12 minutes of Pisces, and reaches with its power until 2 degrees and 22 minutes of Aries, and is of Mars' and the Sun's nature, dry, and means much evil to people.

[Who will be] born when Alporabol is rising will receive many goods, will lose it all, but will be lucky and although he does not have enough goods, he will be handsome and healthy. But who will be born during the second hour of its rise will be salacious and handsome.

Who will be born during the third hour will be black, [will] have enough children although some of them will die, [he] will like wine, be proud and angry [and] will die from an accident, in poverty, will walk around with good (?) [salb], [he] will receive a mark form wood or iron, will live healthily for 22 years, thereafter he will get ill, if he recovers he will live 52 years, then he will get ill again, if he recovers he will 72 years.

The evil years are the 6th, 13th, 14th, 17th, 18th, 20th, 25th, 30th, 33rd, 34th, 36th, 40th, 55th, 66th, 80th, and 89th.

All other things he needs to know he shall seek under the 25th star.

Manazil

[Chapter 49] Of the star Alcharga and its effect

The home of this star is in 2 degrees and 23 minutes of Aries, and ends in 15 degrees and 53 minutes of the same sign. It is moist, and of Venus and Jupiter nature, means much luck to people in their old age. It is also called Althalgalmoad and its Lord is Alhemiel.

[Who will be] conceived when Alcharga is rising during the first hour of the day will be clever and win many goods, white, fair, true and healthy, but at some point he will get into terrible trouble, so much that he will lose all his possessions, [he] will be coming to a master's office, and will be aware that many people will want to cause him harm, but they will not achieve this, as much as they try.

But who will be born during the second hour of the day will receive great honours, he will survive his parents, have many children, will be cured of all pains and will be lucky in 'Ostland' in the sea, [he] will have long eyes, his faith is ill [?], [he will] win many things, but also will lose much, he will live healthily [for] 27 years, thereafter he will get ill, if he recovers he will get to 53 years, thereafter he will get ill again, if he survives he will live 65 years, then his last day will approach and he will have to die from lack of blood.

This star also covers the first 6 degrees of Taurus, and who is born under the 6th degree may search for his luck and bad luck, month, day, colour, and other things, under the 28th star.

The evil years are [the] 7th, 12th, 14th, 24th, 25th, 27th, 28th, 30th, 35th, 38th, 40th, 50th, 60th, 70th, 75th, and 89th.

[Chapter 50] Of the star Benalhot and its effect

This star, which is also called Alothan, Alchalch, and Albothan, and whose Lord is Amixelis, can be found in 6 degrees and 30 minutes of Taurus, and ends with its power in 19 degrees and 25 minutes of Aries, is temperate and of Mars and Sun nature, unlucky for people.

[Who will be] born if Benalhot is rising in the first hour of the day will be white, strange, and very rich, ingenious, not too small, not too tall, avoiding many illnesses, healthy, his goods will be more enjoyed by strangers than by his friends, he will have many children out of mischief, he will have marks on his neck and near his eyes, and two on one foot.

But who will be born in the second hour will on his finger or somewhere else on his body have marks, [he] will break a bone, if he recovers it will not happen again. He will be left with all honours and goods of two women, will be mean, which is why he has not got enough, he is longing for goods on water and on land, will win a brave (?) [Sinn] and will be an honourable father to his children. He will experience an adventure, fall into the water, and get out again, and a master will be angry with him which will lose him money but he will still have enough of it.

His luck is towards Orient and South [Mittag], therefore his house and his front door, the foot-end of his bed, and his cattle in the stable with their heads shall point towards these lands.

The best months are March, April, Heumonat, December and January, also when the Moon is lucky in Aries, Capricorn, Leo, Taurus, or in Aquarius, the best days of the week [are] Saturn and Jupiter day.

The best colours of his clothes are red, yellow and gold-coloured, on the cattle the best colours are red, fox-coloured, yellow, apple-grey, brown.

All long-lasting good things he shall begin when the Moon is waxing, especially when he is lucky in Leo, Aquarius, or Taurus.

His bad luck is towards West and North.

The evil months are August, September, October, and Hornung, and when the Moon is in Virgo, Libra, Scorpio and in Pisces. The evil days [are] Moon, Mercury, Venus. But the Moon day is better than the Venus day.

The evil years are the 5th, 8th, 10th, 12th, 14th, 15th, 17th, 19th, 20th, 24th, 28th, 30th, 38th, 50th, 74th, and 90th.

Manazil

Johannes Schöner: Ein nutzlichs Büchlein viler bewerter Ertzney, lang zeyt versamlet und zusammen pracht, Nürnberg, 1528

Look in the common, annual almanac for the day / you want to know the Mansion the Moon is in / and on its right side you will find the sign and degree of the Moon for that same day. This sign and degree / you may look up in the following table of the Mansions in the signs and degrees of the beginning and the end of this Mansion / an if you find the sign and degree of the Moon therein / he will be in that Mansion / according to the degree on the left hand / and the nature of the Mansion to the right side of the degree. An example: I state / that the Moon be in 6 degrees / and 35 minutes of Cancer / this sign / degree and minute / I find at the beginning of the table of the Mansions / and on the left hand side / seven / stating / that the Moon is in the seventh Mansion / its nature is written on the right hand side / which is moist. But if the degree of the Moon in a particular sign would not be in the table / so find out where this degree is included / between the beginning and the end of the Mansion / because the Moon will be in this line of the Mansions. An example / in the year 1528, on the 29th day of March / the Moon is in 8 degrees Leo: 8 degrees Cancer is included between the 2nd degree / and 17 minutes of the beginning / and 15 degrees / 9 minutes of the end of the ninth Mansion. Therefore I say / that on this 29th day the Moon is in the ninth Mansion / whose nature is dry. To know about these Mansions / is of use for many things / and particularly for medicating / as will be shown.

Peter Stockinger

Table of the 28 Mansions of the Moon

1   19* 26 Aries   to 2* 17 Taurus.
Moderate/good to travel/take medicines/new clothes/not keeping things.
2   2* 17 Taurus   to 15 * 9 Taurus.
Dry/good to sow seeds/don't travel across water/buy tame animals.
3   15.* 9 Taurus to 28* 0 Taurus.
Moist/buy/don't make friends/buy large animals/to tame them.
4   28.*0 Taurus to 10* 52 Gemini.
Moist/sow seeds/wear new clothes/beware of weddings.
5   10* 52 Gemini to 23* 43 Gemini
Dry/good to marry/and weddings/good to take medicines/send children to school/good to travel.
6   23* 43 Gemini to 6* 35 Cancer
Moderate/don't sow seeds/don't plant/war/don't start anything good.
7   6* 35. Cancer to 19* 26 Cancer
Moist/good to sow/plough/new clothes/do not travel.
8   19* 26 Cancer to 2* 17 Leo
Moderate/good to take medication/clothes/travel across water/not over land.
9   2* 17 Leo to 15* 9 Leo
Dry/don't go out to sea/don't travel/no clothes/deal in corn.
10   15* 9 Leo   to 28* 0 Leo
Moist/good to get married/do not travel/no clothes/don't deal with large sums of money.
11   28* 0 Leo to   10* 52 Virgo
Moderate/sow/plant/do not set your prisoners free.
12   10* 52 Virgo   to 23* 43Virgo
Moist/good to sow seed/plant/marry.
13   23* 43 Virgo   to 6* 35 Libra

Manazil

Moderate/sow/plough/travel/marry.
14 6* 35 Libra to 19* 26 Libra
Moderate/marry widows/[take] medicine/plant.
15 19* 26 Libra   to 2* 17 Scorpio
Moist/dig watery grounds/do not travel.
16 2* 17 Scorpio to 15* 9.Scorpio
Moist/do not travel/do not take medicines/don't buy/no clothes.
17 15* 9 Scorpio to 28* 0 Scorpio
Moist/buy animals/lead them to the pasture.
18 28* 0 Scorpio to 10* 52 Sagittarius
Dry/sow on the field/buy/take on duties.
19 10* 52 Sagittarius to 23* 43 Sagittarius
Moist/fight/occupy your enemy's property/travel/watch out for ships.
20 23* 43 Sagittarius to 6* 35 Capricorn Moist/buy animals/
this mansion is not good for anything else.
21 6.* 35 Capricorn to 19* 26 Capricorn Moderate/start
sowing/buy fields/sow seeds.
22 19* 26 Capricorn to 2* 17 Aquarius   Moist/
do not marry/new clothes/medication/travel.
23 2* 17 Aquarius to 15* 9 Aquarius
Moderate/medication/clothes/travel/
do not buy large things or make payments.
24 15* 9 Aquarius to 28* 0 Aquarius   Moderate/purge/medication/
for warriors to fight.
25 28* 0 Aquarius to 10* 52 Pisces
Dry/good for wars and fights/good for travelling towards the south.
26 10* 52 Pisces to 23* 43 Pisces
Dry/do not start anything new/because this Mansion is completely suspicious.

27 23* 43 Pisces to 6* 35 Aries
Moist/good for sowing/buy/get married/do not invest money.
28 6* 35 Aries to 19* 26 Aries
Moderate/buy/sow/medicate/get married/ get an annuity or life-annuity/do not take out a loan.

Judgment upon the 28 Mansions of the Moon, English translation of
***Ephemeridum opus ab anno 1532 - 1551*, Tübingen, Hulden Morhart 1531.**

Mansion 1: Alnat (Horn of the Ram) 19*26 Aries.
Mansion 2: Alothaym (Belly of the Ram) 02*17 Taurus.
Mansion 3: Athorage (Pleiades) 15*09 Taurus
Mansion 4: Aldebaran (Head of the Bull) 28* Taurus
Mansion 5: Alchataga (Tips of the Bull's horns) 10*52 Gemini
Mansion 6: Alchaga (Little Star of the Great Light) 23*43 Gemini
Mansion 7: Alargach (Arms of the Twin) 06*35 Cancer
Mansion 8: Anatrachia (-) 19*26 Cancer
Mansion 9: Alcharph (Eye of the Lion) 02*17 Leo
Mansion 10: Angelioche (Neck of the Lion) 15*09 Leo
Mansion 11: Azobrah (Hair of the Lion's Head) 28*00 Leo
Mansion 12: Azarpha (Tail of the Lion) 10*52 Leo
Mansion 13: Alhagre (Dog or Companion of the Virgin) 23*43 Virgo
Mansion 14: Azimech (Ear of the Virgin) 06*35 Libra
Mansion 15: Algarpha (-) 19*26 Libra
Mansion 16: Ahubne (Horns of the Scorpion) 00*02 Scorpio
Mansion 17: Alchil (Crown [lit. Wreath 'Kranz'] of the Scorpion) 15*09 Scorpio
Mansion 18: Altoh (Skin of the Scorpion) 28*10 Scorpio
Mansion 19: Achala (Tail of the Scorpion) 10*25 Sagittarius
Mansion 20: Abnahaga (Beam) 28*43 Sagittarius
Mansion 21: Abeldach (-) 06*35 Capricorn
Mansion 22: Sadahacha (-) 19*26 Capricorn
Mansion 23: Sabadola (The Swallower) 02*18 Aquarius
Mansion 24: Sadahod (Seat of Luck) 15*09 Aquarius
Mansion 25: Sadalachia (Butterfly) 28* Aquarius

Mansion 26: Alphargh (-) 10*52 Pisces
Mansion 27: Alcharga (-) 23*43 Pisces
Mansion 28: Albotham (The Fish) 06*35 Aries

From the Planeten Buch, Straubing 1596:

Look in the common, annual almanac for the day / you want to know the Mansion the Moon is in / and on its right side you will find the sign and degree of the Moon for that same day. This sign and degree / you may look up in the following table of the Mansions in the signs and degrees of the beginning and the end of this Mansion / an if you find the sign and degree of the Moon therein / he will be in that Mansion / according to the degree on the left hand / and the nature of the Mansion to the right side of the degree. An example: I state / that the Moon be in 6 degrees / and 35 minutes of Cancer / this sign / degree and minute / I find at the beginning of the table of the Mansions / and on the left hand side / seven / stating / that the Moon is in the seventh Mansion / its nature is written on the right hand side / which is moist. But if the degree of the Moon in a particular sign would not be in the table / so find out where this degree is included / between the beginning and the end of the Mansion / because the Moon will be in this line of the Mansions. An example / in the year 1597, on the 20th day of January / the Moon is in 8 degrees Cancer: 8 degrees Cancer is included between the 6 degree / and 35 minutes of the beginning / and 9 degrees / 26 minutes of the end of the seventh Mansion. Therefore I say / that on this 20th day the Moon is in the seventh Mansion / whose nature is moist. To know about these Mansions / is of use for many things / and particularly for medicating / as will be shown.

Table of the 28 Mansions of the Moon

1   19* 26 Aries   to 2* 17 Taurus.
Moderate/good to travel/take medicines/new clothes/not keeping things.
2   2* 17 Taurus   to 15 * 9 Taurus.
Dry/good to sow seeds/don't travel across water/buy tame animals.
3   15.* 9 Taurus to 28* 0 Taurus.

Moist/buy/don't make friends/buy large animals/to tame them.
4   28.*0 Taurus to 10* 52 Gemini.
Moist/sow seeds/wear new clothes/beware of weddings.
5   10* 52 Gemini to 23* 43 Gemini
Dry/good to marry/and weddings/good to take medicines/send children to school/good to travel.
6   23* 43 Gemini to 6* 35 Cancer
Moderate/don't sow seeds/don't plant/don't start anything good.
7   6* 35. Cancer to 19* 26 Cancer
Moist/good to sow/plough/new clothes/don't travel.
8   19* 26 Cancer to 2* 17 Leo
Moderate/good to take medication/clothes/travel across water/not over land.
9   2* 17 Leo to 15* 9 Leo
Dry/don't go out to sea/don't travel/no clothes/deal in corn.
10   15* 9 Leo to 28* 0 Leo
Moist/good to get married/don't travel/no clothes/don't deal with large sums of money.
11   28* 0 Leo to   10* 52 Virgo
Moderate/sow/plant/don't set your prisoners free.
12   10* 52 Virgo   to 23* 43Virgo
Moist/good to build/sow/plant/marry.
13   23* 43 Virgo   to 6* 35 Libra
Moderate/sow/plough/travel/marry.
14   6* 35 Libra to 19* 26 Libra
Moderate/marry widows/medication/plant.
15   19* 26 Libra   to 2* 17 Scorpio
Moist/dig watery grounds/don't travel.
16   2* 17 Scorpio to 15* 9 Scorpio

Manazil

Moist/don't travel/don't take medicines/don't buy/no clothes.
17 15* 9 Scorpio to 28* 0 Scorpio
Moist/buy animals/lead them to the pasture.
18 28* 0 Scorpio to 10* 52 Sagittarius
Dry/sow on the field/buy/take on duties.
19 10* 52 Sagittarius to 23* 43 Sagittarius   Moist/fight/
occupy your enemy's property/travel/watch out for ships.
20 23* 43 Sagittarius to 6* 35 Capricorn Moist/buy animals/
this mansion is not good for anything else.
21 6.* 35 Capricorn to 19* 26 Capricorn
Moderate/start building/buy fields/sow seeds.
22 19* 26 Capricorn to 2* 17 Aquarius   Moist/
don't marry/new clothes/medication/travel.
23 2* 17 Aquarius to 15* 9 Aquarius   Moderate/medication/clothes/travel/
don't buy large things or make
payments.
24 15* 9 Aquarius to 28* 0 Aquarius
Moderate/purge/medication/for warriors to fight.
25 28* 0 Aquarius to 10* 52 Pisces
Dry/good for wars and fights/good for travelling towards the south.
26 10* 52 Pisces to 23* 43 Pisces
Dry/don't start anything new/because this Mansion is completely
suspicious.
27 23* 43 Pisces to 6* 35 Aries
Moist/good for sowing/buy/get married/don't invest money.
28 6* 35 Aries to 19* 26 Aries
Moderate/buy/sow/medicate/get married/ get an annuity or
life-annuity/don't take out a loan.

Peter Stockinger

Stöffler's Judgment upon th(e) 28 mansions of th(e) mone (Beinecke MS 558 (16th Century))

The first mansyon of (Moon) beginneth in th(e) 9 degree & 26 minute of (Aries) whose nature is temperate & wha(n) (Moon) is th(er), it is good to take a journey & medicine but it is evil to take a prentyse
The 2 is in 2 gre of (Taurus) dry good to iourny by wat(er) & bie tame beste(s)
The 3 is in 15 gre of (Taurus) moist, good to bie, evill to make frindship.
The 4 is in 28 gre of (Taurus) cold good to sowe sedes & evill to marry
The 5 is in 10 gre of (Gemini) dry, good to marry, to go to scole & medicins
The 6 is in 23 gre of (Gemini) temp(er)ate good to go to warre, ill for good(ness)
The 7 beginneth in th(e) 6 degre of (Cancer) moist of nature,
yt is good to eare, sowe & put on new clothes, it is ill to Journey
The 8 is in 19 gre of (Cancer) misty, cloudy & temperate, good to take medicines, to cloth th(ee) new, & to take a journey by wat(er)
The 9 is in 2 gre of (Leo) dry, good to borrow or lende whete
The 10 is in 15 gre of (Leo) moist, good to go a woing, il to Journey.
The 11 is in 28 gre of (Leo) temp(er)ate good to sowe and plante
The 12 is in 10 gre of (Virgo) moist, good to build, marry, eare & sowe
The 13 is in 23 gre of (Virgo) temp(er)ate, good to marry, & Journey
The 14 is in 6 gre of (Libra) temp(er)ate, good for medicins, & to plante
The 15 is in 19 gre of (Libra) moist, ill to Journey, good to dytche
The 16 is in 2 gre of (Scorpio) moist, it is good to do no good thing
The 17 is in 15 gre of (Scorpio) moist, good to put beaste(s) to pasture
The 18 is in 28 gre of (Scorpio) dry, good to take a(n) office & bye londe(s)
The 19 is in 10 gre of (Sagittarius) moist, yt is evil to enter a Shippe.
The 20 is in 23 gre of (Sagittarius) moist, yt is good to Bie beastes
The 21 is in 6 gre of (Capricorn) temperate, good to sowe long & build.

Manazil

The 22 is in th(e) 19 degre of (Capricorn) moist of nature, it is good to take medicine,
to Journey, to clothe th(ee) new, & evill to marry
The 23 is in th(e) 2 degre of (Aquarius) temperate, it is good to take medicines,
& Journeis, & it is evill to lay on wagers
The 24 is in 15 of (Aquarius) temp(er)ate, fortunate, good for medicins.
The 25 is in 28 gre of (Aquarius) dry, good to Journey southward.
The 26 is in 10 gre of (Pisces) dry, it is ill to begin anythinge
The 27 is in 23 gre of (Pisces) moist, good to bie & sell, sowe & mary
The 28 is in 6 gre of (Aries) temp(er)ate, & like to the 27 mansion.
And if thou wilt go spedely in thy Journey or oth(er) busines set forth in the houre of (Moon) whan she is in a good manshion off these signs (Cancer) (Taurus) (Pisces) or (Sagittarius) & let her be fre from (i)nfortune, & in a good aspect, to a good planet, then is good to do anything, ffor th(e) mone sygnifieth th(e) messenger

The MAGUS or CELESTIAL INTELLIGENCER

by Francis Barrett, F.R.C., 1801 (Book Two, Chapter 33)

Of the twenty eight Mansions of the Moon, and their virtues.

And seeing the Moon measures the whole Zodiac in the space of twenty eight days, hence is it that the wise men of the Indians and most of the antient astrologers have granted twenty eight Mansions to the Moon, which being fixed in the eight sphere, do enjoy (as Alpharus says) divers names and proprieties from the various signs and stars which are contained in them, through which while the Moon wanders, it obtains other and other powers and virtues; but every one of these mansions, according to the opinion of Abraham, contained twelve degrees, and fifty one minutes, and almost twenty six seconds, whose names and also their beginnings in the Zodiac of the eight sphere, are these.

The Mansions in the First Quarter of Heaven

The first is called Alnath; that is the horns of Aries: his beginning is from the head of Aries of the eighth sphere; it causes discords, and journies;

The second is called Allothaim or Albochan, that is the belly of Aries, and his beginning is from the twelfth degree of the same sign, fifty one minutes, twenty two seconds complete; it conduces to the finding of treasures, and to the retaining [of] captives;

The third is called Achaomazon or Athoray, that is, showering or Pleiades; his beginning is from the twenty five degrees of Aries complete forty two minutes, and fifty one seconds; it is profitable to sailors, huntsmen, and alchymists;

Manazil

The fourth Mansion is called Aldebaram or Aldelamen that is the eye or head of Taurus; his beginning is from the eight degree of Taurus, thirty four minutes, and seventeen seconds of the same Taurus being excluded; it causes the destruction and hindrances of buildings, fountains, wells, gold mines, the flight of creeping things, and begets discord.

The fifth is called Alchatay or Albachay; the beginning of it is after the twenty one degree of Taurus, twenty five minutes, forty seconds; it helps to the return from a journey, the instruction of scholars, it confirms edifices, it gives health and good-will,

The sixth is called Alhanna or Alchaya, that is the little star of great light; his beginning is after the fourth degree of Gemini, seventeen minutes, and nine seconds; it conduces to hunting, and besieging of towns, and revenge of princes, it destroys harvests and fruits and hinders the operation of the physician.

The seventh is called Aldimiach or Alarzach, that is the Arm of Gemini and begins from the seventeenth degree of Gemini, eight minutes and thirty four seconds, and lasts even to the end of the sign; it confers gain and friendship, its profitable to lovers, it scares flies, destroys magistracies. And so is one quarter of the heaven completed in these seven mansions; and in the like order and number of degrees, minutes and seconds, the remaining mansions in every quarter have their several beginnings; namely so, that in the first sign of this quarter three mansions take their beginnings, in the other two signs two Mansions in each;

The Mansions in the Second Quarter of Heaven

Therefore, the seven following mansions begin from Cancer, whose names are Alnaza or Anatrachya that is misty or cloudy, viz. the eighth mansion; it causes love, friendship, and society of fellow travellers, it drives away mice and afflicts captives, confirming their imprisonment.

After this is the ninth called Archaam or Arcaph, that is the eye of the Lion; it hinders harvests and travelers, and puts discord between men.

The tenth is called Algelioche or Albgebh, that is the neck or forehead of Leo; it strengthens buildings, yields love, benevolence and help against enemies;

The eleventh is called Azobra or Ardaf, that is, the hair of the lion's head; it is good for voyages, and gain by merchandise, and for redemption of captives;

The twelfth is called Alzarpha or Azarpha, that is the tail of Leo; it gives prosperity to harvests, and plantations, but hinders seamen, and is good for the bettering of servants, captives, and companions.

The thirteenth is named Alhaire, that is Dogstars, or the wings of Virgo; it is prevalent for benevolence, gain, voyages, harvests, and freedom of captives;

The fourteenth is called Achureth or Arimet, by others Azimeth or Alhumech or Alcheymech, that is the spike of Virgo, or flying spike; it causes the love of married folks, it cures the sick, is profitable to sailors, but hinders journeys by land; and in these the second quarter of Heaven is completed.

The Mansions in the Third Quarter of Heaven

The other seven follow: the first of which begins in the head of Libra, viz. the fifteenth Mansion, and his name is Agrapha or Algarpha, that is, covered, or covered flying: its profitable for the extracting of treasures, for digging of pits, it assists divorce, discord, and the destruction of houses and enemies, and hinders travelers.

Manazil

The sixteenth is called Azubene or Ahubene, that is, the horns of Scorpio, it hinders journeys and wedlock, harvests, and merchandise, it prevails for redemption of captives.

The seventeenth is called Alchil, that is the Crown of Scorpio, it betters a bad fortune, makes love durable, strengthens buildings, and helps seamen;

The eighteenth is called Alchas or Altob, that is the Heart of Scorpio; it causes discord, sedition, conspiracy against princes and mighty ones, and revenge from enemies, but it frees captives and helps edifices.

The ninteenth is called Allatha or Achala, by others Hycula or Axala, that is the tail of Scorpio; it helps in the besieging of cities and taking of towns, and in the driving of men from their places, and for the destruction of seamen, and perdition of captives.

The twentieth is called Abnahaya, that is a beam; it helps for the taming of wild beasts, for the strengthening of prisons, it destroys the wealth of societies, it compels a man to come to a certain place.

The twenty first is called Abeda or Albeldach which is a desert; it is good for harvests, gain, buildings, and travellers, and causes divorce; and in this is the third quarter of Heaven is completed.

The Mansions in the Fourth Quarter of Heaven

There remains the seven last Mansions completing the last quarter of heaven; the first of which being in order to the twenty-second, begins from the head of Capricorn, called Sadahacha or Zodeboluch, or Zandeldena, that is a pastor; it promotes the flight of servants and captives, that they may escape, and helps the curing of diseases;

Peter Stockinger

The three and twentieth is called Zabadola or Zobrach that is swallowing; it is for divorce, liberty of captives and the health of the sick;

The twenty fourth is called Sadabath or Chadezoad, that is the star of fortune; it is prevalent for the benevolence of married people, for the victory of soldiers, it hurts the execution of government, and prevents it being exercised;

The twenty fifth is called Sadalabra or Sadalachia, that is a butterfly or a spreading forth; it favors besieging and revenge, it destroys enemies, causes divorce, confirms prisons and buildings, hastens messengers, it conduces to spells against copulation, and so binds every member of man, that it cannot perform its duty;

The twenty sixth is called Alpharg or Phragal Mocaden, that is the first drawing; it causes union, health of captives, destroys buildings and prisons.

The twenty seventh is called Alcharya or Alhalgalmoad that is the second drawing; it increases harvests, revenues, gain, and heals infirmities, but hinders buildings, prolongs prisons, causes danger to seamen, and helps to infer mischiefs on whom you shall please;

The twenty-eighth and last is called Albotham or Alchalcy, that is Pisces: it increases harvests and merchandise, it secures travellers through dangerous places; it makes for the joy of married couples, but it strengths prisons, and causes loss of treasures;

And in these twenty eight Mansions do lie hid many secrets of the wisdom of the antients, by the which they wrought wonders on all things which are under the circle of the Moon; and they attributed to every Mansion his resemblances, images, and seals, and his president intelligences, and worked by the virtue of them after different manners.

Bibliography

Agrippa von Nettesheim, Heinrich Cornelius: *Agrippa's von Nettesheim Magische Werke: sammt den geheimnitzvollen Schriften des Petrus von Abano, Pictorius von Villingen, Gerhard von Cremona, Abt Tritheim von Spanheim, dem Buche Arbatel, der sogenannten Heil. Geist-Kunst und verschiedenen anderen.* Zweites Bändchen, Scheible, Stuttgart, 1855.

Agrippa of Nettesheim, Henry Cornelius: *Three books of occult philosophy written by Henry Cornelius Agrippa of Nettesheim ... ; translated out of the Latin into the English tongue by J.F. (John French)* London: Printed by R.W. for Gregory Moule ..., 1651.

Agrippae ab Netteshaym, Henrici Cornelii: *De occulta philosophie libri tres*, Johannes Soter, Cologne, 1533

Al-Biruni: *Book of Instruction in the Elements of the Art of Astrology,* trans. Wright, Luzac & Co., London, 1934.

Barrett, Francis: *The Magus or Celestial Intelligencer*, Lackington, London, 1801

Bonatti, Guido: *Book of Astronomy*, trans. Dykes, Cazimi Press, Golden Valley, Minn., 2007

Brennand, W.: *Hindu Astronomy*, Straker & Sons, London, 1896

Brenner: *Das Grosse Planetenbuch*, 1559 and 1789

Burckhardt, Titus: *Mystical Astrology According to Ibn Arabi*, Beshara, 1989.

Ethe, Hermann(trans.): Zakarija Ben Muhammed Ben Mahmûd El-Kazwîni's Kosmographie, Leipzig, 1868

Ficino, Marsilio: *Three Books on Life*, trans. Kaske and Clark, Tempe, Arizona, 2002

Fürbeth, Frank: *Johannes Hartlieb Untersuchungen zu Leben und Werk*, Max Niemeyer Verlag, Tübingen 1992.

Gundel: *Dekane und Dekansternbilder*, Wissenschaftliche Buchgesellschaft Darmstadt, 1969

Hartlieb, Johannes: *Das Buch aller verbotenen Künste*, published, translated and with comments by Falk Eiserman and Eckhard Graf, param Verlag Günter Koch, Fulda 1989.

Hartlieb: *De Mansionibus*, 1433[?]

Heidelberger Mondwahrsagebuch, Universitätsbibliothek Heidelberg, Cod. Pal, germ.3

Hommel, Fritz: Deutsche Morgenländische Gesellschaft Zeitschrift, Vol.45, 1891

Ibn Ezra, Abraham: *The Book of the World*, Brill, Leiden, 2010

Ideler, Christian Ludwig (ed.), Al-Qazwini, Zakariya ibn Mahmud: *Untersuchungen über den Ursprung und die Bedeutung der Sternnamen. Ein Beytrag zur Geschichte des gestirnten Himmels,* published by Johann Friedrich Weiss, Berlin 1809.

Klio, *Beiträge zur alten Geschichte*, Dieterich'sche Verlagsbuchhandlung, Leipzig, 1901

Liber Lunae: MS Sloane 3826

Kunitzsch, Paul, and Smart, Tim: *A Dictionary of Modern Star Names*, Sky Publishing Corporation, 2006

Kunitzsch, Paul: *Arabische Sternnamen in Europa*, Harassowitz, Wiesbaden, 1959

North, J. D.: *Chaucer's Universe*, Oxford University Press, Oxford, 1988

Pingree, David (editor): *Picatrix. The Latin version of the Ghāyat al-hakīm, (Studies of the Warburg Institute, vol. 39)*, London, Warburg Institute, 1986

Ramesey, William: *Astrologia Restaurata; or Astrologie Restored Being an Introduction to the General and Chief Part of the Language of the Stars*, 1653.

Ritter, Hellmut and Plessner, Martin (Trans.): *"Picatrix" Das Ziel des Weisen von Pseudo-Magriti*, (Studies of the Warburg Institute Vol. 27), London, Warburg Institute, 1962

Rosenberg, Diana: *Secrets of the Ancient Skies*, Ancient Skies Press, 2012

Selin, Helaine (editor): *Science across cultures: The History of Non-Western Science*, Springer-Science+Business Media, Dordrecht, 2000

Steinschneider: *Über die Mondstationen (Naxatra, und das Buch Arcandam*,

Stucken, Eduard: *Der Ursprung des Alphabets und die Mondstationen*, Leipzig, 1913

Tester, Jim: *A History of Western Astrology*, Suffolk, 1987

Thorndike, Lynn: *A History of Magical and Experimental Science*, vol I – VIII, Columbia University Press, New York, 1923 - 1958

Varisco, Daniel Martin: *The Magical Significane of the Lunar Stations in the 13th Century Yemeni "Kitāb Al-Tabsira Fī'ilm Al-Nujtūm of Al-Malik Al-Sharif*, in: Quaderni di Studi Arabi, Vol. 13, Divination magie pouvoirs au Yemen (1995), pp. 19-40.

Vehlow, Johannes: *Lehrkurs der Wissenschaftlichen Geburts-Astrologie*, Band VII, Sporn Verlag, Zeulenroda, 1936

Vian, Robert: *Ein Mondwahrsagebuch*, Verlag von Max Niemeyer Halle a. S., 1910.

Volguine: *Lunar Astrology, an Attempt at a Reconstruction of the Ancient Astrological System*, ASI Publishers, New York, 1974

Weber, Albrecht: *History of Indian Literature*, Trübner, London, 1878

Weinstock, Stefan: *Lunar Mansions and Early Calendars*, in: The Journal of Hellenic Studies, Vol.69, 1949, pp 48-69

Wellhausen, J.: *Reste Arabischen Heidentums*, Georg Reimer Verlag, Berlin, 1897

Index

Abnormal sexual behaviour: 43
Acrab: 105, 105
Adhafera: 75
agriculture: 47, 248
Al Jabhah: 74, 75
al-Awwa: 33, 88
al-Baldah: 34, 119
al-Bula: 126
al-Butayn: 42
al-Dabaran: 32, 50, 222
al-Dhira: 32, 62
al-Fargh al Thani: 34, 141
al-Fargh al-Mukdim: 137
al-Ghafr: 33, 97
al-Han'ah: 32, 58, 59
al-Haq'a: 32, 54, 57, 222
al-Jabhah: 74
al-Jubana: 33, 100
al-Kalb: 33, 108
al-Na'am: 34, 115
al-Nath: 37, 43
al-Nathrah: 32, 67
al-Sa'd al Dhabih: 34, 122
al-Sarfah: 84
al-Sharatan: 32, 36
al-Shaula: 111
al-Simak: 33, 93, 222
al-Tarfa: 32, 71, 222
al-Thurayya: 32, 46
al-Zubrah: 33, 80
Albaldah: 119, 120
Albali: 127
alchemical operations: 48, 64, 85
Alcyone: 46, 47
Aldebaran: 22, 37, 50, 50, 51, 51, 52, 52, 75, 76, 76, 77, 150, 257
Algenib: 141
Algieba: 75
Alhena: 58, 59
alienation: 40
Alnasl: 116
Alnath: 32, 32, 32, 37, 37, 38, 39, 39, 40, 165, 264
Alpheratz: 141, 142
Alterf: 71, 72
Alzirr: 58, 59
Antares: 75, 76, 76, 108, 109, 151, 193, 193, 194, 194
Aquarius: 56, 119, 123, 127, 129, 130, 133, 134, 138, 152, 152, 152, 174, 174, 175, 202, 202, 224, 224, 226, 243, 247, 247, 248, 248, 252, 252, 255, 255, 255, 255, 257, 257, 257, 261, 261, 261, 261, 263, 263, 263
Aries: 7, 12, 24, 36, 36, 38, 39, 39, 43, 43, 47, 51, 138, 141, 146, 149, 150, 155, 157, 164, 165, 165, 165, 166, 177, 202, 202, 202, 224, 224, 224, 225, 226, 233, 234, 240, 242, 250, 250, 251, 251, 252, 254, 256, 256, 257, 258, 259, 261, 261, 262, 263, 264, 264, 264
Asad: 63
Ascella: 116
Aselli: 67, 68, 168
Auva: 89, 89

Barker: 88, 88, 91, 189
Batn al Hut: 145, 145, 146
Belly of Aries: 42, 42, 44
Belly of the Fish: 145, 145, 147, 200

Botein: 42, 43
Brand: 58, 59
building: 51, 52, 52, 56, 56, 85, 90, 105, 109, 111, 120, 134, 138, 215, 243, 261
Butterfly: 133, 257
buying: 17, 39, 47, 56, 61, 64, 85, 102, 109, 116, 120, 124, 127, 134, 138, 209, 232, 237, 248

Cancer: 7, 17, 55, 59, 63, 67, 67, 71, 72, 75, 150, 168, 168, 202, 202, 224, 224, 225, 228, 231, 231, 232, 232, 233, 233, 233, 234, 234, 236, 237, 240, 240, 242, 242, 247, 250, 250, 253, 254, 254, 254, 257, 257, 259, 260, 260, 260, 262, 262, 263, 265
Canis Minor: 63
Capricorn: 7, 112, 116, 119, 123, 123, 127, 129, 130, 152, 174, 174, 224, 226, 231, 232, 234, 235, 236, 240, 242, 244, 244, 245, 246, 246, 247, 247, 250, 252, 255, 255, 255, 257, 257, 261, 261, 261, 262, 263, 267
career: 30, 65
Castor: 62, 63, 63, 184
Changer: 84, 84, 86, 188
City: 119, 119, 121, 195
Claws: 100, 100
clothes: 17, 39, 42, 47, 48, 51, 60, 64, 65, 68, 72, 78, 79, 81, 85, 90, 102, 109, 120, 120, 124, 127, 130, 181, 191, 193, 201, 205, 227, 227, 229, 230, 231, 231, 233, 235, 237, 247, 248, 252, 254, 254, 254, 254, 254, 254, 255, 255, 255, 259, 260, 260, 260, 260, 260, 261, 261, 261, 262
Covering: 97, 97, 191, 191
Coxa: 81
Crib: 67, 67, 68, 69, 185
Crown of Scorpio: 104, 267
cure illnesses: 98
curse enemies: 78
cutting hair: 39, 72, 81, 98, 105, 109
Dabhi: 123, 123
Denebola: 84, 85
Desert: 119, 119
discord: 52, 52, 72, 72, 98, 99, 102, 105, 109, 124, 265, 266, 266, 267
divorce: 98, 120, 134, 183, 266, 267, 268, 268
Draining: 137, 141
Dschubba: 105, 105

enmities: 73
enmity: 40, 52, 95

fire: 41, 44, 47, 48, 48, 58, 74, 87, 92, 143, 202, 205, 208, 210, 212, 213, 224, 227, 231, 235, 238, 239
First Drawing: 137
First Spout of the Bucket: 137
Follower: 50, 50, 53
Forearm: 62, 62, 63, 65
Forehead: 74, 74, 79, 104, 104
Fortunate of the Fortunate: 129, 129
Fortune of the Hidden: 133, 133, 136
Fortune of the Slaughterer: 122, 122
Fortune of the Swallower: 126, 126
friendship: 55, 60, 61, 64, 68, 68, 69, 95, 99, 99, 106, 106, 117, 139, 265, 266

Gap: 67, 67, 69
Gemini: 17, 43, 47, 50, 54, 55, 55, 56, 58, 59, 62, 62, 63, 150, 150, 167, 168, 202, 202, 224, 224, 225, 230, 231, 233, 235, 237, 242, 247, 248, 248, 254, 254, 254, 257, 257, 260, 260, 260, 262, 262, 265, 265
Giedi Prima: 123, 123
Giedi Secunda: 123, 123
Glance: 71, 71, 73

Good Luck Star of the Tents: 133
good luck: 44
goodwill: 51, 56, 99, 99
Graffias: 105, 105

hair cutting: 56, 64
harmony: 56, 78, 95, 98, 101, 130, 147
harvests: 60, 60, 64, 72, 86, 90, 90, 95, 102, 113, 120, 135, 135, 135, 142, 143, 147, 265, 266, 266, 266, 267, 267, 268, 268
health: 56, 139, 147, 204, 204, 226, 226, 227, 265, 268, 268
Heart of Scorpio: 108, 267
Heka: 55, 55
hindrance: 72
Horns of Scorpio: 100, 100
hunting,: 48, 60, 60, 265
hunting: 47

Iklil al Jabhah: 33, 104, 104, 105
illness: 16, 16, 61, 66, 80, 83, 87, 103, 107, 122, 124, 127, 136, 208, 209, 211, 211, 212, 214, 215, 217, 218, 232, 236, 237, 238, 239, 241, 242, 246, 246
journeys: 39, 40, 40, 43, 47, 47, 56, 56, 60, 64, 68, 72, 78, 81, 95, 98, 99, 102, 109, 116, 120, 124, 130, 134, 139, 142, 146

Kaus Australis: 116
Kaus Borealis: 116
Kaus Medius: 116

laxatives: 40
Leo: 17, 27, 63, 68, 71, 72, 74, 75, 81, 84, 84, 85, 97, 97, 150, 151, 151, 151, 151, 168, 168, 169, 171, 171, 171, 177, 202, 202, 202, 224, 224, 224, 234, 234, 235, 235, 236, 237, 240, 242, 242, 244, 247, 252, 252, 253, 254, 254, 254, 254, 257, 257, 257, 257, 260, 260, 260, 260, 262, 262, 262, 266, 266
Lesath: 112, 112
Libra: 7, 17, 56, 89, 94, 98, 98, 101, 101, 104, 105, 108, 145, 151, 172, 172, 175, 202, 202, 224, 224, 226, 229, 237, 237, 238, 239, 239, 240, 240, 242, 243, 246, 252, 254, 255, 255, 257, 257, 260, 260, 260, 262, 262, 266
Lion's Mane: 80, 80
Little Star of Great Light: 58
love: 41, 45, 48, 53, 58, 61, 61, 61, 63, 68, 68, 69, 70, 78, 78, 90, 91, 94, 95, 95, 99, 105, 106, 128, 139, 139, 139, 140, 193, 202, 205, 206, 207, 208, 208, 209, 218, 224, 228, 228, 230, 230, 231, 232, 234, 248, 265, 266, 266, 267
lovers: 64, 86, 124, 265
Lower Handle: 141, 175

Many Little Ones: 46, 46, 49
Mark: 58, 58, 59, 61
Markab: 138
marriage: 39, 43, 47, 51, 56, 78, 85, 90, 90, 94, 101, 127, 130, 134, 142, 146, 146, 200
medicine: 25, 52, 60, 64, 64, 68, 90, 95, 105, 120, 124, 124, 127, 130, 135, 142, 255, 262, 263
medicines: 29, 40, 56, 60, 60, 90, 95, 102, 109, 146, 254, 254, 255, 259, 260, 261, 262, 263
Meissa: 54, 55
menstruation: 113
merchandise: 82, 102, 102, 130, 134, 146, 266, 267, 268
Mesarthim: 12, 37, 39
messengers: 85, 134, 134, 135, 268
Mirach: 146

misfortune: 41, 56, 85, 105, 121, 138, 142, 194
money: 45, 91, 124, 142, 148, 206, 212, 221, 228, 238, 252, 254, 256, 260, 261

Neck of the Lion: 74, 257
Nunki: 116

Orion: 54, 55, 55, 55, 150, 167, 167, 183, 183, 183
Ostriches: 115, 115, 116, 173, 173, 194

partnership: 68, 94, 123, 142, 146
partnerships: 39, 47, 51, 56, 60, 64, 72, 78, 81, 101, 112, 116, 127, 130, 134, 139
peace: 21, 64, 147
Pisces: 17, 28, 130, 134, 138, 141, 145, 146, 177, 226, 228, 236, 237, 238, 240, 242, 248, 248, 249, 250, 250, 252, 255, 255, 256, 258, 258, 261, 261, 261, 263, 263, 263, 268
planting: 39, 47, 81, 85, 95, 109, 113, 135, 136
Pleiades: 12, 46, 47, 50, 51, 150, 151, 155, 155, 155, 155, 164, 166, 166, 167, 179, 180, 180, 180, 181, 181, 181, 181, 182, 182, 182, 184, 185, 193, 257, 264
poisonous animals: 52, 241
Pollux: 58, 59, 62, 63, 63, 184
Porrima: 89, 89
Praecordia: 108
Praesaepe: 67, 68
Procyon: 62, 150, 168
profit: 64, 102, 123
Propus: 59
prosperity: 64, 68, 82, 85, 85, 90, 146, 192, 266

Rainy Ones: 22, 46, 46
Regulus: 75, 75, 75, 76, 76, 77, 151

revenge: 47, 60, 60, 65, 109, 110, 134, 209, 215, 233, 243, 265, 267, 268
Ribbon: 145, 145, 175
Royal Stars: 51, 75, 75, 108

Sa'd al Ahbiyah: 34, 133, 133, 134
Sa'd al Bula: 34, 126, 126, 127, 128
Sa'd al Su'ud: 34, 129, 129, 130
Sadalachbia: 134
Sadalsuud: 130, 130
safety: 56, 64, 124
Sagittarius: 17, 56, 101, 105, 109, 112, 116, 116, 119, 119, 152, 152, 156, 173, 173, 202, 202, 224, 224, 226, 229, 232, 233, 237, 240, 242, 242, 243, 243, 244, 244, 246, 248, 250, 255, 255, 255, 257, 257, 261, 261, 261, 262, 262, 263
Scheat: 138, 138
Scorpio: 17, 94, 97, 97, 98, 101, 101, 104, 105, 108, 111, 112, 155, 155, 171, 171, 172, 172, 173, 224, 226, 237, 240, 240, 241, 243, 244, 246, 247, 248, 248, 252, 255, 255, 255, 255, 257, 257, 257, 260, 260, 261, 261, 262, 262, 262, 267, 267
scorpions: 52, 109, 110
Second Drawing: 141
Second Spout: 141, 141, 143, 200
Seven Sisters: 46
Shaula: 112, 112, 112, 114
Shepherd: 122
Sheratan: 12, 37, 39
sickness: 51, 63, 73
Slaughterer's Joy: 122
snakes: 52, 110
sowing: 47, 51, 60, 64, 72, 81, 85, 95, 102, 112, 120, 134, 136, 142, 146, 255, 256, 261
Spica: 11, 93, 94, 151, 170, 171, 189
spouses: 40, 78, 95
Star of Fortune: 129

Sting: 111, 111, 194, 194
Swallowing: 126
Syrma: 98

Tail of Scorpio: 111
Taurus: 39, 43, 47, 50, 50, 50, 51, 55, 141, 146, 150, 150, 155, 166, 167, 202, 202, 202, 224, 224, 224, 225, 226, 228, 229, 229, 231, 232, 243, 247, 248, 251, 251, 252, 252, 254, 254, 254, 254, 257, 257, 257, 259, 259, 259, 260, 262, 262, 262, 263, 265, 265
trade: 47, 64, 81, 82, 90, 102, 130, 143, 146, 146, 186, 188, 243
trading: 142
travel by water: 48, 56
treasures: 43, 52, 52, 91, 98, 99, 114, 212, 216, 238, 244, 264, 266, 268

Unarmed: 93, 93, 96
Unfolding: 133

Vindemiatrix: 89, 89
Virgo: 16, 56, 72, 75, 81, 84, 88, 88, 89, 93, 93, 94, 97, 98, 149, 151, 151, 151, 170, 171, 171, 177, 202, 202, 224, 224, 226, 228, 235, 236, 236, 237, 240, 242, 242, 247, 252, 254, 254, 254, 257, 260, 260, 260, 262, 262, 266, 266
Virgo's Ear of Corn: 93, 93
voyages: 39, 40, 47, 64, 68, 72, 82, 90, 112, 134, 266, 266

washing: 56, 64, 140
wealth: 51, 82, 113, 117, 157, 227, 228, 267
welfare: 56, 95
wells: 43, 52, 52, 98, 99, 99, 179, 265
White Spot: 54, 54, 57

Zaniah: 89, 89
Zavijava: 89, 89
Zosma: 81, 81
Zuben Elgenubi: 101, 101
Zuben Eschemali: 101, 101

www.ingramcontent.com/pod-product-compliance
Lightning Source LLC
Chambersburg PA
CBHW080634230426
43663CB00016B/2862